CONTENTS

FOOD FOR SPORT

JUDY RIDGWAY

First published in Great Britain in 1994 by Boxtree Limited, Broadwall House,
21 Broadwall, London SE1 9PL

The right of Judy Ridgway to be identified as Author of this Work has been
asserted by her in accordance with the Copyright, Designs and Patents Act
1988

10 9 8 7 6 5 4 3 2 1

ISBN: 1 85283 537 0

Cover design: Design 23
Illustrations: Raymond Turvey

Typeset by SX Composing, Rayleigh, Essex
Printed and bound in Great Britain by Cox & Wyman, Reading, Berkshire

A CIP catalogue entry for this book is available from the British Library

1
INTRODUCTION

If the maxim 'You are what you eat' is true, then what kind of diet gives our top sportsmen and women the winning edge to produce those amazing feats of speed, strength and endurance? In *Food for Sport*, Judy Ridgway answers that question, looking at the science of sports nutrition in a clear, concise way, but more importantly translating the scientific data into practical information to be used by anybody who follows an active lifestyle – something we are all being encouraged to do.

Eating a balanced diet is therefore important for everyone: young or old, male or female, Olympic or recreational athlete. It seems a happy coincidence that the types of foods we should eat to improve physical or sporting performance are those that are best for health – there is no conflict. The book guides us through everyday eating for an active lifestyle, to fuelling our sporting activities, and ends with advice for the competitive athlete. There is specific advice for the young, for women, and for vegetarian athletes. Controversial topics such as sports drinks, protein supplements and ergogenic aids are tackled so that the reader can make an informed choice about whether to include such items in the diet.

What sets this book apart from any others on the subject of sports nutrition is the depth of practical information. Many people are aware of the healthy eating messages – to eat less fat and sugar, to eat more starchy foods and fibre and perhaps to have less salt. Far fewer people know how to turn this into actual meals – for instance what foods to choose, how much of each food to eat and how to make these meals interesting and enjoyable. The lifestyle of anyone taking part in regular physical activity can be hectic and though what we eat and drink plays a crucial part in supporting training and competition, time spent on planning and preparing food can be minimal. The squash player who has a quick snack lunch and goes straight from work to play an important match, stays for a few beers and arrives home too late to be bothered with eating is not unusual. Neither is the schoolchild who skips lunch to get some extra shooting practice in before the team football practice after school. In both cases sporting performance could be improved by paying more attention to diet, not only in what is eaten and drunk but also when it is consumed.

Food for Sport is full of tips, menu plans and recipes. Variety is all important in the diet and this book introduces you to a wide range of foods which fit well into the active lifestyle diet. The recipes cover all meal and snack occasions, and many can be prepared in minutes. Symbols indicate whether recipes are suitable for vegetarians and whether they can be frozen, and a nutritional breakdown of each recipe is given to help you build up the right proportions of nutrients in the diet.

Your diet is important every day of the year, because what you eat and drink directly affects your ability to train and recover from training as well as affecting your ability to compete and keep on competing. Following the advice in *Food for Sport* may not turn you into an Olympic athlete but along with your regular physical activity it will help you towards reaching your own peak of health and fitness.

Jane Griffin
Consultant Nutritionist to the British Olympic Association

2
EVERYDAY EATING FOR AN ACTIVE LIFESTYLE

There is no doubt about it – you are what you eat. Food provides the nutrients you need for growth and renewal. It also provides the energy required to live life to the full. The better the diet, the more energy you will have and the fitter you will be.

In addition, the right food can play an important part in reducing the risk of contracting a whole host of twentieth-century illnesses, such as coronary heart disease, high blood pressure, cancer of the bowel, diabetes, tooth decay and diverticulosis.

For sportsmen and women food is even more important. Depending on your sport, it must fuel anything from short bursts of intense activity to sustained effort for hours. It must also build and maintain muscle power, hone reaction times, boost stamina and increase endurance.

Physical training goes a long way to achieving these goals but the very best results can only be achieved through a combination of professional training *and* good nutrition.

So what constitutes a generally healthy diet and how should you modify it to suit the needs of your particular sporting activity?

2.1 EATING FOR BETTER FITNESS

The most generally accepted current guidelines for healthy eating suggest that everyone should:

- eat less fat
- eat more cereals and starchy foods
- eat more fruit and vegetables

Fat is loaded with calories. 25g/1oz butter or margarine has almost 10 times as many calories as 25g/1oz boiled potatoes, and too many calories mean excess body weight.

Experts also believe that eating too much fat is one of the factors involved in the high incidence of coronary heart disease in the West. (Smoking and lack of exercise are other factors.) There have recently been a few dissenting voices, but whatever the facts turn out to be, fat is certainly a contributory factor in obesity, and a cut-back on this ground alone seems reasonable.

However, it is not sufficient simply to reduce the amount of fat eaten. Some of the saturated animal fats in the diet (butter and lard) may need to be replaced with polyunsaturated vegetable fats (sunflower oil and corn oil) and monounsaturated vegetable fats (olive oil).

Research into the effect of eating different kinds of fat on blood cholesterol levels (an important indicator of coronary heart disease) suggests that saturated fats have a detrimental effect and push blood cholesterol levels up, while polyunsaturated and monounsaturated fats do not. (For more information on how this works see pages 19-22.)

Extra cereals and starchy foods, such as bread and pasta, rice and potatoes, are needed to make up some of the energy lost by eating less fat. Active sports people also need them to fuel their muscles.

In addition, these foods provide fibre which is also believed to play an important part in keeping blood cholesterol levels down, in helping to control blood sugar levels and in maintaining a healthy gut.

Like cereals, fruit and vegetables are important both for their fibre content and for their vitamin and mineral content. Some of these vitamins act as anti-oxidants. The precise role of anti-oxidants in the body is not yet fully understood but they, too, are thought to play an important part in the prevention of coronary heart disease.

Rather more controversial are calls to:

- eat less sugar
- eat less salt

Sugar contains no useful nutrients, only energy. Eating large amounts can lead to obesity and tooth decay.

Too much salt can cause high blood pressure and this in turn is associated with heart disease and strokes. The problem here is that not everyone is affected in this way and there is no way of predicting who will be.

Cutting down on salt alone does not guarantee a reduction in the risks, but with the average intake of salt running at two whole teaspoons per person per day it would not do any harm. The question of salt and sport is looked at in more detail on pages 166-167.

Rather than trying to cut down too much on salt (or sodium) it could be useful to pay more attention to the amount of potassium eaten. This mineral is thought to help guard against hypertension and make artery walls stronger.

Composition of Food

There are seven different categories of essential materials that the body needs to work properly and these are known as nutrients. Each has its own set of functions. Many nutrients are found in different sorts of food and on the whole it does not matter which kind of food supplies them, provided that you get them. Other nutrients are only available in a limited number of foods.

These essential nutrients are carbohydrate, protein, fat, vitamins, minerals, dietary fibre and water.

Essential Nutrients and Their Functions			
	Energy producer	*Growth and renewal*	*Regulation of body processes*
Carbohydrate	*		
Fats	*	*	
Proteins	*	*	
Vitamins		*	*
Minerals		*	*
Dietary fibre			*
Water			*

Carbohydrate

Carbohydrates include both sugars and starches. Starches are usually found together with other nutrients and are now more frequently referred to as 'complex carbohydrates' or 'unrefined, natural carbohydrates'.

Pure or refined sugar provides energy alone and contributes no other nutrients. For this reason carbohydrates have traditionally been viewed as the most fattening of foods. If the body takes in more energy than it can use up, the surplus is converted into reserve stores in the unwelcome form of body fat (see page 81).

However, refined sugar and glucose and fructose powders are about the only pure carbohydrate around. Most carbohydrate foods are extremely useful sources of other nutrients such as protein, vitamins, minerals and fibre. Two slices of bread, for example, provide a significant proportion of the body's daily protein requirement as well as a supply of fibre, calcium, iron and vitamins B and E.

Furthermore, research now shows that rather than

being something to avoid, high-carbohydrate foods are the athlete's best friend. The reason for this is that they provide all-important fuel for working muscles. Sportsmen and women may need not only to increase their carbohydrate intake in line with current guidelines but also to use it for the bulk (literally!) of their diet.

> Cakes, biscuits and pastries may look like attractive sources of complex carbohydrates but they are often full of fat and simple sugar too. When in training, try to choose low-fat sweet snacks like Date and Nut Halva (page 344).

'Sugar' is synonymous with sucrose (the familiar table sugar in everyday use), but there are many other sugars in food. After sucrose the most common are glucose, fructose, maltose and lactose. They are sometimes called 'simple carbohydrates'.

Some sugars are naturally integrated into the cellular structure of food. These sugars are known as intrinsic sugars to distinguish them from extrinsic sugars which are dissolved in the water content of food or have been added to it.

The difference in the location of the sugar in food is important because it influences the ease with which sugars are absorbed into the body and turned into energy after eating. Extrinsic sugar will enter the bloodstream more quickly than intrinsic. But extrinsic sugar also causes teeth to decay more quickly because tooth-decay bacteria in the mouth can use it more easily to grow and multiply.

Intrinsic sugars include those contained in fruit and vegetables. Extrinsic sugars include those in milk and milk products, fruit juices, honey and table sugar.

All sugars are chemically related and taste more or less sweet. And this is where the pitfalls arise. Sugar has an attractive taste, so you still can find room for the chocolates even after you have already eaten a three- or four-course meal.

Simple-carbohydrate foods such as sugar, jam, honey

Food Sources of Simple Carbohydrates

Sugar (sucrose)
Glucose
Fructose
Honey
Syrup and maple syrup
Black treacle and molasses
Jams and jellies
Marmalade
Sugar-coated cereals
Milk
Drinking chocolate
Barley sugars, mint cake, Turkish delight,
honeycomb and other sweets and chocolates

Food Sources of Starch or Complex Carbohydrates

Flour
Bread
Pasta
Polenta
Porridge
Rice
Potatoes
Bananas
Beans and lentils
Sweetcorn kernels
Apples
Dried fruits

Breakfast cereals are very variable in starch content, so check the nutritional information on the pack or see page 198.

Where possible eat wholegrain or wholemeal products for extra nutrients such as fibre, vitamins and minerals.

and soft drinks are considered to be less nutritious than complex carbohydrates but they can have an important part to play in the diet of runners and others with high energy requirements (see page 99). Of course, care should be taken with these foods for they promote tooth decay, but sugar is most active in this role up to the age of 20 and children are much more at risk than adults. (In adults gum disease is more likely to cause loss of teeth than dental caries.)

Protein

After water, protein is the largest single constituent of the body. Around 17 per cent of the body tissues are made up of protein. So if you weigh 70kg or 11 stone, about 12kg or 2 stone of that will be protein.

Protein is present in the bones, skin, nails, hair, tendons and arteries, but the lion's share – some 40 per cent – is found in the muscles. It is not surprising that at one time athletes were convinced that protein was of paramount importance to them.

This view was reinforced by the fact that protein foods do indeed play an important part in growth and in tissue replacement and strength. All body proteins, wherever they are, are continually being broken down and replaced. Some of them are discarded daily and an equivalent amount must be provided in the diet.

But the quantity required, even for muscle-building athletes, is not all that large. Most people on a Western diet eat a good deal more protein than they need and excess protein is stored in the body not as protein but as fat.

This fact has largely put paid to the idea that top sports people need to consume vast quantities of red meat or protein supplements before going on to beat world records and earn gold medals (see page 161).

Unlike fat and carbohydrate, no natural food is pure protein. Meat, contrary to popular belief, is not in fact the richest source of protein. Parmesan cheese and low-fat soya flour both contain a higher percentage of protein than meat.

Fish, other kinds of cheese, eggs and nuts (particularly peanuts) and dried beans and peas are all reasonably good sources of protein. Even cereals and milk contain protein. Milk becomes a good source if it is consumed in large quantities or used in the form of dried milk powder.

However, it is not just the quantity of protein contained in food that decides how useful it will be in body-building. The quality of the protein is equally important.

Not all proteins are the same. The protein in milk differs from that in cereals and the protein in liver is different to that in eggs. But all proteins are made up of a combination of chemical components called amino-acids. These amino-acids are released into the bloodstream during digestion (see page 66) and are carried to wherever they are needed to be reassembled into body proteins.

Some amino-acids can be produced naturally in the body, so it does not matter whether they are regularly included in the diet or not. But eight of them cannot be manufactured by the body. If the building of new body proteins is to continue, these eight essential amino-acids must be provided by the protein foods eaten in the diet.

All the essential amino-acids are present in most foods, but unfortunately they do not necessarily occur in the ideal proportions for the body to use. There are usually one or more amino-acids present in disproportionately small quantities.

This means that if, for example, half of the ideal proportions of one of the essential amino-acids is missing from a protein, the body can only use half of all the other essential amino-acids present. The rest are wasted or used to supply fuel. (The deficient amino-acid is called the limiting amino-acid.) It also means that twice the amount of such a protein would need to be eaten to fulfil daily requirements.

The highest-quality proteins would be those in which there was no limiting amino-acid and all the amino-acid was usable by the body. In practice there is no such protein, although the protein in eggs comes close to it. Meat fares reasonably well on the usability side of the scale,

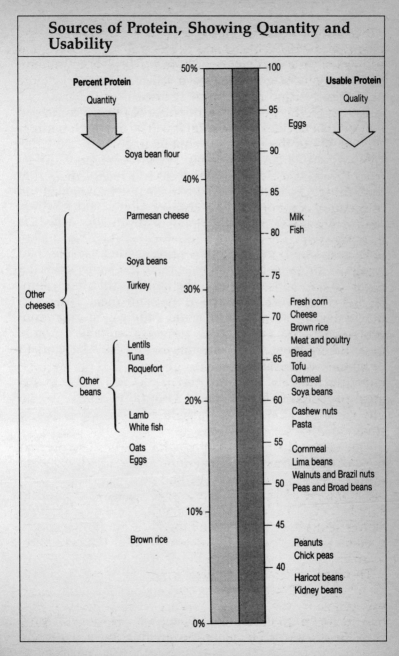

Sources of Protein, Showing Quantity and Usability

Percent Protein

Quantity

50% — 100

Usable Protein

Quality

95

Eggs

Soya bean flour

90

40% — 85

Parmesan cheese

80 Milk
     Fish

Soya beans

75

Turkey 30% —

70 Fresh corn
     Cheese
     Brown rice

Other cheeses

Meat and poultry
65 Bread
     Tofu
     Oatmeal
     Soya beans

Lentils
Tuna
Roquefort

Other beans

20% — 60 Cashew nuts
             Pasta

Lamb
White fish

55 Cornmeal
     Lima beans
     Walnuts and Brazil nuts
50 Peas and Broad beans

Oats
Eggs

10% — 45

Brown rice

Peanuts
Chick peas

40 Haricot beans
     Kidney beans

0%

although milk, cheese and eggs all come higher up (see box on the previous page).

Some vegetable proteins approach the level of meat and these include those in soy beans and whole rice. The rest of the vegetable proteins fall rather further down the scale and you would need to consume quite large amounts of them to cover daily requirements.

However, you eat food, not single proteins, and this gives a natural mix of different protein sources. Vegetarians can augment their protein intake by making sure that they eat two or more complementary protein foods at the same time. The trick is to match a protein food which is rich in one particular amino-acid with another which is deficient in it.

This results in more protein being made available than would have been the case by eating the same foods on separate occasions. It used to be thought that these combinations needed to be eaten at the same meal. However, nutritionists now believe that the body can store amino-acids until the next meal provides suitable protein partners for them. The combination can thus be worked out on a daily basis.

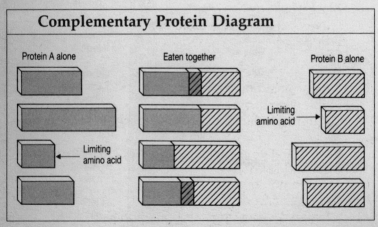

Complementary Protein Diagram

Protein A alone   Eaten together   Protein B alone

Limiting amino acid

Limiting amino acid

A good example is baked beans on toast. Combining these two foods can increase the amount of usable protein by more than 30 per cent of the total achieved by eating them separately. More ideas are given in the Protein Partners recipe section on page 267.

Fat

Fat has taken over from carbohydrate as the worst word in the nutritional vocabulary, but some fat is essential to life. Fat acts as a carrier for the fat-soluble vitamins such as A and E as well as for vitamins D and K (see page 43). It also plays a part in cell structure. Body fat acts as a form of insulation and protection round the body's main organs.

The problem is that we need only a relatively small amount of the essential fatty acids for good health. Otherwise the body can manufacture fats from protein and carbohydrates.

Few people set out to eat a fatty diet, but fat is surprisingly tempting – think of the smell of a roasting joint, the appeal of a cream cake and the craving for chocolate. Fat carries the flavour of food and it helps to lubricate it.

Food Sources Rich in Fat

Butter
Margarine
Olive and other vegetable oils
Dripping
Lard
Suet
Fat on meat (crackling)
Skin on poultry
Fat in meats like bacon, ham, pork, lamb and beef
Oily fish such as herring, mackerel, sardines, tuna and salmon
Cream and cheese
Sausages and salami
Vinaigrette dressings and mayonnaise
Peanut butter

For more sources of invisible or hidden fat see page 41.

Fat in food can be visible, as in the fat on a steak or butter on bread, or it can be invisible, as in cakes, biscuits and pastry. Half the weight of roast and salted peanuts is fat.

Fat is mainly concerned with energy supply. It offers more than twice the calories per gram of carbohydrate or protein. But it is slow to digest. This can be useful because it helps to stave off hunger pangs. On the other hand, it can be a problem for sports people if they still have fatty food in the stomach when they are performing.

It is worth remembering here that all types of fat contribute the same amount of energy. So polyunsaturated margarine and so-called 'light' olive oil are actually just as 'fattening' as butter and cooking oil.

When fat is digested it breaks down into cholesterol, fatty acids and phospholipids.

CHOLESTEROL
Cholesterol is present in all animal foods except egg white. It is also manufactured naturally by the body, which makes twice as much cholesterol every day as is eaten in the normal diet. Cholesterol is an essential component of the blood and is found in all body cells, including hormones. In addition, it has a role in the formation of bile acids in the liver and these help to absorb fats.

However, excessive amounts of cholesterol in the blood are thought to be associated with the development of atherosclerosis or coronary heart disease. This is a condition in which fatty deposits cling to the inside walls of the blood vessels leading to the heart and interfere with the flow of blood.

The link between cholesterol in the diet and cholesterol in the blood is still very uncertain. Some people appear to be unaffected by cholesterol in their diet, others develop high levels of cholesterol in their blood without eating excessive amounts of it in their food. As a result of these anomalies less emphasis is now put on reducing cholesterol in the diet. The spotlight has moved on to the fatty acids.

Eggs, liver, kidneys and fish roe (including tara-masalata) are particulary rich in cholesterol, as are some shellfish such as lobster, shrimps and scampi. When eggs took the brunt of the anti-cholesterol lobby, sales fell. This seems illogical when you consider that eggs provide a protein which is almost fully usable by the body (see page 15).

FATTY ACIDS
There are around 20-plus fatty acids which occur naturally in fats. These can be divided into two main types:

Saturated fatty acids: These are usually solid at room temperature and are derived mainly from animal sources such as butter and cream, although both palm oil and coconut oil contain quite high concentrations of it. (These oils are often used in biscuits, and other ready-made foods, so double-check the labels.)

Unsaturated fatty acids: These are usually liquid at room temperature and come mainly from plant sources. They include most vegetable oils. Some fish are also rich in unsaturated fats and chicken also has a surprisingly high proportion (over 50 per cent).

Unsaturated fatty acids are divided into monounsaturated (olive and avocado oil) and polyunsaturated (sunflower, rapeseed and corn oil among others).

The body can manufacture for itself most of the fatty acids we need but there are three which it cannot manage. These are called the essential fatty acids and they are all polyunsaturated. They are *linoleic acid*, found mainly in vegetable oils, *linolenic acid*, found mainly in fish and seafood, and *arachidonic acid*, found in liver, kidneys, beef, pork, lamb, chicken and turkey. Incidentally, arachidonic acid can be synthesized by the body from linoleic acid and so vegetarians are not at risk from lack of this essential fatty acid.

The amount of fat needed to supply these essential acids in adequate amounts is as little as 1 tablespoon of polyunsaturated fat a day.

Omega-3: This is the name coined for the essential fatty acids found in oily fish such as herring, mackerel and sardines and to a lesser extent in tuna and salmon.

Recent medical evidence suggests that an increased intake of these particular fatty acids may reduce the risk of arterial blood-clotting which can lead to thromboses and heart attacks.

Eskimos, who eat large amounts of fish containing Omega-3, appear to have a lower risk of heart disease and stroke than the rest of us.

Current healthy eating guidelines (see page 35) not only recommend eating less fat, they also suggest moving away from saturated fat towards more unsaturated fat. In the USA doctors are currently advocating one-third saturated fat, one-third polyunsaturated fat and one-third monounsaturated fat.

This is something of a change from the early recommendations to switch to polyunsaturated alone. The reasons lie in the most recent research into the way in which the body uses fatty acids and how this in turn affects the development of coronary heart disease.

Blood cholesterol levels, which have been shown to have a strong correlation to heart disease, also seem to be directly related to fat consumption. However, it is the fatty acid content of the dietary fat rather than the cholesterol content which is important.

There are two types of blood cholesterol, known as HDL (high-density lipoprotein) and LDL (low-density lipoprotein). HDL is regarded as beneficial because it is thought to carry artery-clogging fats away from the heart for disposal by the liver. LDL, on the other hand, is thought to encourage fatty deposits. It is important, therefore, to maintain high levels of HDL in order to prevent the build-up of cholesterol in the arteries.

Saturated fats increase levels of LDL. Polyunsaturated

The Chemistry of Saturated and Unsaturated Fats

Fatty acids are made up of carbon atoms arranged in long chains with hydrogen atoms attached to them. If the fatty acid has no double bonds and is full up with hydrogen, as in the example below, it is called a saturated fatty acid.

```
H   H   H   H   H   H   H
C – C – C – C – C – C – C
H   H   H   H   H   H   H
```

If, on the other hand, a fatty acid has one or more double bond, and so room for more hydrogen atoms, it is called an unsaturated fatty acid. Where there is only one double bond in the chain (see example below) it is called a monounsaturated fatty acid and where there is more than one double bond it is called a polyunsaturated fatty acid.

```
H   H           H   H   H
C – C – C = C – C – C – C
H   H           H   H   H
```

The double bonds in unsaturated fatty acid molecules allow other molecules such as oxygen to be added to the chain. In this case the fat will become rancid. However, these bonds can also be used by the body to add other nutrients which can be carried around the body and used in cell building or other functions.

fats, on the other hand, seem to lower cholesterol generally, but this means that the beneficial HDL is lowered along with the LDL. Monounsaturated fats lower the level of LDL but leave HDL untouched.

Other factors which improve HDL levels are regular

exercise and maintaining ideal body weight, both of which will be equally important for success in your chosen sport. Some studies show that long-distance runners and endurance athletes have naturally elevated levels of HDL and lowered levels of LDL.

Hydrogenated Fat

Food manufacturers have been very quick to exploit the experts' advice and polyunsaturated margarines and shortenings soon followed vegetable oil on to the market. Millions of people have switched from butter to margarine, and lard and suet have had such a bad press that they might almost have been banned.

It now looks as though this change might have been a little premature. The polyunsaturated fats used in these artificial spreads have to be processed by the manufacturer to produce a vegetable fat which is solid at room temperature.

Hydrogen atoms are added to the double bonds of the polyunsaturated fats to convert them into solid (hydrogenated) fats but in the process trans-fatty acids are formed. There is some evidence to show that trans-fatty acids have a similarly undesirable effect on blood cholesterol to that produced by saturated fats. Research is continuing in this area.

PHOSPHOLIPIDS

Lecithin is the best-known phospholipid and egg yolks are the richest source. Lecithin occurs in both plant and animal products. In the former it is usually polyunsaturated and in the latter saturated. It is present in soy beans and is used commercially as a stabilizer and emulsifier.

In the body it is found in blood and in the protective sheath around nerves. The body can also manufacture its own lethicin and so it is not an essential nutrient. Various claims have been made for lecithin, particularly that it has a role in preventing fat gain, but these have not been substantiated.

Vitamins and Minerals

Vitamins and minerals are present in food in minute quantities yet their absence can cause major deficiency symptoms. Medical science is only just beginning to discover exactly how these nutrients work in the body but each discovery points to an important role for them in almost all body functions.

Sports people in particular need to pay attention to eating vitamin- and mineral-rich food. For example, niacin, one of the B-group vitamins, combines with other chemicals in the body to form co-enzymes, and in this form is essential for extracting energy from carbohydrate and fatty foods.

Vitamin D is essential in allowing calcium to be extracted from the small intestine into the bloodstream, and this in turn is very important in muscle contraction as well as in blood-clotting, bone-building and the functioning of the nervous system.

For more information on the major function of vitamins and minerals see the Source Chart on pages 26-31.

Vitamins are organic compounds which are either fat-soluble or water-soluble. Fat-soluble vitamins (A, D, E and K) can be stored in the fatty tissues of the body, but water-soluble vitamins (B-group, C, folic acid, pantothenic acid and biotin) are carried in the circulatory and urinary systems from which they are easily excreted. This means that they need to be supplied every day.

Antioxidants

Vitamin C, vitamin E, beta-carotene (the pigment found in fruit and vegetables which is converted to vitamin A in the body) and

---

selenium (a mineral found in foods such as seafood, meat and grains) are now known to be powerful antioxidants.

Research is increasingly pointing to a very important role for antioxidants in counteracting the effects of free radicals (often groups of oxygen atoms) which attack cell walls and may cause other damage.

Anti-oxidants may also be important in the prevention of both coronary heart disease and cancer. They are also thought to have an important role in strengthening the immune system and fighting infection generally.

Experts disagree on exactly how much of each of the major vitamins and minerals you need to eat. The current recommendations for the UK are given in the Source Charts on pages 26 to 31.

The question of very large doses of certain vitamins is discussed in Section 6.5. However, it is known that too much vitamin A harms the liver and causes blurred vision and headaches. Too much vitamin D can cause kidney stones.

Minerals are inorganic compounds which are divided into macronutrients (of which you need more than 100mg a day) and micronutrients or trace elements (of which you may only need a few micrograms and no more than a few milligrams a day). Incidentally, the quantity of a mineral required does not reflect its importance to the body. Iron, for example, is only required in relatively small quantities but it is an essential nutrient.

Minerals and vitamins are measured in grams (g), milligrams (mg) and micrograms (ug).

1000ug = 1mg   1000mg = 1g

When minerals are dissolved in liquid they are sometimes referred to as electrolytes (Sports Drinks, page 151).

Iron is stored in the liver and calcium is stored in the bones but it is still important to include sufficient quantities of these and other minerals in your daily diet. This is particularly important for athletes in hard training because several minerals work with vitamins to extract energy from food.

Inadequate iron intake results in loss of strength and endurance, easy fatiguability, shortened attention span and loss of visual perception. This kind of lowered haemoglobin level in athletes is known as sports anaemia. Contributing factors are:

- decreased absorption by gut
- increased destruction of red blood cells and excretion through urine through deficiencies in B12, folic acid or iron
- athletes' low energy intake – not eating enough
- natural response to endurance training – increased blood volume for same number of red blood cells
- sweating loss
- menstruation loss

Dietary Fibre

Implementing the current healthy eating guidelines by adding more cereals and fruit and vegetables to the diet will automatically help to increase the amount of fibre you eat, for fibre is contained in the cell walls of plants.

The greatest concentrations of fibre are usually found in the skins of fruit and vegetables and in the outer coating of whole cereals such as wheat and rice. Oats, kidney beans and sweetcorn are particularly rich sources of soluble fibre.

> Foods high in fibre are not necessarily stringy or rough in texture. Even smooth foods like bananas (3g per 100g/3½oz) and avocados (2g per 100g/3½oz) contain some fibre.

Food Sources and Functions of Vitamins

Vitamins	Some food sources	Some functions in the body	Vulner-ability	RNI
Fat Soluble				
Vitamin A (Retinol)	Liver, butter, margarine, cheese canteloup melons, leafy vegetables such as spinach, carrots, yellow fruit, milk eggs, broccoli.	• Maintenance of healthy growth and development. • Maintenance of healthy vision and the ability to adapt to poor light. • Maintenance of healthy cells in the skin, gut and respiratory tract. • Contains antioxidants in the form of beta-carotene.	Air	Men: 700 µg Women: 600 µg
Vitamin D (Calciferol)	Eggs, butter, margarine, fish oil, manufactured by the body in the presence of sunshine.	• Essential to healthy bone and teeth formation. • Aids in the absorption of calcium and phosphorus from the diet.	Light Air	M: – W: –
Vitamin E (Alpha-tocopherol)	Wheatgerm, vegetable oils, peanuts, sunflower seeds, wholegrains, leafy vegetables, eggs, almonds.	• Acts as a natural antioxidant for fatty acids, proteins and vitamins in the body. • Essential for red blood cell production.	Air	M: – W: –

Vitamin	Sources	Function	Destroyed by	RNI
Vitamin K	Liver, meat, soybeans, green leafy vegetables, cauliflower.	• Important in blood clotting. • Important in the functioning of some bone and kidney proteins.		M: – W: –
Water Soluble				
Vitamin C (Ascorbic acid)	Blackcurrants, green peppers, rosehips, watercress, tomatoes, parsley, broccoli, citrus fruits, beansprouts, potatoes, tropical fruit.	• Essential for the healthy growth of cells and connective tissue. • Helps to increase resistance to infection. • Acts as a natural anti-oxidant. • Facilitates the absorption of iron. • Plays a part in wound healing.	Air Water	M: 40 mg W: 40 mg
Vitamin B$_1$ (Thiamin)	Meat (especially pork), yeast, wheatgerm, nuts, all vegetables, oatmeal	• Important in carbohydrate metabolism and energy production. • Maintenance of healthy nervous system, a healthy heart and healthy growth.	Heat Water	M: 1 mg W: 0.8 mg
Vitamin B$_2$ (Riboflavin)	Milk, butter, eggs, organ meats, green leafy vegetables, yeast, bananas.	• Important in fat and protein metabolism and energy production. • Necessary for growth and development. • Concerned with healthy vision.	Water Light	M: 1.3 mg W: 1.1 mg

RNI = Reference Nutrient Intake (see page 35)

Food Sources and Functions of Vitamins

Vitamins	Some food sources	Some functions in the body	Vulner-ability	RNI
Niacin	Meat, liver, fish, peanuts, instant coffee, yeast, watercress, eggs, dried fruit, cheese.	• A vital component of co-enzymes concerned with energy processes. • Helps to improve circulation and maintain proper brain activity.	Water	M: 17 mg W: 13 mg
Pantothenate Acid	Meat, poultry, fish, yeast, egg yolks, peas and beans, yogurt, cereals.	• Plays an important part in the metabolism of carbohydrates, fats and proteins. • Important for increasing resistance to infection and in the proper function of the respiratory system.	Heat Light	M: – W: –
Vitamin B_6 (Pyridoxine)	Most high protein products, yeast, wholegrains, peanuts, eggs, bananas, avocados, milk.	• Aids in both glucose and protein metabolism and energy production. • Maintenance of healthy nervous system. • Important in resistance to infection.	Water	M: 1.4 mg W: 1.2 mg
Vitamin B_{12}	Liver, meat, dairy food, sardines, eggs, soybeans, beansprouts, bananas.	• Important in the formation of genetic material. • Promotes the growth of healthy blood cells. • Relieves muscle fatigue and increases energy. • Important in strengthening the immune system.	Water	M: 1.5 µg W: 1.5 µg

	Some food sources	Some functions in the body		RNI
Folic Acid	Liver, meat, fish, walnuts, carrots, spinach, watercress, orange juice, wholemeal, melon.	• Works with Vitamin B$_{12}$ in the formation of red blood cells. • Essential for the formation of genetic material such as DNA. • Strengthens the body's immune system.	Water Light Heat Air	M: 200 µg W: 200 µg
Biotin	Meat, fish, vegetables, nuts, eggs (also produced by the bacteria in the intestines).	• Important in the metabolism of carbohydrates, fats and proteins. • Plays a role in nerve cell growth and function.		M: – W: –

Food Sources and Functions of Minerals

Minerals	Some food sources	Some functions in the body	RNI
Macronutrient Calcium	Milk, cheese, particularly Stilton, yogurt, pilchards, leafy vegetables.	• Essential for healthy bone structure and teeth formation. • Important in muscle contraction and in the transmission of nerve impulses.	700 mg
Chlorine	Table salt.	• Maintenance of electrolyte and fluid balance.	
Magnesium	Most foods except sugar, fats and convenience foods.	• Involved in the regulation of protein synthesis, muscle contraction and body temperature regulation. • Essential co-factor in most energy production pathways.	

Food Sources and Functions of Minerals

Minerals	Some food sources	Some functions in the body	RNI
Phosphorus	Milk, cheese, poultry, eggs, fish, meat.	• Essential to the normal functioning of B group vitamins. • Important role in the final delivery of energy to all cells including muscles in the form of ATP. • Important in the formation of bones and teeth.	550 mg
Potassium	Abundant in most foods.	• Important in muscle function and nerve transmission. • Plays an important part in carbohydrate and protein metabolism. • Maintenance of body fluids and the acid base balance of the blood.	3500 mg
Sodium	Table salt, soy sauce, seafood, dairy products, yeast spreads.	• Very important co-role with potassium in all functions above. • Important in maintaining constant body water balance.	1600 mg
Micronutrients			
Chromium	Very small amounts in meat and vegetables.	• Functions with insulin to help control glucose metabolism.	
Cobalt	Meat, liver, milk, green vegetables.	• Thought to help anaemia and disorders of the nervous system.	

Copper	Meat, fish, vegetables, Brazil nuts, cocoa.	• Component of many enzymes. • Plays a part in haemoglobin formation.	1.2 mg
Iodine	Seafood.	• Essential for the proper functioning of the thyroid gland and thus the metabolic rate.	140 µg
Iron	Liver, lean red meat, dried apricots, kidney beans, leafy vegetables.	• Essential in red blood cell formation. • Involved in the formation of compounds essential to the transport and utilisation of oxygen.	14.8 mg
Manganese	Wholegrain cereals, nuts, bananas, green leafy vegetables.	• Co-factor in carbohydrate metabolism. • Involved in bone structure and in the activity of the nervous system.	
Molybdenum	Liver, beans and peas, whole grains.	• Component of certain enzymes.	
Selenium	Chicken, fish, canned tuna, wholegrain cereals, molasses, cashew nuts.	• Component of an anti-oxidant enzyme concerned with protecting cells from free radicals of oxygen.	60 µg
Zinc	Meat, liver, eggs, wholegrain products, beans and peas.	• Component of many enzymes. • Aids in healing wounds. • Co-factor in protein and carbohydrate metabolism. • Role in healthy growth.	7.0 mg

It used to be thought that there was only one type of fibre and that it was not digested by the enzymes in the stomach and intestine. In fact, there are two types of dietary fibre, soluble and insoluble.

Soluble fibre *is* partially broken down during digestion. It is thought to be helpful in reducing cholesterol levels in the blood. It combines with cholesterol in food and assists in its elimination from the body. Soluble fibre also delays the uptake of sugar into the blood, allowing a moderate uptake over an extended period of time.

Insoluble fibre assists the passage of foods through the body. It takes up water and acts as a bulking agent in the stomach. It also increases the rate at which food passes through the body and at the same time helps to remove toxic substances, thus helping to prevent diseases of the bowel.

Fibre or NSP?

Experts want to replace the word 'fibre' with the phrase 'non-starch polysaccharides' or NSP. Thus you may find fibre listed as NSP on a food manufacturer's list of ingredients.

Important though fibre is in the diet, you can have too much of a good thing. Some people may experience discomfort in the form of wind if they eat too much fibre, though this is not to be confused with an early reaction to increasing fibre levels from a very low base. The gut should get used to recommended levels.

Too much fibre also appears to reduce the availability of iron, calcium and zinc in food. However, this should not be a problem at normal levels.

Professional sports people in intensive training may also find that a high intake of complex fibre-packed carbohydrate food is just too bulky to eat (see page 94).

Good Sources of Dietary Fibre

Aim to eat at least one or two different items on this list at each meal.

Food	Serving size	Fibre content
Wholemeal pasta	cooked from 75g/3oz dry pasta	9.7g
Baked beans	small tin (130g)	9.5g
Dried apricots	4 halves	6.0g
Porridge	made from 75g/3oz dry oats	5.5g
Bran flakes	1 small bowl (25g/1oz)	5.2g
Muesli mix	4 tablespoons	5.0g
Wholemeal bread	2 slices (50g/2oz)	4.0g
Jacket-baked potato	1 medium (100g/3½oz)	3.5g
Sweetcorn kernels	3 tablespoons	3.4g
Peas (boiled)	3 tablespoons	3.1g
Wheat bran	1 tablespoon	2.5g
Roasted peanuts	1½ tablespoons	2.4g
Orange (peeled)	1 medium (125g/4oz)	2.4g
Brown rice	Cooked from 75g/3oz dry rice	1.5g

Water

Water is usually the forgotten nutrient yet it is as essential as any food. Without it you cease to function. About 60 per cent of your total body weight consists of water. The muscles are 72 per cent water and fat is 20-25 per cent water, so the more muscular you are, the greater your total body-water.

The distribution of the water in the body is usually

described as intracellular – fluid inside the cells – and extracellular – fluid outside the cells such as blood plasma, saliva, eye fluids and so on.

Water is derived not only from the fluids you drink but also from most foods. In addition, water is produced as a result of metabolic reactions in the body.

Water Content of Food	
Food	*Percentage Water*
Milk	88-91 per cent
Fruit and vegetables	75-90 per cent
Meat, fish, eggs	50-75 per cent
Cheese and bread	40 per cent
Flour, cereals and nuts	5-15 per cent
Fats and sugar	0 per cent

Water is lost through urine, through the skin in the form of sweat, via the lungs and in faeces. In normal circumstances the body loses around 2 litres/4 pints of water a day and this needs to be replaced. For more on water balance, dehydration and sports see page 103.

Recommended Daily Amounts
Ideally all the essential nutrients should be included in the diet in the correct proportions. But the problem is that the experts do not agree on exactly what is the right amount for each nutrient. Britain, Germany and the USA have all issued various guidelines but the recommended daily amounts for particular nutrients do not always correspond. Nor do they all cover the complete range of nutrients discussed above.

The World Health Organization (WHO) has published an important document on *Diet, Nutrition and the Prevention of Chronic Diseases*. Its recommendations on proportions of essential nutrients are as follows:

Carbohydrate
55 per cent of the energy value of the diet

Protein 10-15 per cent of the energy value of the diet

Fat 30 per cent of the energy value of the diet

> Japan is one of the few industrialized countries to come near to the WHO targets. The Japanese diet consists of 50 per cent complex carbohydrates and 24 per cent fat. This compares with 27 per cent complex carbohydrate and 42 per cent fat in the UK.

In the UK new Dietary Reference Values (DRV) have been issued to replace the old Recommended Daily Amounts (RDAs). The most useful are Reference Nutrient Intakes (RNIs). These are the amounts which are considered to be sufficient for 97 per cent of the population. They are lower than the RDAs used in the USA. This is partly because the USA sets levels for the entire population.

RNIs for vitamins and minerals are given in the Sources Charts on pages 26 to 31.

Mediterranean Diet

The phrase 'the Mediterranean Diet' is one which frequently crops up when people talk about healthy eating, but what exactly is it?

In fact there is no single Mediterranean diet. Rather, it is a way of eating which is reminiscent of foods typically found in the diets of Southern Europe. Cereals and starchy foods form the basis of the meal – pasta in Italy, rice and potatoes in Spain, bread, rice and cracked wheat in Greece and the Middle East. Fruit and vegetables feature prominently, with plenty of fish and a little meat for interest. The fat is olive oil and garlic is used almost universally.

Population studies in the 1950s showed that people who eat this kind of diet (particularly Southern Italians) were much less likely than people in the rest of Europe to suffer from coronary heart disease and the other ills of the Western world.

Exactly which factor in the diet was giving the protection was not investigated but the diet itself seemed to be important. Since that time the food eaten in the Southern Mediterranean has moved nearer to that in other areas and the incidence of heart disease has started to rise.

2.2 MEAL PLANNING FOR A BALANCED DIET

It is all very well knowing the theory behind the healthy eating guidelines but you do not eat nutrients in the form of protein, fats and carbohydrates, you eat food in the form of meals. So how can you translate the recommendations outlined in 2.1. into everyday eating?

Ideally each meal should contain some of all the essential nutrients and certainly they should all appear on the table at some time during the day. So the first step towards a healthy balanced diet is to eat as wide a range of foods as possible.

Avoid eating the same foods day in, day out, however much you like them, for they may not be providing all the nutrients you need. Incidentally, allergy specialists agree that it is the foods which are eaten every day which are most likely to cause problems.

Thus if you need to increase the amount of complex-carbohydrate foods in your diet, do not just eat more bread or potatoes, use rice, pasta and beans as well and experiment with different cereal foods such as couscous, oats or quinoa (an unusual grain from South America, see page 290).

Supplement this variety of foods with a knowledge of the key components in everyday foods such as bread (carbohydrates, protein, fibre, vitamin E and calcium), butter (saturated fat, vitamins A and minerals), chicken (protein, saturated and polyunsaturated fats and niacin), oranges (fibre, water, vitamin C), and so on. For more information look at the Source Charts in Section 2.1 or buy a copy of the Department of Health booklet, *Dietary Reference Values for Food and Energy and Nutrients for the UK*.

The next step is to plan your meals with the emphasis on fruit, vegetables and cereals, using meat, fish and dairy foods to add interest and fats to add palatability. Suggested menus are given at the end of this section (see pages 50-52).

Food Pyramid

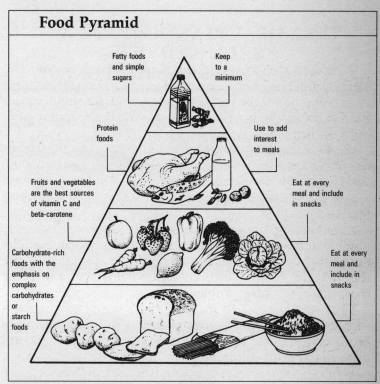

Fatty foods and simple sugars — Keep to a minimum

Protein foods — Use to add interest to meals

Fruits and vegetables are the best sources of vitamin C and beta-carotene — Eat at every meal and include in snacks

Carbohydrate-rich foods with the emphasis on complex carbohydrates or starch foods — Eat at every meal and include in snacks

Choosing Starchy Foods

Few people in the Western world currently eat enough carbohydrate foods or come anywhere near to the 55 per cent of total energy target set by the World Health Organization. The actual figure is nearer 40-45 per cent. When sugar is removed from the calculation this figure falls to 27-32 per cent.

Fibre targets are currently set at 18g per person per day and here again most people fail miserably. The average intake is much lower. In practical terms this means that most people need to eat much more complex-carbohydrate food such as bread, potatoes, rice and pasta.

This, coupled with an increase in the amount of fruit and vegetables, should fill both the energy and the fibre gap. Here are some ways of doing this. There should be no need to add plain wheat bran to food.

12 Ways to Increase Carbohydrate and Fibre

- Add interest to bread-based meals by serving a wide range of different breads. Choose from wholemeal, granary, French bread, Italian ciabatta, pitta bread and Middle Eastern flatbread, Indian naan and chappatis, bagels, crumpets and pikelets, cottage loaves, rye bread and pumpernickel, teabread, teacakes, baps and muffins.
- Slice loaves generously or choose thick-sliced bread.
- Try oatcakes, ricecakes, crispbread, water biscuits and Swedish baked rolls for a change.
- Eat more potatoes in their jackets and try some of the other starchy vegetables such as sweet potatoes, yams and plantains.
- Use potatoes to make potato cakes, tortilla and Rosti (page 323).
- Eat more rice and pasta. Try wholegrain or brown rice, which has an interesting nutty texture – most brands are easier to cook than they used to be.
- Experiment with unusual cereals such as bulgar, couscous, oatmeal, millet and polenta (cornmeal) (see page 288).
- Add lentils, beans and dried peas to soups and casseroles or serve as a side dish.
- Add chopped fresh or dried fruit to your wholegrain breakfast cereal or muesli.
- Make milk-shakes with low-fat milk, yoghurt and bananas.

- Eat apples, pears, bananas or no-soak dried fruits like apricots and prunes if you want a between-meal snack.
- If you bake, use wholemeal products for their fibre content. Keep white flour for sponge cakes, Yorkshire pudding and white sauces.

Take care when applying these ideas to family food. The target of 18g of fibre per day does not apply to children. It is thought that the advantages of fibre are related to body size and so children should be eating proportionately less.

If you are in intensive training and need to eat even more carbohydrate-rich foods see Carbohydrate Loading (page 155) and foods with 5g/2oz of carbohydrate (page 101).

> Forget any idea that starchy foods are fattening. It is the butter on the bread or the sauce on the pasta that will make you fat!

Avoiding Fat

The World Health Organization suggests that fat should provide around 30 per cent of the calories in the diet. In most Western countries the figure is nearer 40 per cent (compare this to Japan where it is only 24 per cent). This means that Westerners need to cut their fat intake by as much as a quarter. This is equivalent to about 2 tablespoons of oil or a match-box size piece of solid fat every day.

Set out below are some ways of doing this. You do not have to follow every one of these suggestions, three or four of them may be sufficient to bring your fat intake into line with the recommendations.

Look at the kinds of fatty food you eat regularly and start by cutting down on these. For example, there is not much point in changing to a low-fat cheese if you only eat cheese once a week. Far better to change from whole milk to low-fat skimmed milk, particularly if you use milk in tea and coffee and on breakfast cereals.

Fat Content of Cream and Yoghurts	
	g/100g
Low-fat yoghurt	1.0
Greek yoghurt	
(strained cows)	9.0
(set cow's)	4.0
(set sheep's)	7.5
Single cream	21.2
Double cream	46.0

Nor do you have to cut particular foods out of the diet altogether. White meat and fish are lower in fat than red meats but this does not mean that you have to avoid your favourite steak completely. Simply restrict that particular choice to once a month or so.

12 Ways to Cut Down on Fat

- Use a low-fat spread rather than butter or margarine *or*, if you prefer not to eat hydrogenated fat (see page 22), spread butter very thinly on bread or toast.
- Dress vegetables with fresh herbs, lemon juice or yoghurt instead of butter.
- Change to semi-skimmed or skimmed milk.
- Eat more fish and poultry.
- When you eat red meat, choose lean cuts and smaller portions and remove all visible fat before cooking. Skim off fat from casseroles, stews and gravy.
- Grill, steam or microwave rather than fry and drain off all excess fat. When necessary use a pastry brush to lubricate with oil rather than pouring oil over.
- Avoid ready-prepared meat products unless they are specifically low-fat. Check the nutritional information on the labels carefully to find out grams of fat per 100g/3½oz or grams of fat per serving.
- Replace cream with plain yoghurt – even the delicious Greek yoghurt has a good deal less fat than cream.
- Cut down on fat in recipes – one tablespoon of oil in a non-stick pan will easily sauté the ingredients for large

soups and casseroles. Take particular care with Chinese stir-fry recipes.

- Replace vinaigrette dressings or mayonnaise with yoghurt- or lemon-based dressings.
- Use lentils, beans and cereals to stretch or substitute for meat in casseroles, pasta sauces and savoury bakes. A good traditional example is chilli con carne.
- Choose low-fat hard cheeses or cottage cheese in place of full-fat cheese. Edam and Camembert are lower in fat than Cheddar or Stilton.

It is the habitually high-fat diet that is the problem, not the occasionally fatty item that is eaten.

Beware Hidden Hazards

In today's busy environment people do not always have the time – or the inclination – to do all their own cooking. As a result ready-prepared convenience foods have grown tremendously in importance. These foods often include a lot of fat, sugar and salt, a fact which can easily be overlooked when calculating the amount of these foods you eat or want to eat.

You can control the amount of fat, sugar and salt you use at the table and in your own cooking but you cannot control what is added to processed food by the manufacturer.

There are also a number of unprocessed foods which do not seem to be very fatty but which do contain quite a high percentage of fat in their make-up.

Here is a list of foods whose hidden ingredients can greatly increase the percentage of fat, sugar and salt in the diet.

Hidden Fat
Naturally fatty:

Hamburgers	Sausages
Olives	Avocados
Tuna	Salmon

Roast and salted peanuts   Peanut butter
Whole milk

Products with a high concentration of added fat:
Crisps and other deep-fried nibbles
Pastries, pasties, and pies
Chocolates and toffees
Cakes and biscuits (variable)
Cheesecake
Fried eggs
Fish and chips
Lemon curd
Dressings and mayonnaise

Hidden Sugar
Some desserts and ice-cream toppings
Sweet pickles and chutneys
Peanut butter
Cider and beer
Sweet wine, sherry and liqueurs
Soft drinks and flavoured mineral waters
Fruit drinks, squashes and cordials

Hidden Salt
Salt is sodium chloride and it is the sodium which needs to be watched. 400mg of sodium is present in 1g of salt and 5g of salt equals one teaspoonful.

Roast and salted nuts
Crisps
Allbran and bran flakes
Bacon
Kippers and other smoked fish
Baked beans
Canned soups
Cheddar cheese
Soy sauce, tomato ketchup, HP and other sauces and condiments
Selzers, antacids and some laxatives

Reading between the Words on Food Labels

Always check the list of ingredients on the labels of ready-prepared or processed foods. The ingredients are in descending weight order.

Words that indicate sugar:

sucrose	honey
glucose	syrup
dextrose	concentrated fruit juice
fructose	hydrogenated glucose syrup
maltose	caramel

Words that indicate fat:
hydrogenated vegetable fat
vegetable oil of various kinds: remember that palm and coconut oil contain far more saturated fat than other vegetable oils
cheese
full-fat milk powder

Words that indicate sodium:
sodium chloride
salt
monosodium glutamate (MSG)
bicarbonate of soda/baking powder

Making the Most of Vitamins and Minerals

Almost all food contains some vitamins and minerals but to make the most of these nutrients they must be eaten as fresh as possible. Vitamin C, for example, starts to disappear from green vegetables as soon as they are picked.

Air, light, heat and water can all have a detrimental effect on vitamin content, so preparation and cooking methods are very important. The water-soluble vitamins will all dissolve into cooking liquids; vitamin B2 and pantothenate are sensitive to light and vitamins B1 and E are affected by heat. Folic acid is particularly sensitive to any kind of treatment. On the whole, minerals are more stable but they too can leach out into cooking liquor.

Eating food raw is the simplest way of maximizing the vitamin content of your food and some people advocate eating one raw-food meal a day. However, this is not always possible and might limit the range of food that you eat. It is probably sufficient to avoid over-processing fruit and vegetables. Add plenty of salads to your menus and serve fresh fruit in place of elaborate desserts.

Vitamin C in Potatoes

Potatoes contain 21g vitamin C per 100g/3½oz when they are dug up in the autumn. By December the quantity has more than halved and by March it will have reduced to a meagre 7g.

Speed is of the essence in preserving vitamins, so peel and chop your vegetables as quickly as possible and eat or cook them at once. Fast cooking methods also help to conserve vitamins. Grilling and stir-frying are both excellent, but beware of using too much fat in stir-frying.

In Chinese restaurants the food is plunged into really hot fat and removed almost at once. It is difficult to achieve the same effect in the domestic kitchen. Instead, try using a single teaspoon of cooking oil in a non-stick wok or frying pan. If the food needs more lubrication use stock, not fat.

Here are some more ideas for conserving vitamins and minerals.

12 Ways to Conserve Vitamins and Minerals
- Choose fresh, firm vegetables. Old and battered ones will contain few vitamins.
- Buy fresh fruit and vegetables regularly. Do not keep them for days on end.
- Scrub rather than peel fruit and vegetables. Very often

the vitamins and minerals are concentrated just under the skin. This is true of both apples and potatoes.

- If you must peel potatoes, do so after they have been cooked rather than before.
- Don't leave fruit or vegetables to stand in rinsing water. Vitamin C and B-group vitamins will dissolve out and be lost.
- Prepare vegetables and fruit just before they are to be eaten or cooked. Vitamins will be lost through the cut surfaces if they are left to stand around.
- Don't discount frozen vegetables – they could be even 'fresher' than fresh vegetables. Manufacturers boast that their produce is frozen the day it is picked. This is rarely true of the vegetables you buy at the supermarket.
- Choose wholegrain products where possible. They contain very many more vitamins and minerals than refined products. White bread is the only exception to this rule as iron, calcium, thiamine and nicotinic acid are replaced by law.
- Do not cook vegetables in large quantities of water. Steaming conserves vitamins and minerals much better. If you do have to boil vegetables keep the liquid to a minimum and reserve the cooking liquor to use in soups, stocks and casseroles.
- Use a microwave oven if you have one to cook anything which might normally be steamed. A microwave is very good for cooking fish and vegetables. Serve the cooking juices with the food.
- Do not keep vegetables warm for too long after cooking or they will start to lose vitamins.
- Wrap meat, fish and vegetables in foil parcels and bake in the oven. This retains both flavour and nutrients. Serve the cooking juices with the food.

To be at their most effective, vitamins and minerals need to be taken in the correct proportion to each other. The B-complex vitamins, for example, seem to act far better together than they do in isolation.

The study of these kinds of relationship is very much in its infancy and precise proportions are unknown, but here are some food and nutrient combinations which could help to enhance your diet. Some of them may be even more important to vegetarians or if you need to enhance your intake of a particular nutrient.

Iron and Vitamin C
Iron from plant sources is more effectively absorbed in the presence of vitamin C.
- Orange juice with iron-enriched breakfast cereals or toast
- Watercress and orange salad
- Grilled liver with broccoli
- Summer pudding (bread and blackcurrants)
- Rice and beans with curly kale or braised cabbage

Vitamin D and Phosphorus and Calcium
This combination is important in bone-building
- Sardines (all three nutrients from one source, provided that you eat the bones)
- Almond Cake (eggs and almonds)
- Cheese soufflé (eggs, milk and cheese)

Folic Acid and Vitamin B12
Folic acid works with vitamin B12 to form red blood cells and protect against anaemia
- Liver (naturally occurring combination)
- Eggs florentine (eggs and spinach)
- Duck and orange salad
- Carrots and spinach with meat dishes

Vitamin B6 and Vitamin B12
Vitamin B6 is necessary for the efficient absorption of vitamin B12
- Most high-protein foods plus eggs and bananas (naturally occurring combination)
- Beansprout and peanut salad
- Liver sausage sandwiches

Phosphorus and B-Group Vitamins

Phosphorus is essential to the functioning of the B-group vitamins

- Milk, eggs and cheese (naturally occurring combination)
- Vegetables with cheese sauce

Vitamins A and E

It is thought that vitamin E may protect against the loss of effectiveness of vitamin A

- Bread and cheese
- Liver sausage sandwiches
- Dried apricot crumble (wheatgerm)
- Carrot and peanut salad

Conversely, some foods can have an adverse effect on each other. For example, oxalic acid in spinach, beetroot and rhubarb can inhibit the absorption of calcium and magnesium by combining with them in the gut and thus rendering them useless to the body.

Phosphorus in nuts, pulses and wholegrain cereals occurs in the form of phytic acid and this can combine with minerals like calcium, iron, zinc and magnesium in the same way as oxalic acid. Soaking pulses like beans and dried peas and old-fashioned bread-making methods which involve leaving the bread to prove decrease the percentage of phosphorus held as phytic acid. The body seems to adapt to the phytic acid in wholegrain cereals and calcium absorption improves.

The Healthy Store Cupboard

The right kind of store cupboard can be extremely useful to the busy sportsman or woman. You should be able to rustle up a quick snack or even a meal without having to go shopping.

Use your store cupboard to augment your daily or weekly fresh food shopping, keeping interesting flavouring ingredients to pep up your everyday cooking.

Basics

- Rice and one or two kinds of dried pasta plus one of the following: bulgar, cracked wheat, couscous, millet, quinoa, buckwheat, polenta or cornmeal, Chinese egg noodles and Japanese noodles. (For cooking instructions see page 242.)
- Plain and wholemeal wheat flour plus one of the following: rice flour, fine oatmeal, potato flour, semolina or ground rice
- Rolled or porridge oats
- Baked beans and red kidney beans plus one of the following: lentils, marrowfat peas, chickpeas, haricot beans, cannellini beans, butter beans, blackeye beans, borlotti beans
- Canned tomatoes and sweetcorn
- Wholegrain crackers, rye crispbread, plain biscuits
- Herbs and spices
- Tomato purée
- Dried skimmed milk powder
- Raisins and dates plus one of the following: dried apricots, prunes, nectarines, bananas, figs
- Selection of frozen vegetables
- Tomato and orange juice

Interesting Flavour Ingredients

- Dried mushrooms and sundried tomatoes
- Olive and vegetable pastes such as artichoke, tapenade or anchoiade
- Pesto, horseradish or cranberry sauces
- Worcestershire sauce or tomato ketchup
- Marmite or other yeast extracts
- Nuts: choose from almonds, hazelnuts, walnuts, pinenuts, brazil nuts
- Seeds: choose from sunflower, sesame and pumpkin
- Canned tuna, salmon and sardines
- Tomato and basil pasta sauces
- Canned anchovies or anchovy essence

Take care with the quantities you decide to store. Foods which are packed in jars or cans will keep in good condition for some time but grains, nuts and seeds do not keep for ever. Their fat content makes them go rancid after a time. Dried beans and peas also go stale. Dried fruit may crystallize or start to deteriorate.

Breakfast, Lunch and Dinner

You do not need to eat three square meals a day to have a well-rounded and healthy diet, but the traditional pattern of breakfast, lunch and dinner probably fulfils the nutritional requirements as well as any. However, there is some disagreement on the relative importance of these meals.

It has been suggested that you should eat like a king at breakfast, a prince at midday and a pauper in the evening. Others advocate a light breakfast and supper, with the main meal at midday. In fact your eating patterns are more likely to be dictated by your lifestyle. Many athletes have to have a meal late in the evening after completing their training.

In this section I have given suggested menus for normal healthy eating, with breakfast, one main meal which can be served in the evening or at lunchtime according to circumstances, and a lighter meal.

Menus for different eating patterns according to training regimes are given in Section 4.1. Ideally, each meal should include, in the same proportions, something from each of the layers in the Food Pyramid on page 37.

Breakfast

Breakfast is an essential meal for everyone, including those trying to lose weight, and skipping it can be one of the worst nutritional mistakes you can make. Going without breakfast leads to loss of concentration in the late morning, a shortfall of energy for lunch-time activities and a feeling of irritability.

Breakfast replenishes the glycogen stores in the liver which may have been used up keeping blood sugar levels constant overnight. Breakfast is even more important when eating a high-energy sports diet (see Section 4.3). Early-morning training may change the time you have breakfast but you still need something before you train and a good meal afterwards.

The quickest and easiest breakfast choice is a bowl of breakfast cereal. Brands of cereal vary quite a lot. Choose a wholegrain cereal with low sugar content. (See pages 198 and 199 for a comparison of the nutritional content of breakfast cereals.)

Certain brands are fortified with some or all of the following nutrients: iron, calcium, vitamin B2 or vitamin B12. If you do not eat red meat, go for extra iron. If you do not drink milk or eat dairy products, go for extra calcium and if you are vegan, go for all of them. Athletes on a high-energy diet may need to include rather less fibre and rather more sugar.

Some experts suggest that you should eat a third of your daily calorie intake for breakfast but this is not very easy if you are in a rush. The following menus offer around 500 calories each.

EVERYDAY HEALTHY BREAKFASTS

Menu 1
Glass of orange juice
Bowl of breakfast cereal
or Swiss Muesli Bowl
(page 200) with skimmed
milk
Banana

Menu 2
Glass of orange juice
2 slices of wholemeal toast
thinly spread with
butter
Apple and mixed dried
fruit and nuts

Menu 3
Glass of orange juice
Bowl of porridge or
cooked oatbran with
skimmed milk and raisins
Indian Toast (page
209)

Menu 4
Glass of orange juice
Bean and Potato Hash
(page 210)
Monterey Muffin (page
207)

MAIN MEALS

The timing of this will depend very much on your lifestyle and training programme.

Menu 1
Tomato soup with crusty bread
Grilled chicken with stir-fried vegetables and boiled potatoes
Mango slices with yoghurt

Menu 2
Minestrone soup with crusty bread
Spaghetti bolognese with green salad dressed with yoghurt
Fruit sorbet with wafer biscuits

Menu 3
Tomatoes Stuffed with Herb Millet (page 241)
Peppered Cod Steaks (page 258) with green vegetables and mashed potatoes
Fresh fruit salad

Menu 4
Tomato salad with minted yoghurt
Austrian Horseradish Lamb (page 266) with Pan-fried Corn and Peppers (page 318) and new potatoes
Banana Walnut Crumble (page 332)

Menu 5
Lentil, Carrot and Watercress Soup (page 237)
Seafood risotto with tomato and green bean salad
Apple fool with shortbread biscuits

Menu 6
Avocado pear with hummus
Mexican Chicken (page 279) with green salad
French Apple Batter Pudding (page 330)

LIGHT MEALS

Use this meal to fill in any nutritional gaps from the main meal of the day. You may feel that you need to add more starchy food or perhaps foods which are rich in vitamin C, calcium or iron.

Menu 1
Jacket-baked Potatoes
(page 227) with ratatouille
or baked bean topping
and a bread roll
Slice of melon

Menu 2
Vegetable soup

Welsh Rarebit

Menu 3
French onion soup with
crusty bread and cheese
Wedge of teabread and a
tangerine

Menu 4
Curried Pasta Salad (page
315) and crunchy salad
Apple, pear and sweet
biscuit
Yoghurt

Menu 5
Tuna salad roll or Pan
Bagnat (page 221)
Banana and dried fruit

Menu 6
Spiced Lentils (page 275)
Fresh fruit salad with
orange juice

2.3 FILLING IN AND EATING OUT

It is not too difficult to eat a balanced diet when you have
time to plan and shop ahead. But when you are pushed
for time or if you are tired and hungry it is easy to let
things slip and grab the nearest food to hand. This frequently means processed or ready-prepared foods which
all too often can have a high fat and sugar content.

Snacks and Rushed Meals

'Grazing' is the word which has been coined to describe
the habitual 'snacker' and this way of eating is becoming
more and more common. The demands of a working
career, family life and a high level of sports activity make it
increasingly difficult to sit down to regular meals, and a
series of snacks and light meals is much easier to manage.

Some sports people have very small appetites and cannot eat as much as they need to support the energy requirements of their sport. Snacking between meals is a sensible way of filling in the gaps.

Snacking is not a problem if you make wise choices. Obviously a day's snacking on bacon sandwiches for breakfast, chocolate biscuits mid-morning, a cheese croissant or a doughnut for lunch, meat pie and chips or French fries in the evening, with crisps and salted peanuts to fill in the gaps, will give you far too much fat and sugar and too few vitamins and minerals.

But if, instead, the choice is a handful of mixed dried fruits and raisins with a banana and milk for breakfast, an apple muffin mid-morning, pitta parcels with tuna and salad at lunchtime, baked potatoes with chilli for dinner and unlimited plain yoghurt and fruit to fill in, most of your nutritional requirements will have been met.

Wise choices include many nutritious and conveniently available foods. Choose from:

12 Healthy Snacks

- Banana, oranges, apples and pears, or any fresh fruit
- Make up your own dried fruit and nut mix, with the emphasis on the fruit, and nibble when you need it
- Tubs of plain yoghurt – add your own chopped fruit if you prefer flavoured
- Homemade biscuits, cookies, buns or muffins made with wholegrains. If stall- or store-bought, choose bran or corn muffins
- Make up your own mix of unsalted nuts, adding seeds like sunflower and pumpkin to taste
- Milk-shakes with fresh fruit
- Raw vegetables such as cherry tomatoes, small cucumbers and baby carrots
- Thermos flask of soup made with dried peas or beans
- Crackers and crispbreads – develop a taste for them without spreads or, if you must, add a low-fat spread
- Homemade Date and Pistachio Halva (page 344) or sesame bars.

- Wedges of homemade Banana Teabread (page 338) or Dutch Pepper Loaf (page 226)
- 175ml/6floz apple, orange or grape juice

12 Healthy Rushed Meals
- American club sandwiches
- Jacket-baked Potatoes with a tasty topping (page 227) (a microwave oven makes these a very quick meal)
- Frozen pizza bases with your own toppings
- Frozen pre-cooked savoury rice, stir-fried with diced cooked chicken
- Corn on the cob with your own toppings
- Pitta bread parcels filled with salad and low-fat cottage cheese, flaked tuna, falafel or feta cheese
- Chinese egg noodles with stir-fried chicken and vegetables
- Grated potato Rosti (page 323)
- Cheese, beans, and eggs on toast, crumpets or oatcakes
- Taco or tostada shells filled with chilli and salad
- Pre-prepared rice and pasta based salads stored in the fridge
- Japanese buckwheat noodles (soba) with miso broth and vegetables

Eating Out – The Healthy and Unhealthy Options

Some people have to eat in restaurants because they spend a good deal of time away from home or because they are travelling to or from a sports venue. Others just like to eat out.

The odd meal out does not really pose any problems unless you are on a strict training regime (see pages 178-181), but if you do eat away from home on a regular basis you may have to take a close look at just what you are eating.

Many restaurants specialize in the kind of food you are unlikely to cook at home, and however tempting, it may well be much too high in fat and too low in complex carbohydrates. So try to choose restaurants which offer more wholesome simple foods, such as vegetarian and health food restaurants.

Once in the restaurant, avoid choosing dishes just because they appeal to you, think about the composition of the main ingredients and how they are cooked. Keep the following foods in mind when looking at the menu and ordering your meal:

Soup: Go for vegetable soups like minestrone, mixed vegetables, pea, leek and potato and mushroom or broth-based soups like consommé, chicken vermicelli, Chinese wonton soup and crab and sweetcorn soup. Avoid bisques and cream soups.

Appetizers: Choose melon, fruit cocktails, tomato juice, light salads (with the dressing on the side for you to add yourself), grilled grapefruit, marinated (not deep-fried) mushrooms or grilled vegetables or prawns.

Seafood, poultry and meat dishes: The plainer the better – avoid rich sauces and butters and ask for gravy on the side. Choose grilled, steamed or poached fish or poultry rather than fried meats, duck or sausages. If you like to have a steak when you are dining out, choose a lean fillet or trim all the fat from a rump or entrecote steak.

Potatoes: Go for baked potatoes, preferably with very little butter or soured cream, or boiled potatoes in their skins.

Pasta: Choose tomato-based sauces rather than cream- or cheese-based ones.

Vegetables and salads: Request plain unbuttered vegetables and undressed salads. Pour on your own oil and vinegar and avoid mayonnaise. Some restaurants now offer yoghurt-based dressings.

Bread: Ask for extra, but eat it plain.

Desserts: Choose fresh fruit, fresh fruit salad or sorbet.

Water: Request a jug or a bottle at the table and drink as much as you like.

Fast Food

If you eat out a lot, this may be more often in a fast food restaurant, café or pub than in a regular restaurant. Unfortunately, the convenience aspect of fast food is outweighed by the fact that most of the dishes are loaded with fat – usually saturated fat – and what few carbohydrates there are are usually in the form of sugar.

> A typical purchase of a large hamburger, French fries and a shake contains over 1300 calories, of which 45 per cent are from the fat.

Fast foods generally lack fibre and are low in vitamins, especially A and C. This can sometimes be offset by the salad bar but these are not usually all that much to write home about as the cut vegetables lose vitamin value as they are exposed to air, light and heat while they sit on the bar. In addition, the dressings can add as much as another 400 calories!

Salt is another hazard. One large burger and French fries can contain as much as 1100mg of salt, around half the recommended daily amount. The drinks on offer, usually sugar-laden soft drinks or fat-filled milk-shakes, present their own problems.

The trouble with all of this is not that any of the dishes will harm you but that you will be left with the problem of filling in the nutritional gaps left by the meal. Finding highly nutritious low-fat foods for the remaining meals of the day could be difficult, particularly as you have already used up at least half your calorie allowance. The likelihood is that at the end of the day you will be lacking some essential nutrients and you will not have come anywhere near your carbohydrate targets.

The Highest-fat Foods

	proportion of calories from fat content
Jumbo sausages	75 per cent
Individual pork pie	65 per cent
Chinese spare-ribs in sauce	64 per cent
Scotch egg	61 per cent
Middle Eastern doner kebab	59 per cent
Kentucky fried chicken	58 per cent
Indian lamb curry	58 per cent
Meat pasty (175g/6oz)	56 per cent
Large burger and bun	54 per cent
Fried fish (cod) and chips	48 per cent
Chinese sweet and sour chicken and fried rice	46 per cent

If you have to eat a fast-food meal, here are 12 ways to increase the carbohydrate content and decrease the fat.

- Order a second bun with your burger. Replace the fat-filled base of the hamburger bun with half of the extra bun and discard the greasy base. Eat the other extra half plain.
- Remove all the coating and the skin from fried chicken and just eat the meat. Order extra rolls for more carbohydrate.
- Choose grilled fish in the fish and chip restaurant and replace chips with mushy peas and bread.
- If possible, stick to the salad bar, with chilli and baked potatoes. Go easy on the salad dressings.
- Choose either deep-pan or thin and crispy pizzas but be careful with the toppings. Order extra vegetable toppings such as peppers, mushrooms and sweetcorn rather than extra cheese, pepperoni or sausage. Avoid the garlic bread!
- Take care with your choice of toppings for baked

potatoes. Choose chilli, ratatouille, baked beans or yoghurt mixed with lean ham and corn rather than creamy cheese toppings.

- Choose shish kebab or skewered lamb in pitta bread in preference to doner kebabs. Ask for extra salad.
- Go for chilli or macaroni cheese in the pub rather than sausages or steak pie. Ask for extra potatoes, boiled – not chips!
- Choose a ploughman's platter at the pub with Edam or Brie and leave the butter. Ask for extra tomatoes.
- Request sandwiches that put the emphasis on the bread rather than the filling. Refuse mayonnaise and moisten the sandwich with diced tomatoes or cucumber.
- Choose iced buns or muffins at tea time rather than cream cakes or pastries.
- When in real difficulties look for a 'breakfast-all-day' menu and choose boiled, poached or scrambled eggs with plenty of toast or pancakes.

Drinks

Water is *the* ideal drink but it is certainly not an interesting one. In some areas it has been cleaned to such an extent that it tastes strongly of chlorine. As a result people have turned to mineral waters, fruit juices and soft drinks, coffee and tea and, of course, alcohol to quench their thirst.

Mineral Water
Over the years mineral water has become a generic term for all bottled water. However, not all bottled water is natural mineral water, it may just be bottled mains water – albeit an even cleaner version of what comes out of the tap.

In Europe natural mineral water must, by law, come from an officially recognized source that is protected from all risk of pollution and be bottled at this source. It must not undergo any treatment other than that necessary to remove particles. It must contain naturally occurring minerals and there must be a typical mineral analysis printed on the label or available on request.

If a water is labelled 'natural spring water' it must come from an underground source that flows naturally to the surface but it does not have to meet the same stringent criteria as mineral waters. It is, of course, thoroughly clean because it is treated to be so.

Some water is carbonated to make it sparkle. This is done by adding carbon dioxide to the water. Natural mineral water may have a little fizziness from carbon dioxide naturally dissolved in it but even this needs to be enhanced to get real bubbles.

In the past the high mineral content of some mineral waters like Apollinaris, Ramlosa and Vichy was considered to be very beneficial to health, and some important health spas grew up on the basis of their spring waters. Today the pendulum has swung the other way and waters with the lowest mineral content like Volvic are those which are recommended.

It was thought that the bubbles in fizzy water helped to empty the stomach more quickly but this has not been substantiated. So most sports people choose their bottled water for the taste and in line with their preference for fizz or no fizz. Watch out for the fact that many flavoured mineral waters contain sugar.

Fruit Juice and Soft Drinks

Pure fruit juice offers a good source of liquid with simple carbohydrates, vitamin C and potassium. They are a very useful adjunct to the diet both at breakfast, particularly as they will aid in the absorption of iron if you have chosen an iron-fortified cereal, and as a between-meal snack. If the flavour is too concentrated to drink in quantity, simply dilute the juice with water.

Pure fruit juice must by law contain 100 per cent juice with no peel or seeds. Long-life juice is the most popular. It has a shelf-life of three to four months. Chilled short-life juice has a far better taste but it must be drunk within eight to ten days of purchase. But best of all is freshly squeezed juice. This has a very short life – ideally it should be drunk as soon as it is squeezed – but you cannot beat it for flavour and texture.

Take care not to confuse fruit juices with fruit drinks. These include squashes and high-juice squashes, cordials and whole-fruit drinks. The latter contain the whole fruit, pith, pips and peel, very, very finely ground.

Percentage fruit content of 'fruit' drinks	
Pure fruit juice	100 per cent juice
High-juice squash	45 per cent juice
Fruit squash	25 per cent juice
Cordials	25 per cent juice
Whole-fruit drinks	5-10 per cent juice

Most of these drinks contain added sugar and in cordials, at least, the sugar content can be very high. A few contain added vitamin C. Most squashes contain sulphur dioxide to preserve the fruit and allow a reasonable time to use the product once it has been opened.

Sugar is the problem with most of the popular soft drinks. A 330ml/11floz can of cola contains the equivalent of eight lumps of sugar and appreciable amounts of caffeine, although some manufacturers produce caffeine-free cola. Except for vitamin C- and vitamin E-enriched drinks, there are no other nutrients in most soft drinks.

With diet soft drinks the sugar problem is avoided but the artificial sweeteners used in its place may be even more detrimental. This is a controversial area (see page 110).

Coffee and Tea
Some people say that they cannot survive without their regular cups of coffee. Others never drink the stuff, consuming copious cups of tea instead. Others avoid both.

Coffee, like tea and cola, contains the stimulant caffeine. Many research studies have attempted to link coffee or caffeine with increased risk of the various modern diseases. So far, there are no confirmed correlations. Indeed, one report seems to indicate that coffee drinkers are in a better position than non-coffee drinkers.

However, drinking tea or coffee can interfere with the absorption of iron and that could be a problem for anaemic sports people. But if you drink the coffee an hour or more before eating, the effect disappears.

Pregnant and nursing mothers and ulcer patients seem to be the only people who normally need to take care with drinks containing caffeine. If you are healthy, a moderate amount of coffee (say one or two cups a day) is unlikely to harm you.

It is not a good idea, though, to use coffee instead of food or to keep yourself alert. Some fresh air and a quick walk or a good night's sleep will be much more effective.

If you are in strict training it might be worth changing to de-caffeinated coffee or limiting your intake for a while. Caffeine can act as a diuretic and if you are drinking coffee to replace water lost from the body this effect could defeat the object.

Caffeine is also a substance banned by the International Olympics Committee (IOC) and care needs to be taken before a sporting event. However, the limit is set at the equivalent of around six to eight cups of coffee taken within two to three hours of the event (see page 169).

Alcohol

Experts are divided in their opinons on the merits or otherwise of alcoholic drinks but they all agree that taken in moderation alcohol is enjoyable and not damaging to the health. But the key word is MODERATION.

To the UK medical profession, moderation means no more than 14 units (more of these later) per week for women and no more than 21 units for men. To French doctors and some American researchers it means as many as five units a day or 35 units per week. To the sports person it may mean as little as two or three units a week or total abstinence during intensive training and competition.

Of course you do not drink units of alcohol, you drink beer, wine, aperitifs, gin and whisky according to your taste or to suit the mood of the occasion. Units of alcohol are simply a convenient way of measuring and comparing the amount of alcohol in each of these various drinks.

The diagram below shows one unit of alcohol in terms of popular drinks.

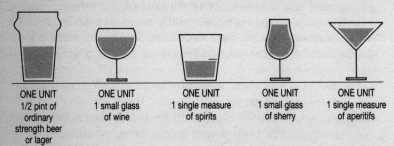

| ONE UNIT | ONE UNIT | ONE UNIT | ONE UNIT | ONE UNIT |
| 1/2 pint of ordinary strength beer or lager | 1 small glass of wine | 1 single measure of spirits | 1 small glass of sherry | 1 single measure of aperitifs |

One unit equals 10ml or 8g of alcohol. So large glasses of wine and half-pints of cider contain one and a half units of alcohol.

The UK guidelines represent the current thinking on safe drinking; they are not sacrosanct limits above which you will start to harm yourself. Indeed there is increasing evidence to show that this level of alcohol is positively beneficial and that even those who, like the French, might drink five units a day are just as healthy, if not healthier than teetotallers.

Of course people vary in their capacity to tolerate alcohol and body weight is an important factor. Indeed French doctors work on body weight and offer one gram of alcohol per kilogram of body weight per day so that you can work out for yourself how much you can safely drink.

For sports people, it is not sufficient just to consider the effect of the alcohol in drinks. The calorie content and its potential effect on weight, the fact that these calories cannot be used in providing energy and the dehydrating effect of alcohol are all vitally important. Thus the decision whether or not to have a drink will be a much more complex one for athletes.

> Always drink the same volume of water as alcohol when you have a drink. This helps to avoid dehydration.

When looking at the calorie content of different drinks, remember that it is the alcohol which is providing the majority of the calories in the drink, not the sugar. Thus a medium-sweet German wine with an alcoholic content of 8 per cent by volume will generate fewer calories than a strong but dry red wine from Spain or Portugal which may have an alcoholic content of 13.5 per cent. Of course, really sweet wines, such as Asti Spumante, *will* have added calories from the sugar.

Alcoholic drinks may provide a psychological boost but they do not offer very much in the way of nutrients. At best, a glass of red or white wine contains about 10-15 per cent of the iron you need in a day, and half a pint of light ale will provide about 7 per cent of two B vitamins – riboflavin and nicotinic acid. And that's about it!

However much or however little you decide is the correct amount of alcohol for you and your training programme, it makes a difference when and how you drink it. Food is an important factor in slowing absorption of alcohol. Drink on an empty stomach and you will soon feel the effects. Metabolic rate is also important, which means that women, with their naturally slower rate, cannot tolerate as much alcohol as men.

People often underestimate the amount of time that it takes the body to process alcohol. On average it takes at least one hour for the liver to reduce blood alcohol by 15g/100ml. So if you go to a party and drink five or six glasses of wine, blood alcohol will rise to about 150mg/100ml or 70g above the legal limit and it will take nearly five hours to fall back to that limit and longer to clear the blood completely.

Because it takes so long for blood alcohol levels to fall, it is easy for someone who has a couple of drinks at lunchtime and another after work to go over the limit for driving.

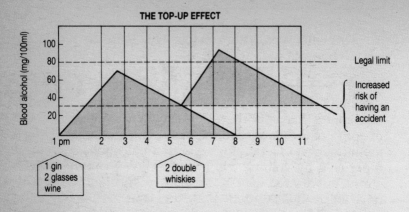

THE TOP-UP EFFECT

Blood alcohol (mg/100ml)

Legal limit

Increased risk of having an accident

1 pm 2 3 4 5 6 7 8 9 10 11

1 gin 2 glasses wine

2 double whiskies

Alcohol is a diuretic, which means that it stimulates the body to produce more urine and you start to become dehydrated. The sensible course, therefore, is to keep alcohol to an absolute minimum when you are in serious training, perhaps allowing yourself a drink on a rest day or on a special occasion. Even small amounts of alcohol can cause the body to dehydrate, and the last thing you want is to be in a dehydrated state when training or on the big day.

Indeed, if you regularly train in the mornings it would be sensible not to drink the night before. If you do, you could start training in a dehydrated condition. In addition, the liver's capacity to maintain blood sugar levels after consuming alcohol is severely limited. Training with a hangover can precipitate hypoglycaemia.

Do not make the mistake, either, of rushing off after an event to have a few pints, even if you want to celebrate or drown your sorrows. If you are already in a state of dehydration it does not seem very logical to drink and make matters worse.

Make your first drink a long, cool, non-alcoholic one. Then, if you want, have a lager or two. Lager or beer is a better choice than wine or spirits because it has a lower ration of alcohol to liquid. But take care with some of the new lagers coming on to the market – they can be very strong indeed.

3
THE SCIENCE OF EATING FOR SPORTS SUCCESS

Whether you are attending dance class, going to the gym, cycling to work or playing squash, you require a great deal of energy. You will need even more if you are to attain your full potential. This is true for both recreational and world-class sport.

3.1 FOOD AND ENERGY

The food that you eat is the sole source of this energy. To get the best performance from yourself you need to understand how food and energy are linked.

Energy is measured in kilojoules and the pre-metric term calories (more commonly known in science as kilocalories). In scientific terms a kilojoule/kilocalorie (kcal) is the amount of heat or energy necessary to raise the temperature of 1000g of water through 1°C.

Different food types vary in their energy output. The body can extract:

4kcals per gram from carbohydrates
4kcals per gram from protein
9kcals per gram from fats
7kcals per gram from alcohol

The rate at which the extraction takes place varies from person to person and from moment to moment.

Converting Food to Nutrients

The food you put into your mouth does not go to work directly. First it must be broken down into its component nutrients. The digestive system acts as a processing plant, breaking down complex foods into much simpler molecules which the body can then absorb and use for body-building and renewal and for producing energy.

During digestion nutrients are broken down into simpler substances called substrates:

- Carbohydrates are converted to monosaccharides (glucose, fructose and galactose)
- Proteins are converted to amino-acids
- Fats are converted to fatty acids and glycerol
- Vitamins and minerals remain unchanged

The digestive process begins in the mouth. The food is broken up by chewing and is mixed with enzymes (substances which do not themselves change but which make chemical processes more efficient) contained in the saliva.

Once the food is swallowed it passes down the oesophagus to the stomach. Here it is mixed with the gastric juices and the whole mixture is churned to a thin acidic liquid. Very little is absorbed through the stomach wall. The notable exceptions are alcohol and fast-absorbing drugs such as aspirin.

Knowledge of the amount of time food remains in the stomach can be very important to the sports person. High-fat meals take longer to leave than light carbohydrate snacks and this will obviously affect a pre-event eating pattern.

The general rule of thumb is to allow:

- Three to four hours for a large meal to leave the stomach
- Two to three hours for a smaller meal
- An hour of so for a snack

However, these are very individual decisions. You may

well experience a difference depending on whether you are about to train or to compete. The psychological effect of 'competition nerves' can have a very real impact on the stomach!

The sports you are taking part in can also affect the amount of time you leave between eating and exercising. For example, racing cyclists can manage to eat quite close to high-intensity exercise.

But by and large your aim is to have your stomach as empty as possible before you start exercising. This is because blood is diverted to your muscles during the intensive exercise and away from the stomach. The digestive process slows down and any food left in the stomach will feel uncomfortable. This will be more of a problem in some sports than others. Runners and boxers can feel the effects particularly.

Liquid foods leave the stomach faster than solid food. Some sportsmen and women find that liquefied meals are useful before an event.

From the stomach the digesting liquids move through the first section of the small intestine. This is called the duodenum and it is one of the most active of the digestive organs. Bile from the liver starts to work on the fats and pancreatic juices from the pancreas and intestinal juices from the wall of the duodenum itself continue the process of reducing carbohydrates and proteins to forms which can be absorbed into the body.

Little absorption takes place in the duodenum itself. This role is reserved for the very long small intestine. Here substrates are absorbed into the bloodstream. By the time the contents of the stomach have passed through the small intestine and into the colon, absorption is largely complete. Water and minerals are extracted in the colon and the waste is then eliminated.

> There is an amazing 3000 square feet of absorbent surface in the gut – almost the size of a baseball court.

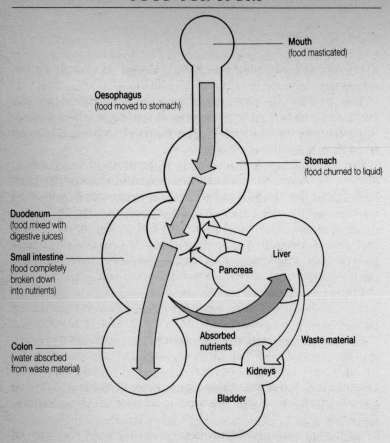

Mouth
(food masticated)

Oesophagus
(food moved to stomach)

Stomach
(food churned to liquid)

Duodenum
(food mixed with
digestive juices)

Small intestine
(food completely
broken down
into nutrients)

Liver

Pancreas

Colon
(water absorbed
from waste material)

Absorbed
nutrients

Waste material

Kidneys

Bladder

All the substrates which are used in the production of energy pass through the liver. Some of the glucose, probably the most important nutrient as far as energy is concerned, is immediately circulated round the body. The rest is stored in the liver and skeletal muscles as glycogen.

When energy is required, glycogen is released into the bloodstream in the form of blood sugar. The blood-sugar level is never allowed to drop too low as the brain and nerves need a constant supply to function properly.

The digestive system is very efficient and around 95 per cent of all nutrients are absorbed. However, travellers' diarrhoea, gastric infections and dehydration can cause poor absorption of nutrients.

Energy Systems

The human body releases energy stored in carbohydrate, fat and protein through an oxidation process which is made possible by intricate enzyme activity in the muscle cells. During this process energy is converted into adenosine triphosphate (ATP). ATP is the body's fuel. It is used for all energy-requiring systems.

For example, when a muscle is contracted, ATP molecules are broken down to release some of the energy contained in the bonds which hold them together. This energy is then used to work the muscle (see page 71).

Comparatively little ATP is present in the body at any one time, probably only sufficient to sustain vigorous exercise for a few seconds. During sustained exercise the body has to break down substrates continually to produce more ATP.

The body can produce energy via ATP in a number of different ways. These are usually classified as aerobic (in the presence of oxygen) and anaerobic (without oxygen).

When a molecule of glucose from muscle glycogen is broken down in the presence of oxygen, it yields 38 molecules of ATP. But this takes some time to achieve. One of the by-products of this reaction is adenosine diphosphate (ADP).

Glycogen can also be broken down without the help of oxygen. This yields far less ATP – only two molecules – but it provides a very rapid source of energy. This kind of anaerobic energy production cannot be sustained for very long.

Anaerobic energy production works in two ways. First, creatine phosphate (another energy-producing molecule which is stored in muscle cells) reacts with ADP (from previous aerobic energy production) to produce more ATP. This is a very fast energy-production system but it can only last for a few seconds. It is known as the CP system.

The second system is the lactic acid system and this can operate for up to one to two minutes of muscle activity. Lactic acid is produced when muscle glycogen or glucose

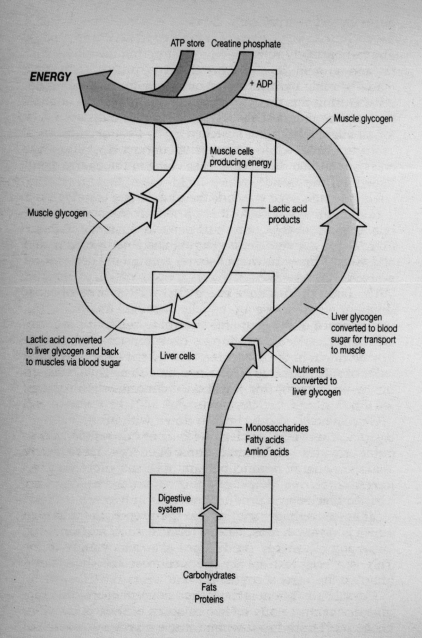

is processed anaerobically. Some of it is transferred via the blood to the liver, where it is converted back into glucose for use again.

During periods of high-intensity exercise such as a single throw, a jump or a 20-metre sprint, the body must be able to produce energy from several pathways in order to meet the requirement. The small amount of stored ATP is used first. This is then backed up by the anaerobic creatine phosphate (CP) system. When the creatine phosphate store runs out, ATP must be generated from the other energy systems.

Lactic acid is not only produced during anaerobic exercise. It is also produced during low-intensity aerobic exercise such as easy jogging or brisk walking. In this instance it is either converted into pyruvic acid on the spot and then into ATP – provided there is enough oxygen around – or it is transported to the liver for conversion to glucose. This constant clearance keeps the muscles free of lactic acid.

As the intensity of exercise starts to build up, the production of lactic acid follows suit. After a period of time the body will be unable to deal with all the lactic acid and it will start to build up in the muscle. Once that build-up reaches a certain point, it will start to interfere with energy production and muscle movement and the exercise will have to stop.

A short rest or even just a slowing of this activity allows more oxygen to become available. This immediately allows the lactic acid to be removed and exercising can continue. Such a slow-down is often known as 'repaying the oxygen debt'.

There is considerable interplay between the different energy systems, but certain sports such as jumping, throwing, downhill skiing, sprinting and weight-lifting rely very much more on the anaerobic energy systems than on the aerobic systems.

Conversely, the aerobic system is what keeps the long-distance runner and endurance-sports people going. (See Sports and their Predominant Energy Systems, page 73.)

Energy Systems I			
	Anaerobic		**Aerobic**
	CP System	*Lactic Acid*	
Rate of energy production	Very rapid	Fast	Slow
Nutrient used	None (Stored ATP is used first then creatine phosphate)	Muscle glycogen (from blood glucose and carbo-hydrates)	Fats Carbo-hydrates plus small amount Protein
Duration of maximum exercise that can be sustained	up to 10 seconds	30 seconds to 30 minutes depending on degree of effort	Hours (virtually unlimited)

However, anaerobic systems are not totally confined to short-duration high-intensity events. They have a very important role to play in mixed demand sports which are 40-60 per cent anaerobic, such as hockey or lacrosse. The anaerobic system may also be used to 'buy time' for the slower-starting aerobic system at the start of a match or a long run which would normally be classed as aerobic.

The anaerobic system may also cut in to assist with energy production when the energy requirement momentarily exceeds the aerobic capacity, for example when a long-distance cyclist is confronted with having to maintain the pace when climbing a hill or when a footballer or rugby player makes a break with the ball.

Sports and their Predominant Energy Systems

During maximum exercise, all systems are used together but one system is often predominant.

	Anaerobic	Aerobic
Aerobics		*
Badminton	*	
Baseball	*	
Basketball	*	
Bowling	*	
Boxing	*	
Canoeing	*	*
Climbing and mountaineering	*	*
Cricket	*	
Cross-country running		*
Cross-country skiing		*
Cycling	*	*
Dance class		*
Diving	*	
Downhill skiing	*	
Fencing	*	
Field events	*	
Field hockey	*	*
Football	*	*
Golf	*	*
Gymnastics	*	
Holiday skiing	*	*
Ice hockey	*	
Jogging		*
Judo	*	
Karate	*	
Keep fit classes		*

Lacrosse	*	
Marathon		*
Recreational swimming		*
Riding, eventing and show jumping		*
Rowing	*	*
Rugby	*	*
Sailing	*	
Squash	*	
Swimming	*	*
Table tennis		
Tennis		
Track running: 100, 200, 440 yards	*	
Track running: 880 yards	*	
1 mile	*	*
Track running: 2 miles	*	*
3 miles	*	*
Volleyball	*	
Walking for pleasure		*
Weight lifting – training	*	
– serious	*	

In some events the predominant energy system will vary, depending on the precise nature of the event. For example, in cycling and swimming there are both sprint and endurance events.

How Muscles Work

Muscles contain thousands of long strands or fibres which are made up of a mixture of thick myocin filaments and thin actin filaments. (Myocin and actin are both proteins which are able to expand and contract.) Muscles shorten and produce movement when the filaments slide across each other.

This sliding is achieved by tiny cross-bridges that extend between the two types of filament. Movement in one location is added to that produced further along the length of the fibre and visible motion takes place. Muscle fibres contract at the command of branched motor nerves.

There are three main types of muscle fibre – slow-twitch, fast-twitch and an intermediate between the two. Differences include:

- speed of control
- resistance to fatigue
- metabolic character

The slow-twitch fibres contract slowly and are slow to fatigue. They have a very rich blood supply and so are very well furnished with the means to keep going during endurance sports. Fast-twitch fibres are fast-contracting and some have a high anaerobic capacity but they are easily fatigued. The intermediate fibres are fast to contract, relatively fatigue-resistant and have a high oxidative and glycolytic capacity.

The way in which the different fibres are called into action generally follows a hierarchical sequence, strarting with the slow-twitch fibres, then the intermittent fibres, and finally the fast-twitch fibres. The speed of movement affects the type of fibres used and the order in which they are used. So too does the force necessary to perform the movement. For example, for rapid lifting of a very light weight the slow-twitch fibres may be the only fibres activiated, while all the muscle fibres will be used for lifting a very heavy weight which has to be moved slowly.

The ratio of slow-twitch to fast-twitch fibres in any individual is inherited and constant. The predominant type is an important factor in success in particular sports and people tend to gravitate towards the sport which they are better at. World-class distance runners and cross-country skiers are usually found to have more slow-twitch fibres. Weight lifters and sprinters tend to have more fast-twitch fibres.

Nutrients and Energy

To work the muscle fibres during exercise you need energy, and the harder the exercise the more energy you need. This energy is provided by the aerobic and anaerobic energy systems outlined on pages 69-74.

Carbohydrate in the form of muscle glycogen and glucose is the only nutrient used in the anaerobic energy system. However, all three nutrients (carbohydrates, fats and proteins) can be used in the aerobic energy system and there is considerable interplay between the ways they are used. Which one is predominant depends upon the rate and duration of the exercise and on the relative availability of each nutrient.

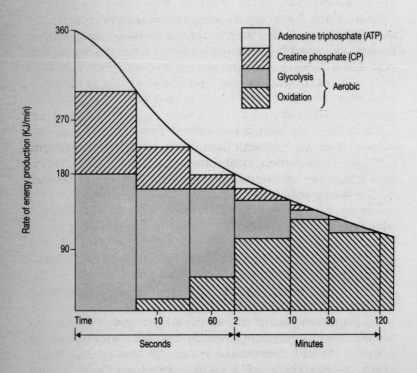

Maximum Exercise for Different Durations Showing Inter-relationship of Energy Systems.

The average person has more than 60 times as much energy stored as fat as he or she has stored as carbohydrate in the muscles and liver in the form of glycogen. It would make sense, therefore, for the body to use up the fat first. But carbohydrates and fats need different amounts of oxygen to release their energy. Much more oxygen is required to metabolize fat than carbohydrate. This makes it a very slow source of energy.

As long as the demand for oxygen does not exceed the amount which can be inhaled, the body will try to conserve the limited amount of energy from the precious store of muscle glycogen and use some of the fat stores. This is what usually happens during comfortable walking, swimming and jogging.

This also holds good during endurance sports such as long-distance cycling, marathon running and cross-country skiing. These activiites cannot be sustained when the stores of glycogen in the exercising muscles run down. The body seems to sense this and uses body fat as much as possible.

As exercise increases in intensity, oxygen is used up more quickly and so the body tends to switch to using its carbohydrate stores (with their lower oxygen requirement and faster conversion rate) for energy instead of fat. Ultimately demand becomes so great that it can only be met by the anaerobic pathways.

Stamina and Strength

The body's energy stores are the link between diet and performance. Most studies agree that the amount of glycogen stored in the muscles before an event is one of the most important limiting factors in performance. The other limiting factor is dehydration (see page 104).

Your glycogen stores determine how long you can go on. When glycogen stores run out you will usually have to slow up. This is sometimes known as 'hitting the wall'. You feel overwhelmingly tired and yearn to quit. Long-distance and endurance-sports people train to put this point off as long as possible.

Glycogen Stores

The average 64-kg/140-lb man has about 530g of carbohydrate stored in his liver, muscles and blood in approximately the following distribution:

Muscle glycogen 450g
Liver glycogen 7g
Blood sugar 10g

In this example there is enough glycogen stored to fuel a 12-mile-plus run.

Increasing the amount of carbohydrates in the diet increases the initial glycogen stores and thus enhances performance. This is particularly important in swimming, long-distance running, soccer and basketball or indeed any sport lasting more than one hour. It is also very important in training.

Studies in the USA have shown that athletes consuming diets offering 40 per cent energy from carbohydrates (the average US and UK diet) failed to recover properly between daily endurance exercise sessions. After three days their glycogen stores were almost depleted. When the diet was changed and carbohydrates increased, glycogen levels recovered in time for the next day's sessions. Experts now recommend a diet containing at least 55 per cent carbohydrates for general training.

Training itself helps sports people to become extremely energy-efficient. They are able to use more fat and spare glycogen. This is because training has a beneficial effect on the capacity of the muscle cells to use fat and to store glycogen.

Aerobic training at sub-maximal levels leads to muscles developing an increased capacity to use fat. Obviously, this is very useful in enabling you to go on for longer before using up your glycogen stores. In addition, the biological changes which occur during training enhance the muscles' ability to store glycogen.

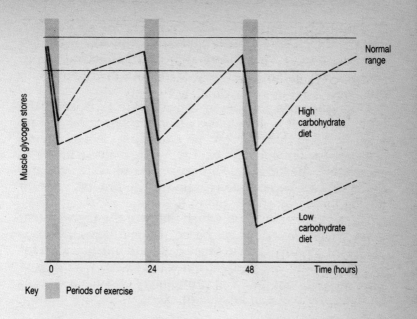

Key ▮ Periods of exercise

Muscle glycogen per 100g/3½oz of muscle

Untrained muscle 13g
Trained muscle 32g

Conversely, every time you run or train, the amount of stored glycogen in the working muscles decreases. If it is not replenished quickly, chronic fatigue will result. Ideally glycogen stores should be replenished within the first hour of completing training or ending a match. This is the time when conversion to glycogen is most efficient.

During preparation for a competition it will be necessary to decrease training levels up to three days prior to the event. This is known as tapering and it helps to maximise the glycogen store in the muscles. During this time carbohydrate intake may also be increased to 65 per cent or even 70 per cent (see Carbohydrate Loading on page 155).

The role of protein as an energy source during aerobic exercise is not really understood. It is used when the stores of muscle glycogen are running out, as might be the case in the last stages of a marathon. The longer the exercise period, the more likely that protein will be used as a source of energy. As a source of fuel protein probably contributes only about 10 per cent of the total energy used for any task.

Protein is used for fuel at considerable expense to the body because it is drawn away from its structural and regulatory roles and this can be damaging. When amino-acids are broken down for energy, waste material has to be excreted by the kidneys. This causes excess water loss and the body will become dehydrated if the process goes on for too long.

This is the rationale on which many of the high-protein quick weight loss diets are based. Protein takes the place of fat and carbohydrate in these diets and must be used for energy. Weight loss occurs from water loss as well as from some loss of body fat. You cannot stay on such a diet for too long nor will you be able to exercise properly on it.

Protein and Muscles

Because protein is the principal muscle-builder it has always been revered by athletes. But protein is used in the bodies of sportsmen and women in just the same way as in everyone else's. So the percentage protein intake recommendations are the same as for the population as a whole.

However, it is now thought that very active sports people do have an increased requirement for protein. The normal dietary intake is around 0.9g per kilogram of body weight per day. Active sports people may need between 1.2 and 1.7g. This still works out at between 12 and 15 per cent of daily calories. If the overall diet meets your energy needs, it is likely to meet your protein needs too.

Eating large amounts of protein is not the way to increase strength. Extra protein does not build muscle, it builds up fat. For muscles to grow they must be stimulated at the cellular level and this is best acheived by progressive high-intensity exercise such as weight-training.

Weight-lifters in particular believe in the value of protein but you cannot lift weights or do heavy work-out sessions if your muscles are deprived of carbohydrates. High-protein diets do not provide muscle fuel and a diet low in carbohydrates means that you will not be able to exercise hard enough to build up strength in the muscles.

There may be an increased need for protein in 'wear and tear' endurance events. But here again the amounts are small and are likely to be covered if energy requirements are met.

3.2 THE ENERGY BALANCE

The energy balance is quite simply the difference between energy input in the form of calories in food and drink and energy output in the form of calories used up in living – body functions, normal activity and exercise. If these are correctly balanced your weight will remain constant and you will be physically fit.

If, however, the energy input is too high and it is not used up in activity it will be stored in the form of body fat. If this goes on for too long the result is obesity. If the energy store is too low, the body will start to use up whatever store of fat it happens to have. This will result in weight loss which if carried too far can lead to malnutrition and ill health.

> The cumulative effect of eating only a little too much every day could prove to be disastrous. In theory, even one extra tortilla chip per day could eventually make you pounds overweight. Equally a small but regular cut-back in your sporting activity with no change in diet could produce the same effect.

So how much energy or calorific input do you need? First of all, energy is required to maintain the fundamental processes of life. The heart must be kept beating, body temperature maintained and the organs kept functioning.

This requirement is called the basal metabolic rate (BMR) and is measured when a person is resting.

Size or body weight has a significant effect on energy requirements. For example, a rugby player weighing 90kg/198lb has to exert 50 per cent more effort to run around the pitch than a team mate weighing 60kg/132lb but he may not have a 50 per cent greater reserve of energy. This illustrates not only the importance of training and diet for particular sports but also the stress which can be placed on the body through obesity.

Because women tend to be smaller and lighter than men their basal rates are lower. There is also a gender difference of around 100 or so calories. Height has only a small effect but research shows that BMR decreases with age. For every 10 years over 25 the energy requirement is reduced by 4 per cent.

As well as covering the BMR, calories are needed for everyday chores such as washing, dressing, eating, walking about, sitting and so on. They are also needed to cover your leisure activities and the work that you do. People doing heavy work will need more calories than those in a sedentary job.

Estimated Average Requirements (EARs) for Energy		
Age	kcal/day	
	Males	Females
15–18 years	2755	2110
19–50 years	2550	1940
51–59 years	2550	1900
60–64 years	2380	1900
65–74 years	2330	1900
75 + years	2100	1810

Sporting activities demand their own energy input. However, they do not require quite as much energy as many people seem to think. The actual energy requirement can vary a great deal.

The number of calories needed for a particular sport depends on the involvement of the muscles and the demands of respiration and heart beat. These in turn will depend upon how efficiently you perform (how skilled you are) and on how hard you push yourself (are you playing for fun or are you pushing to the limit?).

The greater the amount of muscular work, the heavier the weight being moved, the longer the time the activity takes, the more calories are necessary.

Leisurely canoeing on holiday may only need an extra two calories per minute whereas cross-country racing may require an extra 14 calories per minute.

Energy Expenditure in Sports

Calories expended per minute according to weight

| Activity | Body Weight | | | |
	56kg	62kg	68kg	74kg
Badminton	5.4	6.0	6.6	7.2
Basketball	7.7	8.6	9.4	10.2
Boxing in the ring	7.7	8.6	9.4	10.2
sparring	12.4	13.8	15.1	16.4
Canoeing				
leisure	2.5	2.7	3.0	3.3
racing	5.8	6.4	7.0	7.6
Climbing				
with no load	6.8	7.5	8.2	9.0
with 10kg load	7.2	8.0	8.8	9.5
Cricket				
batting	4.6	5.1	5.6	6.1
bowling	5.0	5.6	6.1	6.7
Cycling				
leisure	5.6	6.2	6.8	7.4
racing	9.5	10.5	11.5	12.5
Aerobics				
medium	5.8	6.4	7.0	7.6

Activity	Body Weight			
	56kg	62kg	68kg	74kg
intense	7.5	8.3	9.2	10.0
Field hockey	7.5	8.3	9.1	9.9
Football	7.4	8.2	9.0	9.8
Golf	4.8	5.3	5.8	6.3
Gymnastics	3.7	4.1	4.5	4.9
Judo	10.9	12.1	13.3	14.4
Running				
cross country	9.1	10.1	11.1	12.1
11.5min/mile	7.6	8.4	9.2	10.0
8min/mile	11.9	13.1	14.2	15.4
Skiing				
cross country	6.7	7.4	8.1	8.8
downhill	5.7	6.5	7.1	7.7
Squash	11.9	13.1	14.4	15.7
Swimming				
breast stroke	9.1	10.0	11.0	12.0
fast crawl	8.7	9.7	10.6	11.5
slow crawl	7.2	7.9	8.7	9.5
Table tennis	3.8	4.2	4.6	5.0
Tennis	6.1	6.8	7.4	8.1
Walking at normal pace	4.6	5.1	5.3	6.0

Because so many different factors are involved, the figures given in the chart above can only serve as an indication of the energy likely to be expended during different activities. Everyone will need to work out their own energy requirements with the help of the example opposite or with their coach, qualified sports nutritionist, or dietitian.

Ideal Body Weight

Most sports people are obsessed with finding and retaining the ideal body weight for their sport. They want to optimize their performance and do not want the dis-

Calculation of Energy Required

Example: An active woman of 25 who takes part in competitive fencing. The calculation is for a competition day.

2100	EAR for energy
500	5 bouts of competitive fencing (10 mins)
2600	
(200)	if energy efficient
2400	Total kilocalories required that day

advantage of carrying around any extra pounds. This is particularly important for runners, jumpers and participants in team sports.

Other athletes may need to lose or gain weight to compete in weight-category of matched competitions such as boxing, martial arts and wrestling. Here the winner is likely to be the competitor with the largest muscle mass. The problem may be how to put on muscle not fat, but more often it is the other way round and fat needs to be lost, but not muscle.

Jockeys are another group who need to keep their weight down, and gymnasts and ballet dancers not only need to be fairly slim but often also feel that they must have an extra-thin image.

The first step is to decide exactly how much fat you really are carrying. Very often people have an exaggerated idea of how fat they are. They also underestimate how much fat they need.

Some adipose tissue or body fat is essential to the nervous system and to cell membranes. It is also needed to protect the kidneys and other organs. The average man needs about 13-15 per cent body fat and the average women about 20-27 per cent.

These percentages are likely to be lower for competitive sports people, with men in the range 6-9 per cent and women in the range 12-15 per cent, depending on their sport.

There are a number of ways of deciding whether you are carrying too much body fat.

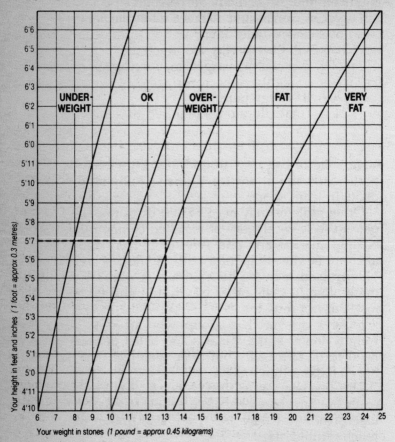

Weight/height charts: The simplest way of assessing whether or not you are overweight is to measure your weight and your height. Armed with these two measurements you can compare yourself with the standard weight/height chart above. This shows a range of 'healthy weights' for different heights. But remember that these charts are only averages. They are not ideal weights.

The problem with this method is that you are not assessing your fatness because you are weighing water, bone, muscle, and bowel contents as well as fat. Most sports people have a higher than average percentage of muscle and even though the body-fat percentage is low the scale can register 'overweight'. Thus a muscular footballer may seem overweight when compared with the chart but will not necessarily be carrying too much fat.

Equally, the 'healthy weight' may not be appropriate for gymnasts or lightweight rowing crews who require a lower weight to compete.

Skinfold or pinch test: A more accuratge assessment of fatness is given by using skinfold callipers (large pincers) to measure the subcutaneous fat below the skin. This is done at four sites on the body, usually at the biceps and triceps, beneath the shoulderblade, and just above the hip bone. There is currently a move to include the anterior thigh as well. The results are used in complicated conversion equations to give body fat percentages.

If this technique is carried out carefully and the correct equations chosen (regarding sex and sporting activity) it can be very useful. However, it is fairly subjective, so it makes sense to have serial measurements made by the same operator.

Underwater weighing: Here the Archimedes principle – which holds that an object submerged in water must be buoyed up by a counterforce equal to the weight of water it displaces – is applied to the human body. Body density is measured by weighing the subject under water. The resultant figure is translated mathematically into percentage fat.

Underwater weighing needs expensive equipment and technically skilled personnel not normally available at a local gym. It also needs a certain amount of skill on the part of the person to be weighed as all air must be expelled from the lungs before going under water.

Biolectrical impedance: This is a computerized system which sends an imperceptible electric current through the body via an electrode attached to the wrists and ankles. The theory is that the amount of water in the body affects the flow of the current. Water is only present in fat-free tissue and so the current flow can be translated into body-fat percentage.

This method has many problems. The readings will be affected if you are dehydrated after a run or work-out or after drinking alcohol. Food in the stomach, premenstrual bloat and carbohydrate loading can all affect the results.

Near-infra-red ineractance: This works by sending an infra-red beam through the upper arm. The amount of light reflected back to the analyser from the bone depends on the amount of fat in the arm. This is then used with other information such as age, sex, weight and height to calculate the body-fat percentage. The problem here is that the fat percentage in the arm may not be the same as the fat percentage elsewhere. However, the method is quick and cheap and is quite popular for this reason.

By and large, body-fat measurements are more useful as a reflection of the changes in your body as you lose fat and gain muscle than as a one-off indication of whether or not you are carrying too much fat. It is probably better to 'listen' to your body. Stop panicking about your weight and consider whether or not you feel right. Your body will usually tell you if you are slipping away from your best weight.

Losing Weight

If, however, you do find that you need to lose weight you must do so in such a way that you do not also lose strength and stamina. This means avoiding excessive measures such as crash diets, fasting, water restriction or laxative abuse. These and other methods only lead to dehydration, weakness and fatigue and consequently poor training sessions and poor performance.

You must make up your mind that any projected weight loss will take time. A safe weight loss is 0.5-1kg/1-2lb per week. Theoretically you should be able to achieve a loss of 0.5kg/1lb per week by eating 500 calories less per day. This is because 0.5kg/1lb of fat is the equivalent of 3500 kilocalories:

500 kilocalories × 7 days = 3500 kcal = 0.5kg/1lb body fat

Unfortunately it does not always work quite like this. Some people adapt to eating less, particularly if they have dieted for a long time or have no excess fat to lose.

Weight and Exercise

Never cut back by more than one-third of your calorific needs to sustain your current weight and activities. If you do not eat enough you will not get the nutrients that you need for full health and prime performance. Far better to diet over a longer period and use aerobic exercise like brisk walking or jogging to help with the weight loss. Indeed, this strategy is the best one in most circumstances.

The best type of exercise for weight control is any form of physical activity you can maintain comfortably for 20 to 30 minutes at least three times weekly. The emphasis should be on duration rather than on intensity. Choose something which you enjoy doing and which will naturally complement your training programme. Increase the amount of time spent on it as you improve.

Minutes Needed to Jog off Particular Foods	
Food	*Minutes*
Medium chocolate bar	52.0
Meat pie	50.0
Medium packet of crisps	40.0
Cream bun	22.4
Salad sandwich	21.6
Carton fruit yoghurt	12.4
Lean chump chop	11.4
Slice of bread	6.6
Knob of butter (1 tsp)	3.6
Stick of celery	1.0

Gaining Weight

In theory you should gain an extra 0.5kg/1lb by eating an extra 500 calories per day for a week (see page 111). But just as some people seem to adjust to dieting, so others find it very hard to gain weight. Some people can eat 500 calories a day more and simply not put on the full 0.5kg/1lb of weight.

This is often due to heredity. You can alter your physique to a certain extent with diet and weight-training but you may have to accept you will never be an Arnold Schwarzenegger.

Most people think that the best way to gain weight is to eat a high-protein diet but this is just not true. Unfortunately a pound of steak does not convert to biceps. Any extra protein required in body-building is likely to be contained in a normal diet. What you do need is extra carbohydrate to fuel muscles so that they can do more exercise and so grow (see page 111).

If muscles are overloaded with weight-lifting or other resistance exercise, the muscle fibre will increase in size. It is exercise that builds muscles, not extra protein.

4
FUELLING YOUR SPORTING ACTIVITIES

Whether you are exercising for fun, jogging or swimming to improve your fitness, or training seriously for organized events, you need to think quite carefully about how you are fuelling the muscle effort involved. After all, you would not think of driving your car to work every day without checking the petrol, oil and water from time to time.

Fuel for muscles, of course, means food, but not just any kind of food. Not only do you need to follow the general guidelines set out in Chapter 2, you should also be thinking about the specific energy requirements of your chosen sport (see page 83).

Should footballers eat more pasta? What is the best time to have the main meal of the day? Should gymnasts avoid potatoes? What is the right kind of snack to grab after spending the lunch-hour jogging round the park? Should you be drinking more liquid and is it OK to include lager?

The answers to these and other questions will not only enhance your performance but help you to organize your life more effectively. But do remember that although food may be there to fuel your activities, it is also there to be enjoyed. Try not to become obsessed and faddy about your food.

4.1 EATING FOR PERFORMANCE

The Ideal Diet

Whatever your sport and whatever your level of training, the ideal diet is one which provides the essential nutrients for good health and enough of the right fuel for the demands of your sport. This means:

- a high proportion of complex-carbohydrate foods with dietary fibre, topped up with simple carbohydrates in some cases
- some fat, but not in excessive amounts
- sufficient, but not excessive, amounts of protein
- sources of calcium, iron and other minerals, as well as the whole range of vitamins
- plenty of fluid

This is very much in line with the current healthy eating guidelines set out in Chapter 2. Sportsmen and women do not need to eat substantially different food to the rest of the population.

Complex-carbohydrate foods form the base of the Food Pyramid on page 37 and it is particularly important for sports people that these foods provide at least 60 per cent of the total energy intake. It is essential, too, to keep fats down to no more than 30 per cent of total energy intake.

With the emphasis on increasing carbohydrate and decreasing fat, it is very easy to lose sight of the importance of fruit and vegetables. These foods are a vital source of vitamins and minerals. The protagonists of the Mediterranean Diet (see page 35) suggest that everyone should eat a minimum of 400g (14oz) actual weight of fruit and vegetables every day.

Protein foods such as meat, fish and cheese are best used to add interest and flavour to meals. They should not be the main attraction as they have been traditionally.

To give some idea of what all this means, the largest serving of food on your dinner plate should consist of complex-carbohydrate foods like rice, pasta and potatoes.

The next largest serving should be vegetables or salad and the smallest portion should be the meat, fish or dairy food.

> Q: Are you guilty of thinking it does not matter what you eat because you exercise regularly?
>
> A: It matters very much, both in terms of keeping fit and in terms of improving your performance. If you are eating the typical British diet, you will not be eating enough carbohydrate to fuel your exercise.

Although there is no difference between the generally healthy diet and the sports diet, the latter is likely to include a larger overall number of calories to fuel the sport involved. A normally active sportsman may require around 2500kcals a day to fuel his activities but the regular squash player, for example, will need to add up to 500kcals extra to fuel his sport.

This means that the 60 per cent of total energy derived from carbohydrate must be calculated on a larger base. In some instances it could be necessary to eat really large quantities of these foods. For example, a serious competitive runner who requires an energy input of 4000kcals a day would need to eat 600g/1¼lb of carbohydrate foods.

Obviously, the amount of food a cross-country runner eats will be very different to the amount eaten by a weight-lifter or a pole-jumper. However, it is quite easy to work out your own needs.

Start by estimating the number of kilocalories you need per day (see page 82). Supposing the answer is 2200kcals, your 60 per cent carbohydrate intake target will be

60 per cent × 2200kcals = 1320kcals from carbohydrate
Divide this by 4kcals per gram of carbohydrate
= 330g carbohydrates per day

Once you are armed with this information you can plan your meals to maximize your carbohydrate intake. Read labels carefully, check the nutritional information given with recipes in this book and work out the carbohydrate content of your own recipes.

If you do this as a matter of course you will avoid the trap that so many sports people fall into when they take good care of themselves just prior to an event but neglect their training diets. If you do not train at the peak you will not compete at it either.

Adding Complex Carbohydrates

Of course, the easiest way to increase your carbohydrate intake is simply to pile extra rice, noodles, potatoes and the like on to your main-course plate. Alternatively you could follow the Portuguese pattern of serving both rice and potatoes at every main meal or the French habit of serving bread as well as potatoes.

But plain starchy accompaniments can become rather boring after a while and you may be tempted to brighten them up with extra fat in the form of butter, olive oil or soured cream. Much better to vary the form in which you take your starchy foods so you do not get fed up with them.

Here's a list of suitable dishes to include in your menus from time to time. Some of them can be bought from supermarket freezer or chilling cabinets. Others are taken from the recipe sections in Quick and Easy Fillers (page 212), All-In-One Dishes (page 277) and Cereals on the Side (page 288). Look for additional ideas in these sections too.

PASTA
Spaghetti with a variety of sauces, Tagliatelle with Garlic Cheese Sauce (page 244), macaroni cheese, Neapolitan Macaroni (page 244), filled pasta such as tortelloni and ravioli, lasagne, cannelloni, Chinese Egg Noodles with Stir-fried Beef and Beans (page 246), Japanese Buckwheat Noodles with Stir-fried Vegetables (page 249).

RICE
Quick Paella (page 287), risotto, Spanish Rice (page 299), rice and peas, Chinese fried rice, Cajan Jambalaya (page 279), American Gumbo (page 234).

OTHER CEREALS
Polenta Plus (page 295) or yellow cornmeal, bulgar, Spicy Aubergine Millet (page 298), Multi-grain Pilaf (page 297).

POTATOES
Potato Stew (page 283), tortilla (page 278), Pommes Anna (page 323), Quick Rosti (page 323), filled Jacket-baked Potatoes (page 227), Italian Potato Pie (page 324), baked sweet potatoes.

PULSES (BEANS OR DRIED PEAS)
Butter beans in parsley sauce, baked beans in tomato sauce, Spiced Lentils (page 275), beanpot, Italian-style Beans (page 320), red kidney bean salad, low fat chilli.

OTHER VEGETABLES CONTAINING CARBOHYDRATES
Sweetcorn, fresh peas and broad beans, beetroot, parsnips and carrots.

Fats and Proteins in Training
Although you must increase your intake of carbohydrate and decrease the amount of fat, you should not run away with the idea that fat should be cut out altogether. Not only would this be very difficult, but fat is essential to life. Aim for no more than 30 per cent of your daily energy intake being accounted for by fat.

If your target is 2200 kcals, you can calculate the allowed fat as follows:

30 per cent × 2200kcals = 660kcals from fat
Divide this by 9kcals per gram = 73g fat per day

The same kind of calculation can be made for protein intake. Here the recommendation is 12-15 per cent of your daily kilocalories. Thus

15 per cent × 2200kcals = 330kcals from protein
Divide this by 4kcals per gram = 82.5g protein per day

This is much less than most people think they need as it is training that builds muscle, not protein (see pages 80/111)

and it is carbohydrates which fuel that training. If you are taking part in power sports the chances are that you will have more muscle mass than runners or jumpers and so you will weigh more. Thus you will need a larger daily kilocalorie base and your 12-15 per cent protein will increase too.

If you persist in the belief that protein is best you will not be able to lift such heavy weights or demand so much from your work-out sessions. Your muscles will be carbohydrate-depleted and you will not be able to exercise hard enough to reach your full potential.

Conversely, you will do your performance just as much harm by eating too little protein. Not only will you be short of protein – an essential nutrient in itself – you will also start to miss out on iron, zinc, calcium and other essential nutrients which are found in meat, fish and dairy produce.

Making it Work

These calculations are very useful but they do need to be interpreted in terms of real food. You can translate a requirement for 50g/2oz fat per day into 50g/2oz of butter, oil or meat fat, but the same cannot be done with protein and carbohydrates. Foods which are rich in these nutrients also contain appreciable amounts of other nutrients too. So 50g/2oz of protein is not supplied by 50g/2oz of beef, lamb or plaice. You would have to eat some bread, pasta, rice, nuts, milk or cheese as well.

Of course, it is one thing to know what you should be eating but it is quite another to do it all the time. When you come home from a hard day's work it is all too easy to grab food that is quick to prepare without thinking about how it fits into your daily nutritional requirements.

It does make it easier if you plan ahead and stock your shelves, fridge and freezer with wholesome foods which are ready to use when you get home. Try to keep as wide an array of possible ingredients as you can so that there will be something you are tempted to eat. It is hopeless trying to eat a balanced and varied diet if you have to buy everything on the way home.

Have a look at the store-cupboard ideas on page 47 and add some of your own favourites. Keep the freezer well stocked too and consider investing in a microwave oven if you do not already have one. If you do not like cooking, make a careful choice from the frozen food and chilling cabinets at the supermarket.

---

12 Easy Ideas from the Supermarket

- Lasagne and cannelloni, particularly with vegetable fillings
- Tagliatelle with seafood sauce
- Spaghetti with tuna and tomato sauce
- Vegeburgers
- Pizza with vegetarian toppings
- Filled jacket potatoes
- Vegetable or mushroom risotto
- Vegetable curry (check label – can be fatty)
- Dhal with lentils or chickpeas
- Saffron or Thai rice
- Chinese noodles (check label – can be fatty)
- Tuscan Bean Soup or Dried Pea Soup

Very often a quick meal is a fast-food meal on the way home. There are five basic faults with fast food:

- too much fat – everything seems to be fried or composed of fatty meat
- lacking in fibre – very little complex carbohydrate and what there is is usually refined
- low in vitamins, particularly A and C – salads likely to be tired or non-existent
- high in salt – not always obvious
- high in sugar – drinks, milk-shakes and sauces.

---

6 Light Meals to Buy Away from Home

If you can, choose these kinds of food rather than hamburgers, fried chicken or fish and chips.

- pitta parcels with Greek salad and lean lamb kebabs or Turkish falafel
- jacket-baked potatoes filled with baked beans, chilli, ratatouille or scrambled eggs
- thick sandwiches filled with chicken, turkey, or cottage cheese and salad – but go easy on the mayonnaise
- tortilla with beans or vegetables
- slice of tomato and cheese pizza
- baps or large rolls filled with tuna, prawns, salmon, and salad

If you enjoy cooking when you have the time, it is a good idea to make double or treble quantity of your favourite dishes and organize a cook-in occasionally at a weekend or on a rest day. Freeze food in one- or two-portion containers for easy thawing. Good standbys include bags of well-flavoured cooked rice, very lightly oiled pasta, sliced wholemeal bread, fish cakes and sliced polenta.

Sample Main Meal Menus for a Normal Training Diet

Menu 1
Mixed bean salad with rolls
Stir-fried chicken with cashew nuts and rice with plenty of vegetables
Fresh peaches or nectarines with ice-cream

Menu 2
Mixed vegetable soup
Lasagne with green salad
Banana Walnut Crumble (page 332)

Menu 3
Spiced Country Salad (page 311)
Chinese Chicken in Foil (page 263) Flageolets with Bulgar (page 274) and carrots

Menu 4
Mixed grilled vegetables
Low-fat sausage or Lentil Toad in the Hole (page 270), green salad and new potatoes

Traditional Rice Pudding
(page 334)

Banana with Cumberland
Sauce (page 329)

Menu 5
Peanut Dip with Baked
Garlic Pitta (page 269)
Tuscan Herby Pasta (page
248) with salad
Cake and Apple Pudding
(page 331)

Menu 6
Cardamom Fish Curry
(page 254), vegetable
curry, raita and dhal,
savoury rice
Fresh orange and
grapefruit segments
with ginger biscuits

Putting on the Pace

If you increase the mileage that you run or the frequency
of your training, you will need to increase the amount that
you eat, still keeping carbohydrate-rich foods as the predominant element. Keep in the front of your mind the
thought that carbohydrates are a sports person's best
friend – they fuel the working muscles.

However, this can become quite difficult to achieve. You
can load the meal with thick soups (see page 232), extra
beans and starchy desserts (see page 326) and of course
this will help. But the solution is to start using both simple
and complex types of carbohydrate. Indeed studies have
shown that both types are needed if an intake of more
than 500g/1lb of carbohydrate is to be achieved.

If you are a slim, healthy adult who is not putting on
weight you can safely include sugar as part of your diet,
but the operative word is part! As you increase the amount
of carbohydrates in your diet you must make sure that you
are not also increasing the overall energy input. This can
be avoided by reducing your fat intake. Look at the ideas
for cutting down on fats on page 40 and step up the number of methods you are already using. You must also be
sure that you are getting the correct amount of protein,
vitamins and minerals.

Three Dozen Quick Ways to Add Approximately 50g/2oz of Carbohydrate or 200kcals to Your Training Diet

Food	Quantity
Fruit and Vegetables	
Apples	450g (3-4)
Apricots, dried	150g
Baked jacket potato	175g (1 small)
Bananas	2 large
Dates, dried	100g
raw	200g
Mango	1 large
Orange juice	500ml
Pears	450g (3-4)
Peeled chestnuts, roasted	175g
Prunes, dried	75g
Raisins	75g
Cereals	
Alpen	2 sachets
Cornflakes	175g
Porridge made with skimmed milk	large bowl
Shredded Wheat	3
Weetabix	3½
Rice (brown)	175g cooked
Pasta (wholemeal)	200g cooked
Pizza (tomato)	200g slice
Bread	
Bread, white	3-4 slices
wholemeal	4 slices
Pitta loaf	1 (large)
French stick	22cm length
Roll, white	2 soft sesame
wholemeal	2 small baps
Crumpets	4

Biscuits and Cakes

Chelsea bun*	1
Digestive biscuits	5
Fig rolls	4
Oatcakes	6
Cereal bars	2-3

Sweets

Boiled sweets	60g
Honey	2 tablespoons (level)
Individual pot fruit yoghurt	1
Dairy ice cream*	200g portion

*Watch the fat content.

Post-training Eating

Training uses up the glycogen store in your muscles and this must be replenished as soon as possible. For the serious sports person it is as important to take as much care in choosing food to eat after training as in deciding what to eat before. If you neglect to do this you will find that your muscles will not work at their best and your performance will start to slip.

It is crucial to consume 50g/2oz carbohydrate in the first two hours after each training session and another 50g/2oz within the next two hours. Good foods to eat include bananas, raisins, sweets and low-fat biscuits. Other ideas are given on pages 158 and 182. However, people are not usually at all hungry immediately following exhaustive exercise and often prefer to drink carbohydrate fluids rather than eat solid food.

You must also make sure that you have eaten your full carbohydrate requirement for the day by the time you go to bed. So your evening meal needs to be a high-carbohydrate meal with a low-fat and protein content.

POST-EVENT MEALS

Menu 1
Pasta or Chinese noodles
with stir-fried chicken
and vegetables
Ice-cream

Menu 3
Guacamole Dip (page
214) (made in advance)
with pitta bread and raw
carrot and cucumber
sticks
Rice with Peas and
Pimiento (page 292)
and green salad
Sliced oranges

Menu 2
Courgette and Fennel
Soup (page 234) (made in
advance)
Bruschetta (page 222)
Fresh fruit

Menu 4
Potato Stew (page 283)
with carrots
Strawberries with yoghurt

Drinks

Sixty per cent of your body is made up of water. If this is
decreased for any reason you become dehydrated. It is
particularly important for sports people to remain as well
hydrated as possible, so try to get into the habit of drinking water or other suitable liquids as a routine throughout
the day. If you do start to lose water from the body, you
will start to lose performance as well.

To be sure of getting enough fluid you will need to drink
at least 10-12 glasses of water a day and you may need
more, particularly in hot or in humid weather. A general
rule of thumb is to drink 1litre/1¾pints for every 1000kcal
that you expend.

Everyone is susceptible to dehydration, so if you are
working, keep a jug or bottle of water on your desk or take
advantage of every work-break to drink plenty of liquid.
Alternatively carry a water bottle with you.

Fluid is important because:

- Fluid in blood transports glucose to working muscles and carries away metabolic by-products.
- Fluid in sweat helps to maintain a constant body temperature through heat loss by evaporation.
- Fluid is also needed for urine to eliminate waste products from the body.

If you drink too little or if you lose too much water through profuse sweating your body will not be able to carry out these tasks efficiently. This will prevent you from exercising to your full potential.

Water loss through sweat

You will lose about 500ml/16floz of sweat for every 300kcals of heat you dissipate. It is not unusual to lose a litre or almost 2 pints of fluid every hour during heavy exercise in hot conditions.

It is essential to drink a large glass (at least 300-450ml/10-15floz) of water just before you start training. This will not cause stomach cramps as is sometimes believed. It may feel uncomfortable at first, but usually the more you drink before exercise the more you get used to it and the less uncomfortable you become.

If you continue to find it difficult to drink quite so much, try drinking a smaller amount every 10-15 minutes during the run-up to the start of training or the event. Use your training to get used to drinking plenty of water.

The amount you can drink depends on the rate at which fluid is emptied from the stomach and this varies considerably from person to person. Cold drinks empty out a little more quickly than hot ones. They also tend to be more palatable, but if you are skiing or ice-skating you might want a warm drink for the psychological benefit it will give.

Water is very good for replacing lost fluid but recent research shows that sweetened drinks with a glucose level of 6-8 per cent are absorbed into the body just as rapidly as water, and they have the added advantage of providing some energy. If sodium is also added to the drink, both the carbohydrate and the water in it will be absorbed even more quickly.

Most of the so-called sports drinks (see page 151) contain both carbohydrate and mineral salt, so if you like the taste they can be useful for quick absorption. Check that the carbohydrate content does not exceed 8 per cent.

You can make your own sports drink by adding a little sugar and salt to your drinking water, about 2-8g glucose and a pinch of salt in 100ml/4floz water will be sufficient. You may not find this mix very palatable on its own, so add some low-calorie flavouring to a strength which you enjoy but do not find cloying in the mouth.

Ideally, you should also drink about 150ml/5floz every 15 minutes during training. Most people carry something to drink with them when training, but the chances are that it will not be enough, so drink as much as you can when you get back, to replace any loss. Do not wait until you feel thirsty. Unfortunately, thirst is not a good indicator of fluid loss.

Signs of dehydration include very dark, scanty urine, a tired and headachy feeling and poor performance. However, your urine may be dark if you are taking vitamin tablets, in which case check the volume.

If you get bored with having to drink so much water, here are some more ideas for fluid intake:

- low-sugar Ribena with apple juice and water
- fresh orange juice with a splash of lemon juice and water
- unsweetened pineapple juice with grapefruit juice and water

More substantial drinks are very useful after exercise when you need to replenish glycogen but don't feel hungry. Banana milk-shake, for example, is ideal.

Watery Foods

Watery foods can contribute quite significant
amounts of water.

Lettuce	96 per cent water
Cucumber	96 per cent water
Melon	94 per cent water
Tomatoes	93 per cent water
Grapefruit	91 per cent water
Watercress	91 per cent water
Carrots	91 per cent water
Strawberries	89 per cent water
Low-fat yoghurt	86 per cent water
Oranges	86 per cent water
Peaches	86 per cent water
Apples	84 per cent water
Cottage cheese	79 per cent water
Grapes	79 per cent water
Bananas	71 per cent water

4.2 EATING TO CHANGE YOUR WEIGHT

If you are to get the best out of yourself you need to be at
the correct weight (see page 86). It is very important to get
sound advice both on what your body weight should be
and on how to achieve it, from a qualified sports nutritionist or dietitian.

Losing Weight without Losing Performance

There are two common fears about losing weight among
sports people. One is that if they lose weight they will lose
strength and stamina. The other, rather more common, is
that they will never be thin enough.

Boxers, light-weight rowers, jockeys and judo wrestlers who need to lose weight to compete in a lower weight classification are amongst the first group and their fear is understandable. However, if weight is lost in the right way, slowly and carefully without resorting to fasting, crash diets and the like, strength will not be undermined.

The second group includes all those athletes who believe that they will always be too fat. This is particularly prevalent among women. If this fear is allowed to go to the extreme it could result in anorexia.

Some fat is an essential part of you (see page 95). Men need about 3 per cent essential body fat and women 12 per cent. (The higher figure for women includes what is known as 'gender' fat which is found in the breasts and pelvic region.) These figures are known as lean body weight and inroads into this fat will seriously impair body functioning and ability let alone capacity for hard training.

In addition to this essential fat the body also contains storage fat around the vital organs and this acts as an energy reserve. For a typical man storage fat accounts for 12 per cent, bumping the total fat up to 15 per cent, and for a typical woman it is 15 per cent, bumping the female total up to 27 per cent. These percentages may be as low as 6-9 per cent and 12-15 per cent for competitive athletes.

If you really do need to lose weight, look at your current diet to see where the unwanted weight is coming from. It is the food that you eat every day which has the most effect on your weight. Write down everything you eat and drink for a week. The latter is very important, for people often forget the drinks.

Assessment of the following factors will help you to start correcting matters. Are you:

- eating too many fatty foods?
- skipping breakfast, or even breakfast and lunch, and filling up later?
- indulging in unnecessary snacks between meals?
- bingeing on cakes or chocolates when you get fed up with healthy eating?

- cheering yourself up with food?
- eating to keep someone else company?
- drinking too much alcohol?

If you can identify at least some of the problems you will find it much easier to make a start on changing your habits. For this is what you need to do. Going on a crash diet is a waste of time. Such diets never last and sooner or later you will come off it.

If, however, you set up a brand-new eating pattern which is enjoyable and enables you to lose weight and compete well, you are much more likely to stick to it. It really is possible to lose weight and continue to enjoy a high-energy sports diet. The secret is to choose the right food and eat it at the right time in the right amounts.

The Right Food

The right food remains a diet rich in complex-carbohydrate foods. Starchy food like bread, potatoes and pasta are not fattening. It is excess fat in the form of butter or margarine on bread and potatoes and creamy or meaty sauce on pasta that is fattening.

Not only do fatty foods contain twice as many calories as carbohydrate foods, they also turn to body fat more easily. In addition the body can burn off the calories from carbohydrates more readily than those from fat. Excess protein will be stored as fat too (see page 80).

If you need to have a snack, you are much better off choosing a plain wholemeal roll or even a plate of crackers than a tub of cottage cheese. It will be much easier to burn off excess calories from the roll or the crackers than from the cheese.

The percentage targets outlined in pages 34-35 hold equally good when slimming. They are just worked out on a lower daily calorie basis. The requirement for 60 per cent of daily calories from carbohydrate remains the same. This is good news as complex-carbohydrate foods have the advantage of a high fibre content (which has virtually no calories). This means that food takes longer to digest, and by filling you up it makes you feel less hungry.

Your overall energy intake will be less but you will still need the same level of vitamins and minerals, so it is important to choose nutrient-dense foods such as unrefined cereals, brown rice, wholemeal bread and plenty of fruit and vegetables.

Avoid foods like cakes, pastries, biscuits and soft drinks for they tend to be high in refined carbohydrates and sugar, low in vitamins and fibre and high in fat – a sure recipe for obesity and tooth decay.

Avoid, too, faddy or drastic diets like the popular high-protein diet. As well as the disadvantages set out on page 88, this diet can be very hard on the kidneys and may lead to dehydration.

Excessively low-carbohydrate diets are equally bad. As well as leaving you fatigued and lacking in energy they can lead to depletion of serotin in the brain. This substance is very important in transmitting nerve messages. If levels drop too low you are likely to crave carbohydrates and go on a binge.

The Right Amount
The amount that you eat should be determined by the kind of calculations set out on page 85. These take account of your basal metabolic rate, your everyday activities and your sporting activities, as well as your current weight and the weight that you are trying to achieve.

If you have got used to eating large platefuls of food at every meal you will need to find ways of distracting yourself from the fact that there is less food – perhaps by adding more salads or using smaller-sized plates.

The Right Time
Distribute your daily calories as evenly as you can throughout the day. Some people think that skipping a meal will help them to eat less but the chances are that you will get so hungry that you will buy a fattening snack to fill the gap. If you spread your calories through the day, eating three small meals plus pre-training snacks, you are

less likely to feel deprived.

Skipping breakfast is a particularly bad way to diet. Your body can burn breakfast calories more easily and efficiently than those consumed at night. No breakfast very often means a doughnut or bacon sandwich mid-morning.

---

12 Ways to Help Lose Weight

- Eat slowly – the brain needs 20 minutes to receive the signal that you have eaten your fill. During that time you could have consumed large quantities without the satiety signal coming into play.
- Start a meal with fruit juice or broth – they take time to eat and decrease the appetite for the next course.
- Cut out the obviously fatty foods in your diet. Cut all exposed fat off meat and remove the skin from chicken. Switch to skimmed milk in tea and coffee.
- Get into the habit of eating plain bread with your meals rather than buttered rolls.
- Use lemon juice or yogurt instead of salad dressing or mayonnaise on salads.
- Do not cut out all your favourite foods. If you do, you are more likely to give in at some stage and go on a binge.
- Keep as few ready-to-eat foods around as possible. Keep them out of sight.
- Try cheering yourself up or distracting yourself with an interesting activity rather than a snack. If necessary, eat your allowed snack earlier in the day.
- Weigh yourself only once a week, first thing in the morning, on the same day and at the same time. This will give you a true basis of comparison.

- Use a smaller plate. This helps control portion sizes and makes what you are serving look rather more.
- Grate cheese to make it go further. This also has a cosmetic effect in salads by making it look as though there is more than there is.
- Serve a large side salad of raw vegetables at most meals. This helps to fill you up and increases your vitamin intake.

Artificial Sweeteners

If you are longing to lose weight but have a sweet tooth, you may be thinking about replacing the sugar in your diet with an artificial sweetener. There are two types:

- Caloric sweeteners or those which provide some calories. These include manitol, sorbitol, xylitol and hydrogenated glucose syrup.
- Non-caloric sweeteners which do not add any calories. These include cyclamate, aspartame (Nutrasweet), ace-sulfame k, saccharin and thaumatin.

Saccharin is about 200 times sweeter than sugar. It has been used for over 50 years and has a good safety record. However, if you drink a lot of soft drinks containing saccharin you could be getting more than is acceptable. Saccharin can leave a bitter aftertaste.

Aspartame (Nutrasweet) is also 200 times sweeter than sugar but there is no aftertaste. On digestion, aspartame breaks down into two amino-acids: aspartic acid and phenylalanine, which are then metabolized like any other naturally occurring amino-acid. Some people are unable to digest phenylalanine which is also present in milk.

Cyclamate is banned in Britain but is freely available elsewhere in the EC, so read the labels when you are on holiday or are training or performing abroad.

Some people feel that if they are used with care, artificial sweeteners have a useful role to play because:

- They can be used by slimmers and diabetics who find it difficult to cut out sugar.
- They allow soft drinks and sweets to be produced which are neither harmful to the teeth nor fattening.
- They allow the production of alternatives to alcoholic drinks.

Others disagree because:

- The long-term effects of consuming large quantities are not yet known.
- There may be adverse reactions in a small minority of people.
- They may stimulate the appetite and if so their effect would be counter-productive.

Gaining Weight or Bulking Up

For the average person, it is much easier to put on weight than to lose it. But this does not really help the footballer, shot-putter or rower who wants to gain weight, because the weight to be gained must be muscle, not fat.

Muscle growth is best stimulated by progressive high-intensive training such as weight-training. This extra exercise must be fuelled by extra carbohydrate foods.

Only a small amount of extra protein will be required and this will probably already be covered by your regular diet. Aim for no more than 2g per kg/2lb body weight per day – any more is likely to lead to fat.

If you want to gain weight you will need to work out a plan of campaign in just the same way as the slimmer. Decide exactly how much extra weight you want to gain and work out how many extra calories you will need to achieve your goal (see page 90).

You can then work out a suitable high-carbohydrate diet. This is probably best done with the help of a qualified sports nutritionist or dietitian who will help you make sure that you are gaining muscle, not fat.

12 Ways to Help Gain Weight

- Plan the extra training and the new diet together. Do not treat them as two separate subjects.
- Take your time. Aim to gain between 250g/9oz and 0.5kg/1lb a week. If your expectations are not too high you will not be tempted to give up too early.
- Spread your calorie intake throughout the day. Try to eat three large meals a day with two or three snacks in between. Do not try to force all the extra calories into two or three meals alone.
- Eat frequently, with gaps not greater than two to three hours between meals or snacks.
- Choose higher-calorie foods: baked beans rather than fresh green beans, cranberry juice rather than orange juice and sweetcorn rather than fresh peas. Small changes like these can make big changes in your weight.
- Choose dense breakfast cereals like muesli or grapenuts and dense breads such as wholemeal, rye and pumpernickel rather than flaked or puffed cereals and fluffy steam-cooked bread.
- Where possible cook with milk instead of water – porridge, muesli, soups and sauces. Use dried skimmed milk in mashed potatoes, soups and baked foods, and to enrich ordinary milk.
- Use wheatgerm, nuts, seeds and dried fruits to boost the calorie content of teabreads, muffins and breakfast cereals.
- You will probably need to increase the amount of fat that you eat, to make the very large quantities of starchy foods required palatable. Choose polyunsaturated

margarine to spread on bread and toast and olive oil to add interest to vegetables and pasta.
- Think of ideas for snack foods that you will enjoy eating even when you are not hungry.
- Make sure you eat plenty of salads for their vitamin content. Convert to high-calorie dishes with the addition of cottage cheese, red kidney beans and chickpeas, chopped nuts, croutons and diced lean meat.
- Experiment with carbohydrate-rich drinks like banana milk-shake.

4.3 RUNNING AND TRAINING ON YOUR STOMACH

Not everyone wants to run the London Marathon but there are plenty of people who go jogging or who train for other sports by running a few hours each week.

Runners and joggers and indeed anyone who is training use both carbohydrates and fats to fuel their exercise but it is the carbohydrate that is the key nutrient. Even the leanest runner has sufficient stores of fat in the body, but the glycogen stores in the muscles (built up by eating carbohydrate-rich foods, see Chapter 2) will only be sufficient for about two hours' endurance work.

Joggers, who run more slowly, will be able to call upon some of their fat stores as well as their muscle glycogen. But most people are also living a busy life at work or coping with a family, so energy stocks will still need to be replenished, though not, perhaps, at the rate of the marathon runner.

For faster runners and those undertaking the volume of training required for long-distance runs, muscle glycogen stores are the first source of energy. It is therefore very important to have glycogen stores at as high a level as possible before a run *and* to replace them immediately afterwards. This obviously affects the timing as well as the content of your meals.

As training intensifies and your everyday activities continue, it may become a bit difficult to fulfil all your requirements from starchy foods alone. The sheer bulk can be a problem so you will need to add some sugar-rich foods to the mix (see page 12).

The rule here is to proceed with care. For example, choose half-coated chocolate digestive biscuits rather than fully coated sweet biscuits. This choice will give you a good mix of some sustaining carbohydrates with some 'quick fix' sugar without too much fat.

Meal-time Guidelines

1. Eat at least two hours before you plan to go jogging or training.

The actual timing of meals is often a matter of preference, but it takes time for all the food you eat to clear your stomach. It can be very uncomfortable, particularly for distance runners, to feel food bumping up and down in the stomach. It can cause nausea or even vomiting. Food normally remains in the stomach two to four hours but this varies according to:

- the individual
- the content of the meal
- the consistency of meal

People vary in their reaction, though, and you will only find the optimum time for you by trial and error. As a general rule, complex-carbohydrate foods like pasta, bread and potatoes are digested more quickly than protein-rich foods like meat or fish. Fats take longest of all. These facts provide another good reason for eating a starchy, carbohydrate-rich meal before a run. Incidentally, rice moves on even faster than other starchy foods. Liquid foods will be digested more quickly than solid foods.

2. Eat as much carbohydrate-rich food as you can manage directly after a run or training session.

Ideally, glycogen stores should be topped up immediately after effort – top athletes eat even before they shower. Eating complex-carbohydrate foods is most effective in replacing glycogen in the first two hours after exercise. The process does continue after that, though at a slower pace. Some athletes prefer a carbohydrate-rich drink in the first two hours and then a full meal after that.

3. Eat little and often at the weekend.

The weekends are more flexible and it is easier to cope with different eating patterns. There is more time, but runs and training sessions are probably longer. It is also very easy to kaleidoscope meals together, with breakfast running into lunch after a late night, or lunch sliding into tea after a session at the pub.

Ideally, eating should be spread out through the day. Consider adding a mid-morning or afternoon snack rather than cutting out meals. If you are training for a marathon, you will most certainly need the extra energy.

This all sounds fairly straightforward, but it may be quite difficult to put into practice. Some people are not able to start their run until well into the evening, others get up at the crack of dawn to jog in the park. The lunch-break may be prime time for others.

Here are some suggested menu plans for different training patterns.

Early-morning Training

FIRST THING
A drink of milky tea, a sports drink or a mixture of fruit juice and water when you wake up, half an hour before training.

BREAKFAST AFTER THE RUN
This is a fairly easy meal because standard breakfast foods are pretty starchy. Eat a bowl of cereals *and* some bread or

toast. Serve the cereals with semi-skimmed milk and add a banana and some dried fruit. If you have time at the weekend, try out Monterey muffins (page 207) or Indian Toast (page 209). Drink tea or fruit juice, avoid coffee.

LUNCH
If you possibly can, carry on the good work with a carbohydrate-based lunch to carry on the glycogen topping-up process started at breakfast.

SUGGESTED HOT MENU
Leek and potato soup

Lasagne with green salad

Banana and yoghurt sundae

SUGGESTED COLD MENU
Lentil Salad (page 238) with radishes

Cold roast chicken with potato salad, tomatoes and watercress and wholemeal bread rolls (page 303)

Wedges of bread and butter pudding

Pack the second menu into a lunch or picnic box and take it to work or to the competition venue. Carry the salads in plastic tubs and wrap the rest of the food in foil and clingfilm.

EATING OUT
Go to a Mexican restaurant and have taco shells with chilli and salad or to an Indian restaurant and have a chicken biryani with naan, dhal and mixed vegetable curry. If you like Chinese food, choose a Cantonese restaurant as they do not include so much deep-fried food as Peking Chinese restaurants.

EVENING MEAL
If you have been able to follow the above advice, a lighter meal will be sufficient in the evening.

SUGGESTED MENU
Tomato, tarragon and yoghurt salad
Prawns and beansprout omelette with tossed green salad
and Wholemeal Rolls (page 303) *or*: Potato and Fennel
Pancake (page 224) with a poached egg and a green salad.
Fresh fruit

Lunch-time Training

BREAKFAST
Start the day with a good breakfast for you may not have
time for as much at midday as you should. If you have
time, include some fruit and perhaps a boiled egg, or
baked beans as well as breakfast cereals and toast. Do not
forget to have a drink.

MID-MORNING
If you had a very early start, a snack now could help to
carry you through the lunch-time run. Try one of the
recipes in Simple Cakes and Sweet Snacks (page 335).
(This is not a good idea of you are overweight.) Drink
plenty of water or fruit juice.

LUNCH
This is the problem area for midday runners. It can be very
difficult to refuel adequately after a lunch-time run. The
run may well take up all of your allotted break and, even if
you do have time, the snacks on sale in the area may not
be very suitable. The answer is to take food which is easy
and unobtrusive to eat at your desk or place of work. Remember to have a long drink.

IDEAS INCLUDE:
Wedges of cheese and Dutch Pepper Loaf (page 229)
Pasta Salad (page 315)
Low-fat muesli bars

EATING OUT
Look at the box on fast-food restaurants on page 56.

EVENING MEAL
It is important to eat all the essential nutrients, but, luckily, you do not have to eat them all at the same meal, so this is the meal at which you can make up any deficit from earlier in the day.

SUGGESTED MENU
Carrot, orange and coriander soup with Wholemeal Rolls (page 303)

Grilled plaice with new potatoes, peas and carrots

Yoghurt ice-cream with mixed berry fruits

or:
Guacamole Dip (page 214) with crudités

Quick Paella (page 287) with a green salad

Tropical surprise (page 328)

Evening training

BREAKFAST
A standard cereal and toast breakfast with some orange juice and fresh fruit.

LUNCH
This is the meal that balances the evening runner's diet, so stick to salads and dishes with a high vegetable content. Finish the meal with fruit.

SUGGESTED HOT MENU
Vegetarian moussaka with mixed salad *or* spinach lasagne with green salad

Cheese and grapes

SUGGESTED COLD MENU
Tuna or egg salad with French bread

Oranges and dates

MID-AFTERNOON

The problem area for the evening runner is the long gap between the midday meal and starting the run. The later the start, the worse the problem will be, and it may make sense to take a good carbohydrate snack into work to eat about an hour before you expect to set off. Choose from the Savoury Snacks (page 212) or Simple Cakes and Sweet Snacks recipes (page 335).

EVENING MEAL

This should of course be a carbohydrate-rich meal to re-plenish glycogen stocks, but some runners are very late finishing the run. You might not be able to start your run until 7.30 and so not get back until 9-9.30 in the evening. You may not always feel like eating a big meal then, but you must eat something.

Try dishes which are not only quick and easy to prepare or reheat, but also easy to eat. Ideas include American-style Apple Rice (page 291) topped with nuts and veget-ables, Multi-grain Pilaf (page 297), Spanish Rice (page 299), Fruit Semolina (page 201) or Swiss Muesli Bowl (page 200).

Are you guilty of playing an evening game of squash when you have not eaten for hours?

You will improve your game tremendously by having a small 'stoke-up' snack around 4 or 5 o'clock. The fifth game is invariably won by the player whose glycogen stores last the longest.

4.4 DEALING WITH SPECIAL CIRCUMSTANCES

Top athletes take it as a matter of course that they will be competing abroad and many of them also spend some of their time training at high altitudes. Members of club teams, too, sometimes have fixtures with similar clubs abroad. Even those who normally only play social games or who jog for fun may decide to have an activity holiday in the Caribbean or go skiing in the Alps.

The different conditions encountered in these venues can have a big effect on performance. However, if you modify your diet to deal with these conditions you can still achieve your top performance.

Effects of Climate

Training and competing in hot weather cause the body to dehydrate and, in extreme cases, to overheat. This can lead to heat exhaustion or even heat-stroke. These extreme conditions need medical care and hospitalization. The situation may be even worse in humid conditions as the effectiveness of sweating is reduced.

If body water is not replaced, the body acts to conserve the remaining fluid by switching off the sweating mechanism and the body temperature will start to rise.

First signs of heat problems
• development of muscle cramps • nausea and faintness Take these signs very seriously and drink water immediately.

If you do have to continue training during a heat-wave or are competing in a hot country, step up the amount of water you drink before, during and after training. Exercise in the cooler times of the day and try to jog or run in the shade. If you can, acclimatize slowly to the conditions, allowing a week or two weeks. Reduce training times during that period.

Competing in cold weather requires more energy than in warm weather. Cross-country skiiers, for example, use as much as 18kcals per minute. So carbohydrate foods need to be stepped up.

It is particularly important not to drink alcohol when competing in really cold climates. Alcohol causes the blood vessels to dilate and lose heat more quickly.

The right kind of clothes will help to keep the body warm. Choose three or four thin layers rather than one to two thick ones and wear a cap or hat. Between 30 and 50 per cent of body heat is lost through the head.

Effects of Altitude

About one in three people are particularly susceptible to changes in altitude. Symptoms include headache, nausea and lethargy. It is obviously important to find out if you are likely to suffer in this way as you may need to allow a longer time to acclimatize. When you are acclimatized you will still need to take more rest. (See page 164 for further helpful steps to take.)

The main dietary requirement is to eat more calories. At altitudes over 5000 feet carbohydrate foods should be increased to as much as 70 per cent of total energy intake. For the best results, start to load up the carbohydrate foods before you leave and pay particular attention to them on the first few days you are at a higher altitude.

Choose foods which are rich in iron and vitamin E such as liver, kidneys and red meat for the former and wholemeal breads, dark green vegetables, eggs and margarine for the latter. You could take some almonds and hazelnuts along to nibble too. Try to eat more and smaller meals.

Extra fluid intake is very important too. The higher the altitude the lower the humidity and the quicker sweat evaporates from the skin. This can lead you to think you are sweating less than usual, which may well in turn influence you to drink less than usual. In fact you should be drinking more fluid than usual – 3-4litres/5¼-7pints – and it is also a good idea to completely cut out coffee and alcohol.

Fatigue

Fatigue is an inevitable accompaniment of prolonged strenuous exercise, but the nature of the fatigue will be influenced by a variety of factors. The most important of these is the intensity of the exercise in relation to the capacity of the individual, and the most effective way to delay the onset of fatigue and improve performance is by training.

There is a proven relationship between the beginning of fatigue and low levels of muscle glycogen. If these are not given a chance to be replenished either by slowing off training or resting, the store of glycogen will be completely used up. This is the point at which the infamous marathon runner's wall occurs.

Muscle fatigue is accelerated by vigorous exercise that overwhelms the aerobic energy production system. At this point little oxygen reaches the muscle cells, lactic acid accumulates and exhaustion occurs (See page 70).

Part of a sports person's training is concerned with learning to judge a running pace which will allow sufficient oxygen to reach the muscles. Alternating hard and easy work-outs will also allow lactic acid to be disposed of by the liver.

Sometimes fatigue is the result of over-training but there is usually more than one factor involved and some could be diet-related. Obviously a diet which is too low in carbohydrates will cause fatigue but other nutrients can also play a part.

A complete diet history could reveal low intakes of vitamins, for example, which might result in tiredness or fatigue before any clinical symptoms are detected. Thiamin, biotin and vitamins B1, B2 and B12 are all associated with energy production and a lack here could be serious. Iron deficiency, too, can result in fatigue.

Hypoglycaemia or low blood sugar levels can also cause fatigue. After a meal the level of glucose in the blood rises and glucose passes into the tissues. (This is one reason why breakfast is so important.) As glycogen is used up in the muscles it is replenished from the blood sugar and this goes down again.

If blood sugar levels fall below normal levels it is possible that you may experience symptoms such as fatigue, mood changes, shakiness, depression and headaches. Some people who eat foods high in sugars or highly refined starches or who go for long periods without food also seem to suffer a drop in blood sugar levels, but this is not as widespread as used to be thought.

If you start to exercise in this condition, blood sugar levels may drop even further and result in decreased performance. Eating the right food at the right time will prevent this from happening.

Another factor which comes into play in high ambient temperatures and humidity is dehydration and thermoregulatory problems. In the laboratory, endurance time may be reduced to less than half that which is achieved at low temperatures. The rate of carbohydrate consumption is the same in both situations, so heat stress rather than glycogen depletion must be the cause here.

5
SPORTS FOR EVERYONE

Exercise is extremely important and everyone, whatever their age or condition, can and should enjoy some kind of sporting activity. The opportunities are almost limitless. For children there are formal sports at school and at sports centres and informal games in the playground, on the beach and in the garden.

These sporting activities may be continued through adult life or new ones added. Keep fit, dance, step and aerobics classes introduce many adults to physical activity for the first time and activity holidays motivate many more. Even walking and cycling to work are valid exercise.

Older people now continue with their sporting activities for very much longer than formerly and veteran sports people are running in marathons, swimming and taking part in track games. There are opportunities too for the diabetic and the disabled.

All this activity needs to be fuelled with the right kind of food (see Chapter 2). A balanced sports diet is essentially the same for everyone, though total energy requirements will of course vary from person to person, depending on the sport and how much effort is put into it.

In addition, special attention may need to be paid to certain nutrients. Growing children will need extra calcium, iron and zinc, while older people may need to watch their fat intake more carefully. This chapter looks at the special needs of these various groups.

5.1 YOUNG SPORTS PERSON'S SPECIAL

Childhood and adolescence is a time of rapid growth coupled with frequent high levels of activity. As a result children have high energy requirements. Unfortunately these needs are too often met by eating more fat and sugar rather than by extra-carbohydrate foods. When the choice of grilled chicken and a jacket-baked potato or a hamburger and chips is offered, the latter is likely to win hands down! The same applies to the merits of a piece of fruit against the offer of a chocolate bar.

The eating patterns of childhood soon become established and bad habits formed now often remain fixed through life. So it is important to encourage sensible eating at a young age. The secret lies in making healthy food as attractive and as exciting as possible. Most children who want to do well in their sport will also respond well to the idea that the right food can help them to win.

The specific energy requirements of an active child depend upon sex, age, height, levels of activity and stage of growth. The latter is a particularly important consideration. Every child goes through a growth spurt when the need for many nutrients will be much higher in proportion to body size and weight than usual.

It makes sense for parents to watch out for this period of rapid growth and adjust the diet accordingly. For girls the most rapid changes normally take place between 11 and 14 years and for boys between 13 and 16, but there is wide individual variation.

The nutrients which are especially needed are:

Carbohydrate

Starchy carbohydrate foods are as important an energy fuel for children as for adults. Indeed children have a higher energy requirement in relation to their body weight. Children who are regularly playing for a school team or who are training for junior athletics events need even more.

The problem is that there is a limit to the actual amount

of food children can eat at a sitting. So it is important to provide foods that are full of nutrients as well as calories. Sugary drinks, cakes, biscuits and sweets provide energy but these foods can also fill the child up without providing much in the way of vitamins, minerals and proteins. Children will always find ways of having some of these, their favourite, foods.

Protein
Protein is essential for growth and children need more protein during their growth spurts than at any other times. However, the average Western diet, with its reliance on milk and milk products, meat and fish, offers a more than adequate amount of protein – even for growing children.

Vegetarians might need to take more care with their children's diet, but it is perfectly possible to put together a protein-rich diet from vegetable sources (see pages 14-15). There could, however, be a problem with a vegan diet for children if the parents are not well versed in nutrition.

Fat
Although most adults need to eat less fat, cutting back too drastically on children's intake can lead to a shortage of essential nutrients. Fat is also needed to fuel some of that excess energy.

Dietary fibre
Constipation is a common bowel problem with children and you should encourage your children to eat plenty of vegetables and wholegrain foods. Unfortunately these are very often just the foods which children will not eat. To minimize this problem, serve as many different sources of dietary fibre as possible and make sure that some are included at every meal. But don't overdo it, children cannot cope with as much fibre as adults. Never serve plain wheat bran to children.

Here are some ways of making fibre-rich foods more popular with your children.

12 Ways to Make Fibre-Rich Foods More Attractive

- If your kids reject wholemeal bread, white bread with added fibre is quite a good substitute. Some children like soft steam-baked wholemeal bread, while others will not eat this but will eat homemade crusty rolls or soda bread. You may have to experiment to see which they like best.
- Make eating vegetables fun for children by offering raw vegetables like carrot and cucumber sticks, radish flowers, cauliflower florets and strips of red and green pepper with dips.
- Introduce your children to different cereal foods such as bulgar, brown rice and millet. Build their interest by telling them a little about the countries these foods come from and how they are served there.
- Include fruit and vegetables in bread and cakes such as Dutch Pepper Loaf (page 226), Carrot Cake (page 341) and Apple and Apricot Teabread (page 339).
- Ensure that vegetables you serve have as much flavour as possible by using the freshest available and by not over-cooking them.
- Offer a variety of different-coloured vegetables either on the same plate or mixed into a colourful medley.
- Do not force your children to eat a particular vegetable. Try again another time and if they still do not like it, cook it in a different way or try it raw. Mounds of raw grated vegetables can look very attractive.
- Encourage your children to put together their own salad mixes from a variety of leaves, tomatoes, cucumber and other

vegetables so that they can leave out items they do not like.

- Freeze bananas for eating like lollipops.
- Use different-coloured melons such as galia, charentais, honeydew and water melon, to make melon balls.
- Dip slices of apple, pear, orange and banana in fruit juice and roll in muesli or toasted ground nuts. Serve with dried fruits in a mixed fruit platter.
- Use wholemeal cereals like oatmeal, brown flour, rye flour and maize (corn) meal in baking bread, cakes and biscuits.

Vitamins

If you are encouraging your children to eat more wholegrains, fruit and vegetables with some of the ploys suggested above, you will also help to ensure that they are getting enough of the B-group vitamins and vitamin C. If, on the other hand, your children are existing on snacks and take-away food or are eating a lot of refined carbohydrate food they may become deficient in these nutrients. Vitamins are essential for good health at all ages but children with their rapid growth rate need even more.

Calcium

Calcium is essential for strong bones and teeth. The best source of calcium for children is milk and growing children should drink about three to four glasses of milk each day. Some children do not like milk on its own but yoghurt and cheese are good sources too.

6 Ideas for Disguising Milk in Cooked Dishes

- Make custard as a change from yoghurt or single cream.
- Make low-sugar ice-creams.
- Serve rice pudding, semolina or fruit porridge made with milk in winter.

- Add milk to soups and sauces.
- Use skimmed milk powder in baking.
- Make frothy milk jellies.

Canned fish such as sardines, pilchards and salmon with edible bones also contain plenty of calcium. Other reasonably good sources of calcium include baked beans, broccoli, dairy ice-cream and white bread.

Iron

Iron is needed for the efficient transport of oxygen from the lungs to the working muscles. Iron needs are much greater during growth and anaemia can be a problem in childhood. If a child is playing or training more than just for fun, screening for anaemia may be advisable at the start of the sports season. The onset of menstruation in girls also increases the need for iron and the possibilty of anaemia. This can become quite a problem among young girls who become demi-veg (no meat) or vegetarian (no meat or fish).

The best sources of iron are red meat, liver and kidneys, though some vegetables are also rich in iron (see page 31). For ways of increasing iron intake see page 46.

Zinc

Zinc is found inside the cells where it is essential for the working of numerous enzymes, including those concerned with the formation of new body proteins for growth and repair.

In parts of the world where the diet is very restricted and where the heat is such that zinc is lost through sweat, some adolescents have been found to suffer from dwarfism and from sexual immaturity.

Zinc is found in red meat. Vegetarian sources include brewer's yeast, cheese, eggs, carrots, peas, potatoes and whole grains. Like iron, it is more easily absorbed into the body if it comes from animal rather than vegetable sources.

Water

The bodies of children and adolescents are not nearly as efficient at regulating body heat as those of adults. They therefore need to replace body fluid more often.

Very often children drink fizzy drinks and squashes rather than water. These drinks are usually full of sugar and do not fulfil the need for fluid as quickly as water would. They also serve to reinforce the child's already sweet tooth.

Offer plain water as often as you can and keep a jug of cold water flavoured with a slice of lemon or orange in the fridge as an alternative to cans of coke.

Eating Patterns

Parents must instil healthy eating habits in their children from a very early age so that eating a balanced diet becomes second nature. Here are some ways to start.

- Try to provide three meals a day at around the same time each day. A routine in early childhood helps to instil the idea that three meals are important.
- Provide nutritious between-meal snacks to discourage your children from buying their own less healthy ones.
- Encourage your children to drink at least two or three glasses of plain water every day.
- Introduce your children to a new food as a regular treat. Do not force them to eat it if they do not like it but try it again at a later date.
- Make chips and fried food into special occasion treats not everyday meals.
- Do not put the salt cellar on the table and keep salt in cooking to reasonable levels.
- Allow sweets after a meal but not before and follow with a good teeth-cleaning session.

It is important to remember that children, even adolescents and teenagers, are just that. It is no good expecting them to think about their diet in the way that an adult sports person might.

There is a general tendency among adolescents to skip meals and rely on snacks and take-away meals. They are susceptible to slick advertising for nutritionally poor foods and peer pressure means they like to eat the same food as their friends are eating.

This means that you will need to pay careful attention to the provision of really healthy school lunches as well as between-meal snacks. Nutritious snacks include milk, fresh fruit, wholemeal toast, peanut butter sandwiches, mashed bananas, cereal bars, wholegrain breakfast cereals with milk, muesli and yoghurt. (See the ideas for adults on page 53.)

Breakfast is a particularly important meal for children and too many kids miss out on this meal. This means that they may go for as long as eighteen hours without food, resulting in lack of concentration during the morning and feelings of tiredness and headache. This in turn leads to snacking on bars of chocolate, crisps or sweet biscuits. A drink and a bowl of cereal or a slice of toast first thing is far better than nothing at all.

Lunch, too, may be skipped if children are keen to get out to the playground or sports field or if they do not like the food provided at school dinners. If lunch is missed they will tire more easily in that most active after-school period of the day.

Since the 1980 Education Act, local authorities are not obliged to provide school meals, though many still do. However, the Act also abolished the need for school meals to meet any nutritional standards and some are very bad indeed.

If you are concerned about your child's lunch-time meal, make an effort to find out what their school provides and if you are not happy with it make a packed lunch to take to school instead. Remember that there is not always time to eat lunch *and* play during the lunch-break, and play might win if the packed lunch is boring.

To help keep your child's interest, pack a number of different items rather than a mound of sandwiches all with the same filling, and do not forget the drink.

12 Ideas to Brighten up your Child's Packed Lunch

- Make mini 'subs' (page 218) by hollowing out and filling small crisp rolls.
- Make small pitta parcels with mini-pitta bread loaves and fill with cottage cheese and salad.
- Add slices of savoury breads such as Dutch Pepper Loaf (page 226) and hazelnut bread (page 340).
- Pack fresh vegetable dippers with small portions of dips in mini-tubs.
- Pack slices of cold pizza, tortilla (page 278) or Oatmeal Leek Savoury (page 296).
- Stuff eggs with chopped watercress or mustard and cress.
- Make rolled sandwiches with ham or cheese or tuna rolled in the centre to make a cigar shape or thicker ones sliced to make catherine wheels.
- Fill small tubs with rice- or pasta-based salads (pages 306-317).
- Stuff vegetables such as tomatoes, cucumber sections or celery sticks with low-fat cheese spread flavoured with fresh herbs.
- Include Oatmeal Scones (page 304) or a slice of Portuguese Cornbread (page 301).
- Sandwich Digestive Biscuits with peanut butter.
- Pack small cakes which are low in sugar and fat for those with high energy requirements. Ideas include Rock Buns (page 337) or Date and Orange Squares (page 335).

To work out the right diet for your child, you must ask the right questions.

- What did your child have for lunch? The evening meal

can be used to balance the day's intake.

- How often does your child play games or practise a particular sport and for how long? This will give some idea of extra energy requirements.
- What time does your child practise and is anything eaten beforehand? What time does he or she finish? The answers will help you to ensure recovery food is on hand.
- Is your child drinking anything during practice and is body fluid being replaced after practice? Should you provide simple drinks to take along to practice?
- Does your child need to lose or gain weight to improve performance or make the team?

Children use more energy at all levels of activity than adults. They are also more likely to be taking part in more than one sport at once, playing hockey at school and swimming or playing tennis at the weekend. For this reason it is important to monitor their weight on a regular basis.

Estimated Average Requirements (EARs) for Energy		
Age	**kcal/day**	
	Males	*Females*
0–3 months	545	515
4–6 months	690	645
7–9 months	825	765
10–12 months	920	865
1–3 years	1230	1165
4–6 years	1715	1545
7–10 years	1970	1740
11–14 years	2220	1845

One of the most common problems among young athletes is an obsession with reducing body fat and losing weight. Gymnasts, ballet dancers and middle-distance runners all feel that they will be more successful if they minimize their weight.

But these young athletes have particularly high energy requirements and if they aim to diet too drastically they will not get that energy. The end-result will be quite the opposite to that which they hope for. Performance will slump and in extreme cases eating disorders such as anorexia or bulimia could develop (see page 136).

5.2 SPORTS WOMEN

Sports men and women both need to follow the same kind of high-carbohydrate, low-fat diet, but female athletes have an increased need for certain nutrients.

Iron

Women need iron far more than men because of the amount of blood lost during menstruation. Quite often female athletes just do not eat enough iron-rich foods. This may be because they are not eating enough food anyway or because they are vegetarian and have not found non-meat substitutes.

Women taking part in endurance sports are more likely to lose iron than other sports women because of a greater turnover of iron. Lack of iron eventually leads to anaemia. All sports women should make a point of knowing which foods are rich in iron so that they can quickly increase their intake if they need to.

There are two types of iron in food. One, known as haem iron, is present in animal products such as meat, liver and kidneys, poultry and fish. It is relatively easily absorbed by the body.

The second type, known as non-haem iron, is found in vegetable foods such as spinach, leafy vegetables, wholegrain cereals and dried fruits, and is not so easily absorbed. However, absorption is increased if you eat foods which are rich in vitamin C at the same time (see page 27). Remember that tea and coffee can reduce the absorption of iron.

Liver is by far the best source of iron. A single serving of liver provides between 10 and 30mg of iron.

Loss of Menstruation

In some sports such as long-distance running, light-weight rowing, gymnastics and ballet dancing the athlete strives for low body weight and body fat and may indulge in an abnormally heavy training programme. This can result in irregular menstruation or even complete loss of menstruation. The latter condition is known as athletic amenorrhoea and is often welcomed by the athlete during the competitive season.

However, recent findings suggest that such a situation should not be viewed so complacently. First of all, it may take some time to re-establish a normal menstrual cycle and this could affect the ability of young female athletes to establish a cycle in later life. The general suggestion that simply discontinuing training and gaining some weight will guarantee a return to normal has yet to be proven.

Even more serious is the possibility that women with amenorrhoea coupled with low body weight and body fat composition can develop osteoporosis in a similar way to post-menopausal women (see page 139). The changes in metabolism associated with amenorrhoea are very similar to the hormonal changes found during the menopause. Both groups lack oestrogen, a hormone which contributes to menstruation and helps to maintain bone density.

Indeed, studies show that amenorrhoeic athletes have less calcium in their bones than female athletes of acceptable body weight and body fat and whose training programme is not so excessive. If you have this condition you may be more prone to stress fractures. You should increase your intake of calcium and iron by including low-fat milk and yoghurt and some red meat. You should also ensure that you get adequate calories from wholegrain cereals and carbohydrate-rich foods. Take advice from your doctor about the need for supplementary calcium and iron.

Eating Disorders

What starts simply as calorie-counting to get the right body weight/body fat ratio can get out of hand and turn into an obsessive fear of eating anything at all. Young women are particularly prone to this kind of problem.

Girls tend to put on fat directly after puberty. This is perfectly normal but unfortunately is not acceptable in sports like gymnastics and ballet where body image is paramount. Nor is it acceptable in sports such as middle-distance running where excessive weight is detrimental to performance.

A well-balanced diet will help in achieving a gradual weight loss without a detrimental effect on performance. Indeed it will improve it if the athlete is carrying genuine excess weight. Unfortunately some girls equate the improvement in performance with the weight loss and they then strive to lose even more.

A lengthy restriction of food can lead to a clear aversion to the food itself and the beginning of anorexia. The first stage of this change can go unnoticed so it is important to watch for any signs that this might be happening.

Symptoms of anorexia include:

- continuing weight loss and regular self-weighing after the desired blance has been achieved
- increasing thinness with arms and legs developing a spindly look
- complaints about being fat even when very thin
- hyperactivity, restless sleep and early waking coupled with an obsession with exercise
- cessation of periods
- insistence that despite above symptoms all is well
- choice of baggy clothes or layers of clothing to conceal thinness

- extreme sensitivity to cold temperatures
- low pulse rate

There may also be other symptoms such as constipation and weakness which are simply due to lack of food.

Another psychological condition is bulimia nervosa. It causes powerful urges to overeat, but overweight is avoided by vomiting, purgatives and periods of starvation.

Both conditions have nutritional repercussions but sufferers do also need psychiatric help. The sad thing about these conditions is that sufferers will eventually get to the stage where they are too thin and too weak to win. Performance is impaired through dehydration and malnutrition and the body loss is ineffective because fluid and muscle are lost as well as fat. There can also be serious long-term effects such as an increased susceptibility to stress fractures.

Pregnancy

Expectant mothers no longer give up their sporting activities the minute they hear that they are pregnant. But if you are pregnant it is even more important than usual to ensure that you are eating a well-balanced diet.

Pregnancy leads to an increased demand for all-important iron and calcium and also for folic acid. The latter nutrient can be found in leafy green vegetables, liver and kidney and peanuts.

Pregnancy affects work output and you should therefore expect the duration and intensity of your sporting activity to decrease. Other changes include an inconvenient need for frequent urination during activity, and your balance and flexibility may alter somewhat.

The general rule in training is to avoid anything new and anything excessive. As pregnancy progresses, more calories are needed to perform the same activities and more fluid required to counteract dehydration during exercise. An approximate weight gain for pregnant women is about 12-15kg/24-30lbs. In general, exercising women gain less than non-exercising women and their newborn babies weigh less.

Breast-feeding

Breast-feeding certainly does not inhibit athletic performance although it may be a bit inconvenient when competing. Indeed, several world records have been set by breast-feeding mothers. However, if you are in hard training you will need to ensure a really high calorie intake alongside increased protein and calcium.

The calorific needs of breast-feeding are estimated to be about 500kcals per day and this should be added to the energy needs of basal metabolism, activity and sport (see page 83).

5.3 SPORTS AND MATURITY

A veteran athlete may be a 35-year-old swimmer or an 80-year-old runner and there are plenty of sportsmen and women between these ages. Here again, they all need a well-balanced diet which meets their own special energy requirements.

As you age you change. Muscle mass decreases and so does physical working capacity. The gut stops being quite so efficient and fewer nutrients are absorbed. Other problems may also develop as time goes on. The older athlete therefore needs to take even more care about eating the right foods in the right quantity.

Metabolic rate slows as you get older and many people tend to gain weight if they continue to eat as they always did. Exercise can help to counteract this trend. The slowing of basal metabolic rate is usually allowed for in energy calculations by reducing the figure by 4 per cent for every 10 years over 25.

As you grow older you also become more susceptible to various disorders such as heart disease (see page 20), cancer of the bowel and diverticulitis. In fact bowel disorders are the most common medical disorder among older people. A high-fibre diet can help to reduce the incidence of these and so it becomes increasingly important to eat a diet high in fibre. (See page 38 for ways of increasing fibre.)

Osteoporosis

The mineral content of bones begins to fall with age and this can lead to osteoporosis or thinning of the bones. Post-menopausal women are particularly susceptible to osteoporosis.

You can reduce your risk of developing osteoporosis by eating a life-long calcium-rich diet and following a regular exercise programme.

---

12 Ways to Boost Calcium Intake

- Use milk to make porridge or muesli at breakfast
- Buy calcium-enriched soy milk.
- Make calcium-rich sandwiches and salads with canned sardines, canned salmon, prawns or grated cheese. Mash the bones into the flesh of canned sardines for an excellent 493g of calcium per 125g/4oz of fish.
- Make yoghurt-based salad dressings (see page 316).
- Eat yoghurt mixed with fresh fruit rather than ice-cream for dessert.
- Eat plenty of dark green leafy vegetables like spinach, kale and cabbage greens.
- Add dried milk powder to hot breakfast cereals and baked cakes and biscuits.

- Look out for tofu processed with calcium sulphate.
- Drink milk-based hot chocolate or cocoa instead of coffee at breakfast or before you go to bed.
- Use blackstrap molasses in flapjacks and fruit cakes.
- Sprinke sesame seeds on salads or cooked vegetables.
- Eat more custards, milk puddings and milk jellies.

Milk and milk products are the very best source of calcium. There is no need to worry about taking too much calcium, the body excretes the excess. People who have difficulty digesting milk need to find alternative calcium sources. Some can manage goat's milk products and though this contains a little less calcium than cow's milk it still compares quite well.

Milk Myths Exploded

- Milk is not difficult to digest unless you are lactose-intolerant.
- Milk does not cause stomach cramping. Cramp is more likely to be caused by lack of milk or of inadequate calcium.
- Conversely, drinking extra milk does not hasten the healing process.
- Milk does not cause a dry mouth or 'cotton' mouth.

5.4 VEGETARIAN SPORTS PEOPLE

There is no reason why vegetarian sports people should not perform just as well as those on a more conventional diet, and indeed they do. Some problems can occur as the degree of vegetarianism increases but real difficulties are only likely to arise if the diet consists solely of refined cereals and sweet or fatty foods.

The varying degrees of vegetarianism are:

Demi-vegetarians
Some people simply decide to cut out all red meat but still eat poultry and fish.

Lacto-ovo vegetarians
These people cut out all meat and fish but eat animal products such as milk, eggs and cheese.

Lacto-vegetarians
Similar to lacto-ovo vegetarians, but exclude eggs.

Vegans
Vegans exclude all flesh foods, all dairy products and eggs, and eat only foods of plant origin.

It is quite possible to obtain all ten nutrients you need without eating meat or fish. Most of the nutrients which are usually gained from meat can be found in other foods.

However, these other foods are often dairy foods and if dairy foods are cut out too, much more care will need to be taken in balancing the diet. Indeed the more restricted the diet, the less likely it is to be nutritionally adequate. Fruitarian and macrobiotic diets, for example, which received a good deal of publicity a few years ago, are deficient in many nutrients and should be avoided.

Some people give up meat and overlook the fact that they still need to have adequate amounts of protein. In the past the first area of concern was the amount of protein in a vegetarian or vegan diet. However, it is relatively easy to use the theory of complementary proteins (see pages 16 and 270) to ensure adequate amounts of protein even for those athletes with increased requirements.

Even if you are not a vegan, you should eat as many different vegetarian sources of protein as you can. Cheese and eggs supply very usable protein but care should be taken not to rely too heavily on them because of their high saturated fat content. The best diet is made up of a variety of protein sources.

Areas of Risk

If you are following a strict vegetarian or vegan diet you should plan for the following nutrients:

Calcium
This is particularly important for vegan children, adolescents and pregnant and breast-feeding mothers. Good sources are fortified soy milk, wholemeal bread, almonds, spinach, spring greens and pulses like beans and dried peas. Tap water in hard-water areas of the country can be useful too.

Iron
This should not be a problem provided that you understand the difference between the different kinds of iron (see page 134) and make an effort to eat foods which are rich in vitamin C at the same time (see page 27). Meals which contain bread, pulses like beans and peas and dark green vegetables are useful here.

Iodine
Iodized salt is the answer to any possible problems.

Vitamin B2 (riboflavin)
Some breakfast cereals contain added vitamin B2. Check the labels in the supermarkets.

Vitamin B12
The main sources of vitamin B12 are animal-based (liver, meat, eggs and milk). It is also present in some plant foods if they have been affected by the micro-organisms which produce it. However, vegans may find it difficult to fulfil their requirements and they should consider buying pro-

ducts such as yeast extract, soy milk and breakfast cereals which have been fortified with this vitamin. Check the labels to be sure they are.

Vitamin D

If you do not eat any dairy products it is very important to spend some time in the sun as this vitamin is synthesized by the body on exposure to sunlight.

Provided all these nutrients are properly catered for there is no reason why infants should not be weaned on to a vegetarian or even a vegan diet. But great care must be taken to ensure that they get enough energy.

By their nature, vegetarian and vegan diets contain larger amounts of cereals, fruits and vegetables than meat-based diets. This means that they tend to be bulkier and vegetarian sports people may have to eat more to get enough energy to fuel their sport.

This does not usually cause any problems for adults but active and growing children may find it difficult to eat enough to get the very large amounts of energy and nutrients that they need to grow properly.

---

12 Ways for Vegetarians and Vegans to Achieve a Balanced Diet

- Do not replace animal-protein foods with eggs and cheese alone.
- Choose wholegrain cereals, flour and pasta.
- Eat more pulses – beans, peas and lentils.
- Grind nuts to make them easier to digest but do not include too many as they are rich in fat.
- Choose calcium-enriched soy milk and other soy products such as tofu and soya margarine.
- Use yeast and yeast extracts for their B-group vitamins.
- Step up the amount of green leafy vegetables you eat.

- Look out for breakfast cereals fortified with vitamin B2 and B12.
- Cut out refined and sugary foods except for the occasional treat.
- Include edible seaweeds and tempeh for vitamin B12.
- Eat plenty of vitamin C and iron-containing foods such as leafy vegetables, kidney beans and dried apricots.
- Increase the amount of water drunk to counter the high fibre intake.

Suggested Vegan Menus For a Day

Adjust the quantities to suit your own energy needs.

1

Vitamin B12-enriched breakfast cereal with calcium-enriched soy milk
Wholemeal toast with soy margarine and marmalade

Pasta Soup (page 273)
Date and Nut Halva (page 344) and fresh fruit

Avocado Pear with Tofu Dressing (page 317)
Vegetable curry with brown rice
Spiced Lentils (page 275)
Baked Bananas (page 333)

2

Glass of orange juice
Bean and Potato Hash (page 210) and grilled tomatoes
Toast with soy margarine and honey
Tea or coffee with soy milk

Wholemeal pitta bread filled with falafel and salad with tahina sauce
Mixed dried fruit and nuts

Vegetable soup with a Wholemeal Roll (page 303)

Jacket-baked Potatoes (page 227) filled with braised mushrooms
Crunchy Salad (page 310) with Tofu Dressing (page 317)
Fresh fruit salad

3
Breakfast cereals with added nuts and raisins
Calcium-enriched soy milk
Hazelnut Bread (page 340) and soy margarine with jam

Club sandwiches filled with Middle Eastern Hummus (page 215) and mixed salad
Carrot and Sultana Muffins (page 206) made with soy products

Stuffed Peppers (page 240)
Tagliatelle with tomato sauce and green salad
Sliced oranges with wheatmeal biscuits

5.5 THE INTENSIVE SPORTS HOLIDAY

Sporting activity holidays seem to be on the increase. In addition to the long-popular winter skiing holiday you can now try canoeing, sailing, riding and trekking, rock climbing, golf and many more. You can also spend a week or two of intensive coaching in your favourite leisure sport such as tennis, football, badminton and so on.

If you are not a regular member of a team and only indulge in social sport at the weekends, the chances are that you will be exercising much more intensively on holiday and over a longer period than is normal for you. In addition, some of the sports on offer are extremely demanding in themselves.

If you are to get the most out of the holiday you will want to put as much as possible into it. However, unless you already exercise regularly and eat the right diet, you are probably not really fit enough to push yourself to the limits without harming yourself.

Most people know that they should get some practice in on a dry ski slope or at the very least to do some exercises to get the right muscles into action before they go on a skiing holiday. Unfortunately very few people actually do even this small amount of preparation and then they are surprised at the high injury rate on the slopes.

The correct diet is equally important in getting fit, not only for a skiing holiday but for any kind of activity holiday. So start by ensuring that you regularly follow the current guidelines for healthy eating set out in Chapter 2. This coupled with regular exercise will start to get you in trim.

Countdown to the Holiday

You will probably have to book your holiday well in advance, and you should start planning for fitness well in advance as well. After all, you want to be as fit as possible when you set off.

Going on an Activity Holiday?

- Concentrate on getting fit.
- Improve body weight if necessary.
- Build up body stores of essential nutrients such as iron and calcium.
- Exercise regularly to make your body more energy efficient.

At least a month before you go, check your body weight. Do you need to lose weight – the most likely – or do you simply need to build up muscle strength and shed body fat?

Either way, you should move on to the kind of training diet outlined in Chapter 4. Increase the contribution of carbohydrate food to your total energy intake from 55 per cent to 60 per cent. Remember that this increase must be at the expense of fat and protein foods. It should not be an overall increase in consumption.

Make sure that the food you are eating is rich in essential nutrients. It is very important to build up the body's stocks to maximum proportions. Have a look at the ways to increase your intake of iron and calcium suggested on pages 31/46 and 139 and follow the vitamin and fibre suggestions on page 38.

During the Holiday

A good many activity holidays are based abroad and you may have to adjust to a new climate (perhaps hotter and more humid) or deal with a higher altitude. The food will be different and you may have to be careful with the water.

The first hazard to your new-found strength and fitness is the journey. If this is by air you could well become dehydrated owing to the low pressure and dry air. To guard against this, avoid dehydrating drinks like tea, coffee and alcohol and stick to fruit juice or mineral water and drink plenty of it.

Take some carbohydrate-rich snacks with you such as fresh or dried fruit, cereal bars and sweets to supplement the airline meals, and stretch or walk around if possible to stop your muscles from stiffening up.

If you are going a very long way, jet-lag can take a day or two from the full participation in your sporting activities but there are a number of steps you can take to combat it.

- Adopt the new local hours as soon as possible – set your watch to the new time on take-off. The meals on board are designed to help you into your new time zone.
- On arrival take meals at the correct time for the new time zone.
- Avoid large meals late at night as this may make sleep even more difficult.
- Change your diet temporarily to eat a high-protein breakfast, perhaps with eggs, and a low-protein dinner.

The protein helps to increase the arousal state which is great in the morning but not good at night.

Once you have acclimatized you should revert to your usual high-carbohydrate breakfast – you will need all the fuel you can get. Eat plenty of cereals and toast before you go out to the slopes, river or sea and take some bananas, nuts or plain biscuits with you to eat between practice sessions. At lunch-time go for carbohydrate-rich potatoes, pasta dishes and plenty of bread. The same goes for the evening meal too.

In some countries you may have to be careful to avoid stomach upsets. This is certainly the case in Egypt, Spain, Portugal, Greece, Tunisia, India and other parts of the Far East (see page 181 for steps to take). Try to drink as much liquid as possible. This is particularly important in hot and humid conditions and at high altitudes. This means as much as 3litres/5¼pints of liquid a day.

Of course this is a holiday, but if you are serious about getting the most out of your chosen activity, you must not go too wild on the 'après-ski' or equivalent evening activities. Tea, coffee and alcohol all have a dehydrating effect.

See pages 120 and 121 for more information on different climatic conditions and high-altitude holidays.

5.6 DISABLED, INJURED OR RETIRING SPORTS PEOPLE

Disabled Sports People

Wheelchair athletes have much the same nutritional requirements as their more mobile colleagues. There is a prime requirement for energy, for the essential nutrients and for water. However, disabled sports people often have to overcome additional problems aggravated or caused by their disability.

Dehydration

Sportsmen and women in wheelchairs are just as likely as runners to become dehydrated. Spinal cord injury, for example, often interferes with normal temperature control mechanisms and circulation may be impaired. This can be aggravated by a reluctance to drink, particularly if there are bladder problems.

Constipation

This can be caused by lack of mobility and it is very important for wheelchair athletes to eat enough fibre to counteract the condition. This is a far better solution than an over-dependence on laxatives as this can result in nutrient deficiency which would certainly be detrimental to sports performance.

Excess Weight

This can result from the wrong diet and from compensatory over-eating. If you are a disabled athlete it is just as important for you to work out your energy requirements as if you were able-bodied. You can then tailor your diet to meet your energy needs. Make sure that the lion's share of your daily energy requirement is met by complex-carbohydrate food and not by fatty foods. Make sure, too, that you are getting sufficient vitamin C, iron and calcium and all the other essential nutrients.

Temperature Control

Because your ability to shiver is limited in a wheelchair you may be particularly vulnerable to low temperatures when taking part in a marathon or any other endurance sport.

Injured or Retiring Sports People

Whether you are resting from sport because injury has forced you into it or because you have decided that the time has come to take life a little more easily and retire from competitive sport, you are likely to face the same problem.

You are used to eating a high-energy diet and have the appetite for it! The problem is that you no longer need it. If you do not do something about this fairly swiftly you will start to put on weight.

This is bad for everyone but if you are laid up through injury it could delay your return to competitive sports as the excess weight will need to be removed first. If you are a team sportsman or woman you, too, would be far better off keeping body weight stationary so that you do not have to go on to an excessive diet at the beginning of the next season.

You will have to pay considerable attention to ensuring that the gain in body weight is minimized. If you are temporarily or permanently 'retired', other forms of exercise can help to fill the gap. Walking, jogging, swimming and social games like tennis, badminton and squash are a big help. However, if you are injured you will have to depend on diet plus your rehabilitation exercises.

Whatever your scenario, you will need to reduce your intake of food, keeping the supply of nutrients high. The good eating habits gained in your pursuit of top performance should not be forgotten once you stop competing. They can help you to go on living a healthy life at the correct weight.

6
POWER EATING FOR PROFESSIONAL PERFORMANCE

Everyone wants to achieve their optimum performance but the pressures on competing athletes are even greater. So much can depend upon a single event or a single match that it is not surprising that any proposed method of improving performance is eagerly grasped. Some of these methods have been tried and tested and found to work but others are questionable to say the least.

6.1 SPORTS DRINKS

Sports drinks have become big business with growing sales not only to sports people but also to the public generally. If you drink them in any quantity they can become a very expensive part of your training programme. So the question is, do they do you any good or would you be better off with water?

Sports drinks contain a variety of ingredients but the crucial one is water. They also contain a carbohydrate source and sodium choloride (common salt). Other ingredients are added but they are of lesser importance and are sometimes only added to give the manufacturer a 'unique selling point'.

The concentration of the drink is very important. It must

be isotonic and this will be stated on the label. The carbohydrate content must not be higher than 4-8 per cent: any more and the rate of water-absorption by the body will slow down, making the sports drink counter-productive.

Isotonic fluids are those which have the same concentration of dissolved particles in them as body fluids (usually about 5-7g per 100ml/4floz). They are absorbed by the body at the same speed as water or slightly faster, depending on exercise condition.

Hypotonic fluids are less concentrated than body fluids (usually about 2-3g per 100ml/4floz). They are absorbed into the body more rapidly than water.

Hypertonic fluids are more concentrated than body fluids. In this instance water will move from the body's fluid into the gut to dilate the ingested solution. This water is secreted rather than absorbed.

Water is the most important ingredient in a sports drink because it is water which helps to build up body fluid before an event and replace it afterwards. Sodium is added to aid absorption of the water and to replace the minerals which are lost during exercise, and the carbohydrate is added for energy.

Adequate hydration before exercise is essential for optimum performance. During prolonged exercise more fluid needs to be taken. This improves performance not only for the top athlete but for everyone who is involved in sport. Rehydration after exercise is also essential. It is required for recovery and the restoration of physical and mental performance.

When deciding exactly what to drink the first consideration will be whether or not you need a drink which will primarily replace liquid, perhaps with a small energy top-up, or one which is designed primarily to boost carbohydrates while at the same time providing some liquid.

This choice will in turn depend upon when you are drinking the fluid.

Before exercise: The primary concern here is to build up fluid. Carbohydrate stocks should be as high as they can be from the last meal. Choose isotonic or hypotonic drinks or water at this time.

During exercise: All the evidence clearly shows that isotonic drinks which contain an energy source in the form of carbohydrates together with sodium are the most effective choice to take during exercise. They can and do improve performance.

After exercise: Liquid is probably the primary essential here but carbohydrate is also required. The answer could be an isotonic drink followed by a carbohydrate snack. This is also the best choice if you are taking part in a tournament and the exercise has to be repeated in a short time.

Sodium is necessary for post-event rehydration and this mineral (often referred to as electrolyte in sports drink information material) should be included in a good sports drink. If little or no sodium is taken, urine production will be stimulated and the liquid you have drunk will not be retained. This will be complicated by the intensity and duration of the sport you are involved in, the ambient temperature and humidity and your own physiological and biochemical characteristics. All these factors will influence whether your primary need is for fluid or for carbohydrate fuel.

It would be useful if sports drinks fell into two categories – those which replace fluid and those which boost energy. Unfortunately they do not. Most manufacturers try to achieve the impossible and do both. But whatever the advertising may tell you, there is no single sports drink which is ideal for all sportsmen and women and all sporting situations.

You will have to learn by trial and error what is most suitable for your various needs. You should also practise using the drinks you choose as part of your training programme.

Sports Drinks Labels

Always check the following:
- Isotonic, hypotonic or hypertonic?
- Carbohydrate levels and type?
- Presence or absence of sodium?

The carbohydrate content of sports drinks may be glucose, sucrose, glucose polymers (sometimes known as maltodextrin) or fructose. The first three all stimulate absorption of fluid. Fructose, however, is slower and therefore does not stimulate so much fluid absorption. If the concentration of the other carbohydrate sources goes over about 8 per cent, absorption slows down.

However, a slightly higher concentration of carbohydrate is possible with glucose polymer. This is made up of several molecules of glucose bound together but it acts as one particle. This means more carbohydrate (and therefore energy) can be delivered without affecting the isotonicity of the drink.

6.2 CARBOHYDRATE LOADING

The longer an event or match lasts, the more important stamina and endurance will be. The glycogen store in the muscles is the limiting factor in prolonged exercise. Once this runs out you will start to tire fast. So the more you can extend the period before glycogen stores are exhausted and fatigue sets in, the better your performance will be.

The simple goal is to have as much carbohydrate in the body as possible during the later stages of an event or match. A high carbohydrate diet (60 per cent of total energy intake) and regular training sessions are both designed to do just this.

Some athletes go even further and start to load their diet with as much as 70 per cent total energy intake coming from carbohydrate. This technique, known as carbohydrate loading, is often favoured by marathon runners and for other events lasting one and a half hours or more.

The theory of carbohydrate loading originated in Sweden in the 1960s. A group of researchers combined training and diet in such a way that the stores of glycogen in the bodies of the athletes taking part reached two to three times the normal level.

This was achieved by first depleting the carbohydrate stores by exercising to exhaustion on a low-carbohydrate, high-fat, high-protein diet. The exercise was then stopped and the diet reversed to build up glycogen stores again. The body's carbohydrate stores were found to fill more completely after the initial cut-back than they would have done in normal circumstances.

The Technique of Carbohydrate Loading
Six Day Countdown
Days 6, 5, 4 – Heavy exercise to deplete glycogen stores in the muscles.
– Exercise must involve muscles that will be used during the actual event. It is no use swimming to exhaustion before a marathon.
– Follow a high-fat/high-protein/ low-carbohydrate diet to stop muscles filling up with glycogen.
– Diet must include about 50g/2oz carbohydrates per day to supply the brain with energy.
Days 3, 2, 1 – Avoid all exercise to prevent using glycogen stores.

> – Follow a high-carbohydrate/
> adequate-protein/low-fat diet to
> rebuild glycogen stores to a
> higher level than before.

This drastic method of carbohydrate loading has a number of drawbacks. First of all, it greatly disrupts the normal training schedule, and you need a lot of will-power not to run at all during those three days before the event. The initial low-carbohydrate diet is difficult to follow too. It can cause tiredness, irritability, low blood sugar and even nausea.

This kind of regime is very extreme and should not be attempted lightly, nor should it be attempted more than three times a year.

You may decide that the modified type of carbohydrate loading developed in the USA would suit you better. With this method the high-fat/high-protein glycogen depletion phase is omitted. Instead, training is cut back gradually or tapered, and a normal diet is eaten in the first half of the week. After three or four days, training is reduced even further or stopped completely and carbohydrate loading starts.

The Technique of Modified Carbohydrate Loading

Six Day Countdown

Days 6, 5, 4 – Train as normal or gradually
reduce training.

– Follow a normal training diet
with just enough carbohydrates
to ensure that muscle glycogen
levels are kept reasonably
steady.

Days 3, 2, 1 – Drastically reduce or stop
training to allow muscle
glycogen reserves to build up.

> – Eat a high-carbohydrate diet with carbohydrates contributing 70 per cent of total energy intake, with adequate protein and low fat to build glycogen stores to a higher level.

The super-saturating effect of this much less gruelling regime seems to be just as effective as the full-blown six-day carbohydrate loading.

Whether you need carbohydrate loading of any kind and how much you need must be worked out on the basis of the energy requirements of your particular sport. It is important to remember that carbohydrate loading is a further shift in emphasis to carbohydrate food, it is not an increase in overall energy intake. The extra carbohydrate eaten must be balanced by less fat and protein food.

It is really only endurance sports like long-distance walking and cycling, cross-country skiing, triathlons and marathons which last for more than one and a half to two hours, that need this kind of loading.

Some tournaments and top-class soccer may also be included here, though carbohydrate loading is difficult if you have a large number of matches spread over a period of time. Professional footballers should save the technique for particularly important matches such as cup ties and internationals.

If it is decided that you should try carbohydrate loading, great care will be needed in planning your meals. Simply stuffing yourself with food will not only not work but will be counterproductive.

Total energy intake must not be higher than in a normal diet. You will not be exercising, so excess calories will simply turn to fat. You need to cut back on protein and fat to make room for the carbohydrates.

A small weight gain of 1kg/2lb is normal. Any more and you have failed! The 1-kg/2-lb increase is due to increased glycogen and the water stored with it. It can be an initial

Sample Menus for Carbohydrate Loading

Breakfast: 1

300ml/10floz fruit juice
Pancakes or drop
scones with 1
tablespoon maple
syrup
1 banana
150ml/5floz skimmed
milk

2

300ml/10fl oz fruit
juice
Portion oatmeal
porridge with 1
tablespoon golden
syrup
300ml/10fl oz
skimmed milk
3 slices wholemeal
toast and marmalade

Snack:

1 Rock Bun (page 337)
and some fruit

Carrot and Sultana
Muffin (page 206)
and an orange

Lunch:

Bean or dried pea-
based soup
2 large baps with
mixed salad filling and
a very little
mayonnaise

Portion pasta with
tomato sauce and
green salad
Slice Carrot Cake
(page 341)

Snack:

1 can soft drink
Slice of Apple and
Apricot Teabread (page
339) with tea

Banana milk-shake

Dinner:

Vegetable soup
Multi-grain Pilaf with
Chicken and Mango
Salad (page 308)
Date and Orange
Squares (page 335)
Glass of milk

Stuffed Peppers
(page 240)
Large portion Chinese
noodles or rice with
stir-fried mixed vegetables
French Apple Batter
Pudding (page 330)

disadvantage but many are prepared to tolerate it at the start because of the benefits towards the end.

Be sensible in your food choices. Don't overload on refined carbohydrates or on fruit – difficulties could be constipation and diarrhoea respectively. However, simple sugars can be used to help fill in the gaps. Too much fibre can also cause problems, so choose familiar foods to which you know your reactions. Some athletes use carbohydrate supplements as drinks or add them to other food as one might add sugar.

For shorter events, training plus an ordinary high-carbohydrate diet should be sufficient to build up your capacity to store glycogen. If, in addition, you also taper training just prior to the event, you should have the reserves you need.

The same holds good for matches which last less than two hours. Squash, badminton and table tennis matches do not last long enough to make it necessary to do more than ensure a high intake of carbohydrates on the day prior to the match. Carbohydrate loading can add 1-1.5kg/2.3lb to your weight and players of these games are unlikely to be happy with that.

6.3 PROTEIN FOR PERFORMANCE?

In many sports muscle is regarded as the key to winning and too often prime steaks are seen as the way to provide that muscle. However, the belief that extra protein automatically helps build muscles is misguided.

The recommended amount of protein in a healthy diet is calculated on the basis of an average of 0.9 grams of protein per kg/2lb of body weight per day. Sedentary adults may need a little less and adults building muscle may need a little more – perhaps 1.2 to 1.7 grams per kg/2lb of body weight (see page 90).

Recent studies, though controversial, do seem to show that both endurance and strength/power athletes require slightly more protein in their diet than other sports people. Certainly long-distance runners and cross-country skiers experience a greater degree of 'wear and tear' as a result of their sports.

The quantities of protein involved in these extra needs is very small. The following menus form the diet of a 70-kg/140-lb strength/speed athlete needing 1.7 protein per kg/12lb of body weight or 119g protein per day.

Breakfast:
3 tablespoons fruit and nut muesli 4.6g protein
2 slices wholemeal toast 8.3g protein

Lunch:
2 slices wholemeal bread 8.3g protein
1 small can tuna in brine 23.5g protein
1 × 50-g/2-oz carton fruit yoghurt 6.2 protein

Evening Meal:
Roast chicken breast (large portion) 34.5g protein
Pasta (large portion) 12.6g protein
Peas (large portion) 5.7g protein

600ml/1 pint semi-skimmed milk for cereal and drinks 19.3g protein

Total protein = 123g

This example shows how much protein comes from foods which are good sources of carbohydrates.

In the course of eating more food to get their training needs, most endurance and power sportsmen and women will automatically get the extra protein they require.

Increase in muscle size and strength comes from a combination of training and a diet providing carbohydrate energy to train hard and recover from training.

Exchanging this diet for one which is high in protein rather than carbohydrate will lead to increased dehydration – lowered calcium levels, earlier fatigue and reduced performance. Quite the opposite of what is intended.

Problems with Too Much Protein

- Lack of essential carbohydrate fuel
- Increased urine production with consequent inconvenience and possible dehydration
- Increased risk of stress fractures due to accelerated calcium excretion
- Likely to lead to too much fat in the diet with consequent risk of increased body fat and heart disease.

Protein and Amino-acid Supplements

There are a variety of protein and amino-acid supplements on the market. They come in all shapes and sizes as tablets, liquids and powders. The latter are often made up of a mixture of protein and carbohydrate. The amount of protein differs from product to product (½gram in a tablet to 20g in the liquid type). Some contain all the amino-acids required to make up a usable protein, others only one or two.

These products are invariably expensive and they are a waste of money because the theory on which they are based is false. Protein simply does not build muscle as such.

Even if protein supplements were valuable, most of them contain less protein than you might easily get from much cheaper protein foods like tuna fish, soy beans or eggs.

Supplements which contain the amino-acids arginine and ornithine are thought to stimulate the release of growth hormones which in turn enhances muscle synthesis. However, there is no proof that the small amounts of amino-acids provided by the supplements have any effect on growth-hormone levels or on body condition.

Another concern is that the use of single or unbalanced amino-acid supplements may interfere with the absorption of certain essential amino-acids. When the body's proportion of amino-acids is unbalanced, or if an essential amino-acid is missing, negative nitrogen balance can occur with subsequent loss of protein from the body. Such risks seem unwarranted when the correct sports diet will provide enough protein for muscle synthesis.

Some sports people do find it difficult to consume enough food to meet their energy requirements, but a balanced liquid meal with all the essential nutrients in the right proportions is a much better bet than protein supplements.

6.4 THE QUICK ENERGY FIX

There is no such thing as a quick energy fix. Nor is there anything magic about glucose or fructose. They can be useful when the body's glycogen stores are really low, for example, during the last stages of an endurance race. But at other times sugar will be no more useful than any other carbohydrate food in boosting energy levels. The energy production systems will continue to work in the normal way.

At one time sugar and sweet snacks were not recommended in the hour or so before playing in a match, going on a training run or taking part in any strenuous exercise. However, recent studies have not supported this advice. During experiments some athletes were given quite strong sugar solutions to drink before taking part in prolonged and strenuous exercise and others were given plain water. There was no difference in the performance of the two groups.

Indeed other research suggests that for sporting events lasting longer than two hours (about the length of time it takes to use up most of the glycogen in the exercising muscles), taking a high sugar snack immediately before you start may be helpful.

Sugar at this stage seems to help in providing energy for the later stages of the event. If you decide to try this practice out it is advisable to do so in a mock competition and remember to have a suitable drink with the snack.

Some athletes prefer an extra energy fix after they have been exercising for about an hour or so. Sugar enters your bloodstream very quickly during exercise and can enhance your stamina. Some people like fruit juices, others prefer biscuits, even sweets. Experiment to see what suits you best. Take care with the amount that you eat and spread it over a period of time. Quite often sports drinks are the best answer.

Sugar taken in large quantities encourages fluid to drain from other parts of the body to the digestive system. This can cause cramps, nausea and diarrhoea. Research suggests that 60g of carbohydrate is the maximum the body can deal with per hour.

6.5 VITAMIN SUPPLEMENTS

Most sports people have vitamin supplements on their shopping lists. The supplements are taken in the belief that extra vitamins may lead to better performance. This belief is reinforced by the claims of some of the supplement manufacturers.

Some manufacturers have even gone so far as to market specific supplements for specific sports. The theory is that just as you play soccer and golf with different balls and use different parts of the body, so you will have different vitamin requirements!

In fact there is no evidence to suppose that golfers' requirements are any different from those of a soccer player. Nor is there any evidence that vitamin supplementation by those who already have an adequate intake has any effect on physical working capacity. Exercise does not burn up vitamins. Vitamins are catalysts that are needed for the metabolic processes to occur.

However, a deficiency of any vitamin caused by low intake or increased loss or a combination of both can lead to poor performance. For this reason many people often take a daily multi-vitamin supplement as a kind of insurance policy to ensure that they are getting what they need.

In an ideal world sports people should get all the vitamins required for optimal performance from their food. But research shows that too often sports people do not always eat a very well-planned diet. Of course, the best way to correct this would be to improve the diet.

When this is not possible, a case might be made for supplementation. Supplements may also be necessary when travelling in an under-developed country where the food may be less than adequate.

Vitamin supplements may be useful when;
<ul><li>You are training for a marathon – vitamin C</li><li>You are training or competing at high altitudes – vitamin E</li><li>You are training or competing in high temperatures or high humidity – vitamin C and B-group vitamins</li></ul>

Some researchers believe that sports people are particularly prone to vitamin deficiency because of the physical stress involved in many sports. It has been suggested, for example, that marathon runners should take vitamin C supplements to help combat chronic muscle fibre damage.

There may also be a case for taking vitamin E supplements at high altitudes. This is because studies show that vitamin E has a beneficial effect on physical performance and a partially protective effect on cell membranes at high altitudes. In hot climates extra vitamin C can enhance heat acclimatization and extra B-group vitamins are needed to replace those lost through excessive sweat.

If you do think that you are deficient in vitamins and minerals for any reason, write down everything that you eat for the period of a week. You can then have your diet analysed by a qualified sports dietitian or nutritionist to see if it really is deficient in any nutrients.

Such people can also advise you on which foods will help to improve the situation. You may need vitamin or mineral supplements in the short term but in the long term it is better to change the diet. A bad diet with supplements remains a bad diet.

Top 10 Fruit and Vegetable Choices

Dark and colourful fruit and vegetables tend to contain more nutrients than paler ones.

Fruit	*Vegetables*
oranges	broccoli
bananas	green pepper
canteloup melon	spinach
apricots	carrots
peaches	tomatoes

Supplements should be taken under the supervision of your doctor or dietitian. A carefully planned and well-balanced multi-vitamin supplement is unlikely to do you any harm but if you decide to jump on the latest bandwagon and concentrate on one particular vitamin or mineral, you could do yourself some damage.

Many sports people who prescribe supplements for themselves believe that if a small amount of a vitamin is good for you, a larger amount is even better. This is just not true. Over-dosing on Vitamin B6, for example, can cause severe loss of muscle coordination, and there are question marks over the long-term excessive use of vitamins B1 and B3.

There is also the notorious case of the man who consumed so much beta-carotene he turned yellow. In fact carotene is not toxic. However, retinol, which is also found in vitamin A, can cause liver damage if excessive amounts are consumed for too long. Very large doses of retinol are also dangerous during pregnancy and can result in birth defects.

It is difficult to overdose on vitamin C as it is regularly removed from the body, and vitamin E is thought to be safe in doses as high as 30 times the minimum amount. However, the long-term effects of excessive antioxidant intake is not known.

6.6 MINERAL SUPPLEMENTS

Minerals are very often included along with vitamins in multi-mixes of various kinds. They may also be taken on their own, but you need to be as careful with minerals as with vitamins.

Salt Tablets

A good many sports people take salt tablets on a regular basis to prevent cramp. The actual mechanism involved in cramp is not fully understood but there is no evidence to suggest that muscle cramp can be prevented or cured by taking salt tablets.

On the contrary, not only will salt tablets not help, they may actually be harmful, particularly if you are losing body fluids by sweating.

As you sweat you lose a lot more water than salt. Thus the salt left in the body becomes more and more concentrated.

If you then swallow salt tablets you will only be making matters worse. It is much more important to replace the water loss. What salt has been lost in the sweat will soon be replaced at your next meal.

Hard regular training, games of squash or aerobic classes all result in a small loss of salt through sweating. But sweat contains only a very small amount of salt and this quantity decreases as you get fitter or as you acclimatize to heat. As your fitness improves you also start to produce a more dilute sweat.

Salt and Sweat

Even if you are a relatively untrained athlete you would need to sweat approximately 3litres/5¼pints a day just to get rid of the excess salt in the Western diet. If you are fully trained, that figure rises to 6 litres/10½pints!

Iron Tablets

Iron is a component of haemoglobin, the protein that transports oxygen from the lungs to the working muscles. If you are deficient in iron you are likely to tire easily.
Sports people who are particularly at risk include:

• Teenage athletes who are growing fast
• Sportswomen who lose iron through menstruation
• Vegetarian sports men and women who may have a poor intake
• Marathon and endurance sports people who may lose iron through sweat

Like all minerals, iron is best provided through the diet (see page 31/46 for ways of boosting your iron intake), but iron tablets may be used instead.
The drawback with tablets is that, like most supplements, they are best taken with meals and preferably with the right kind of food. Tablets will be less effective if they are taken with tea or coffee as caffeine can inhibit the absorption of iron.

Effects of Excess Minerals	
Mineral	*Effect*
Calcium	No reported effects
Phosphorus	Can cause reduced blood calcium
Potassium	No reported effects
Chlorine	Vomiting
Sodium	High blood pressure and possible fluid retention
Iron	Affects the interaction with zinc?
Zinc	Nausea and diarrhoea and poor absorption of other minerals

6.7 ERGOGENIC AIDS

An ergogenic aid is a food or drug which offers the hope of greatly improved performance. Megadoses of vitamins (see page 163), wheatgerm oil, bee pollen, bicarbonate of soda, caffeine and pangamic acid are among the best known.

These and other products hold out the promise of greater and greater performance and play on the hopes of getting 'that little bit extra' which will result in a place on the team or even a gold medal.

The question is, do they work and are they safe? The first question is particularly difficult to answer. There is rarely any real confirmation or research. It is usually all hearsay, persuasive advertising and personality endorsement. But the fact that one of the 'greats' uses a particular product does not actually prove that the product works.

In addition, ergogenic aids are expensive and some have side-effects which can be quite severe. Some of the dangers are known but with a new product the side-effects are still unknown.

It is sometimes argued that even if a particular product

does not work as claimed, it can still improve performance thorugh the placebo effect. Thus if you think something will benefit you, that very thought is enough to achieve the desired result. This psychological positive thinking can be enough to gain the small improvement which may be crucial to your performance.

On the other hand you could be lulled into a sense of false security and ignore the real factors which are influencing your performance. You could also become hooked on the idea that you need a particular aid to secure your best. This is both costly and inconvenient and probably useless.

If you do decide to experiment with ergogenic aids, be sure that you know what is in them. One product, for example, contains sufficient caffeine to put you over the IOC limits, but this is not indicated on the label.

Bee Pollen

It is claimed that bee pollen increases energy levels and enhances physical fitness but it has been extensively tested and no proper study has shown that it improves performance in any way at all. On the other hand sensitive athletes can develop serious allergic reactions to it.

Bicarbonate of Soda

The limiting factor in the performance of high-intensity anaerobic sports like swimming, running and cycling events between 30 seconds to two minutes in length is the build-up of lactic acid.

The theory is that the alkaline bicarbonate of soda will act as a buffer to the lactic acid build-up. Positive results have been reported but much more research is needed as side-effects have also been reported.

Caffeine

Caffeine is thought by some to spare muscle glycogen stores by promoting the use of fat as fuel. This is achieved by releasing free fatty acids into the bloodstream from storage sites in the body. Caffeine also stimulates the brain and some athletes believe that it can increase alertness and reaction times, both of which are important elements in many sports.

However, caffeine is recognized a a stimulant by the IOC. The rules allow up to 12ug/mg which is about six to eight cups of coffee consumed in two to three hours. This is a great deal of liquid to consume in the time and if caffeine is detected it can safely be accepted that the sports person took it deliberately.

Large doses of caffeine could also be dangerous to those who do not normally drink large amounts of coffee. Caffeine can cause irregular heart-beat. It can also lead to excessive excretion of urine which is inconvenient and can lead to dehydration, particularly in hot weather.

Ginseng

Ginseng is supposed to protect against tissue damage. It does contain active stimulants but the commercial preparations of it rarely retain these natural agents and even if they do they will usually be taken in such negligble amounts that they are unlikely to do any good. If you do try ginseng make sure that no other substances are mixed with it such as ephedra, a chinese herb which contains pseudo-ephedrine (a banned substance). You should also know that some long-term users of ginseng are known to suffer from nervousness, insomnia and depression.

Royal Jelly

This is a substance produced by the worker bees and fed to the queen bee. It is claimed to increase strength but there is no scientific basis for this claim.

Creatine Supplements
Tests are currently being carried out on supplements containing creatine phosphate. The idea is that the creatine phosphate will increase the concentration of this substance in muscle cells which in turn will mean a larger energy store

---

available for short bursts of high-intensity exercise and so greater resistance to fatigue (see page 69). Creatine phosphate also helps to speed up the transfer of energy from the site of production to where it is actually needed.

The studies carried out so far point to this being an ergogenic aid which really does work. However, the toxic effects and long-term side-effects of taking such a supplement are as yet unknown. In addition it is quite possible that the substance could be banned as unethical.

However effective an ergogenic aid might be, there is no substitute for a thorough, well-planned training programme and the right diet. These, together with adequate rest and sleep and the right mental approach, remain the most important ways to perfect performance.

7
COUNTDOWN TO WIN

The training diet is designed to ensure that you have the fuel to maintain your weight and level of sporting activity in the most efficient way possible.

Equally important to the serious sports person is the competition diet. This is designed to get glycogen levels to their highest peak at the start of the event and to replenish them afterwards.

The training diet lays the groundwork and is common to all sports people but the competition diet varies somewhat depending upon whether you are involved in endurance sports, short-duration sports or intermittent high-energy exercise.

7.1 PRE- AND POST-EVENT EATING

There is no magic pre-event meal which will ensure success every time. Everyone has their own food preferences and aversions, all of which contribute to the psychological as well as the physical build-up to an event. You have to work out for yourself whether you can cope with a large meal or manage just a bowl of cereal and a banana.

The same goes for the amount of time you need to leave between eating and the start of the event. Some people leave a couple of hours, others four or even five. Quite often this will depend upon the sport you are involved in.

In those sports where the body moves up and down, like running and ball games, there is likely to be more post-eating abdominal distress than in sports such as cycling where the body is more stable.

What is agreed is that you should eat something before an event if you possibly can. This meal is not really eaten for fuel - your muscle glycogen stores should have already been filled to capacity by the previous day's eating. It has other important functions such as:

- Ensuring that your liver glycogen stores are also filled to capacity
- Helping to prevent your blood sugar from falling too low and so helping to ward off hunger and weakness during the event
- Helping to settle your stomach by absorbing gastric juices and removing any pangs of hunger
- Ensuring that your fluid levels are as high as possible
- Boosting your psyche with the knowledge that your body is well fuelled

The pre-event meal must be one with which you are comfortable. Choose food which is familiar and which you know you enjoy. Avoid trying out something new on the day of the event and remember that your pre-event nerves may exaggerate your reaction to food. If you sometimes experience discomfort with certain foods this reaction could well be much worse on the big day, so avoid them.

Ideally you should have a light meal two or three hours before the event and to ensure that it really does give you the benefits listed above, concentrate on complex-carbohydrate or starchy food. Fatty foods will slow your digestion and too much sugary food could affect your blood sugar and insulin levels.

Water is particularly important. You will not starve to death during an event but you could very well dehydrate to a level that might affect your health. Drink extra water the day before – anything from four to eight extra glasses. Then drink at least two to three large glasses of water about two hours before the event and drink another one or two glasses five to ten minutes before the start. You should have built up to this level of water consumption during training.

---

12 Do's and Don'ts for Your Pre-event Meal

- Plan the meal round plenty of high-starch, low-fat foods like bread, muffins, potatoes, pasta, rice or breakfast cereals.
- Avoid fatty foods like cheese, eggs, sausages and hamburgers, and don't plaster your bread or potatoes with butter (or margarine).
- Add small servings of low-fat, protein foods like scrambled eggs, cottage cheese, slices of turkey or chicken or a glass of skimmed milk but don't settle for these on their own.
- Allow more digestion time than you do for general training. The intensity of the event will affect your capacity to tolerate undigested food in the stomach.
- Once you've eaten, try to relax and allow the food to digest.
- Experiment with liquid meals during training but do not use them unless you are really sure that they will suit you.
- If you think that you will be unable to eat very much on the big day eat an extra-large bedtime snack the night before. This is also very useful if the event is early in the morning.
- Always choose familiar food which you know you like.
- Try not to get too hooked on the feeling that you have to have one special food – you may not be able to find it at the event venue and if you are travelling away from home it may not be possible to take it with you.

- If the event lasts for more than one and a half hours have something sweet to eat such as mint cake, honeycomb or Turkish delight, or have a carbohydrate drink, within five to ten minutes of the start.
- Drink plenty of water during the run-up to the event or whatever time suits you personally.
- Never leave the pre-competition meal to chance. It should be planned well in advance. This applies whether you are at home or away.

If you are at home, choose cereals and milk, muffins, porridge with milk, dried fruit salad or indeed any of the foods which you might ordinarily eat at breakfast. These food make excellent pre-competition meals at any time of the day.

If you are staying away from home, a breakfast-type meal may be the only one you can find which is suitable. Other good choices include sandwiches with low-fat fillings, pasta with tomato sauce, fresh fruit and rice and pasta salads.

During the Event

In long-lasting intensive sports the carbohydrate you eat before the event will not be sufficient to see you through to the end. However, this only applies when you push yourself to the limit. A good game of cricket or a round of golf is not going to get you into this state but the marathon might.

Carbohydrate supplements made up into drinks can be the answer. They can really help your body to spare muscle glycogen. However, fluid levels are also a priority during prolonged exercise and adding sugars to the fluid leads to delays in the time the stomach takes to empty.

So when fluid replacement is very important, as in hot weather conditions, and when dehydration is likely to cause fatigue before your carbohydrate stores let you down, you are better off drinking water or an isotonic drink with 2-8 per cent carbohydrate.

On the other hand, if you are competing in a marathon or triathlon in cold weather when fluid replacement is not quite as important as eking out your limited glycogen stores, a carbohydrate supplement drink will be useful. Some athletes use a glucose polymer solution. This has less retarding effect on stomach emptying than the equivalent amount of glucose and it may provide an answer to meeting both needs.

Start to fuel early on in the event and continue to take small amounts of carbohydrate at frequent intervals. You will still need to keep a balance between the rate at which fluid empties from your stomach and your need for added energy during the event.

Are you guilty of not drinking during an event because you are not thirsty?
Take up to 150ml/5floz of slightly chilled water every 15 minutes, at the end of each game or when the event allows, and make sure you are well hydrated before the start of the game.

Post-event Eating

After a hard event or a tough competition the first priority is to replace the fluid you have lost. This should be done immediately. Do not wait until you feel thirsty. Even if you have been taking some fluid during the event the chances are that you will still have lost more than you have drunk.

To be absolutely sure of rehydrating properly take your own water bottle to every event. This way you will never be caught out. Do not rely on the organizers or your coach to provide fluid.

Water is the easiest choice for replenishing body fluids but sports drinks can be used as well. The sugar and minerals contained in the best sports drinks enable the body to absorb more fluid more quickly (see page 152) and start to replace the glycogen. Diluted juices, broths and watery fruit like melon and grapes can also be used. Continue to drink more water than usual for a day or two after the event. The body may need as much as two days to get back into fluid balance.

Recovery from exercise also depends upon replenishing your glycogen stores. Do this by eating either complex- or simple-carbohydrate foods. Quite often athletes do not feel at all hungry after an event, indeed quite the opposite, so simple-carbohydrate foods like biscuits, sweets, honey, jam and even sugar may tempt you when other foods do not. You must certainly have something to eat within two hours of the finish.

If you are competing in a tournament or in several heats in one day, eat something immediately after the end of each stage.

Tournament Meals

Less than an hour between rounds:
Stick to liquids such as isotonic sports drinks or high-carbohydrate drinks

One to two hours between rounds:
A light snack including cereal bars, dried fruit, crackers, oatcakes, fruit loaf, muffins (pages 204-207), or toast

Two or more hours between rounds:
Sandwiches made with honey or bananas, Olive Bread (page 305) and tomatoes, milk and fruit

---

However late you finish you must have something to eat, but you do not have to cook. Sandwiches or baked beans on toast with a salad, fruit and a glass of low-fat milk will do very well. Alternatively buy in some ready-made dishes from the supermarket (see page 97) and add a salad, bread roll and fruit.

Equally important after a hard event is rest. A good car-bohydrate-rich diet will build up glycogen stores again but rest enhances the recovery process. The muscles need a day to build their stores back up after a hard match and up to several days after a marathon or triathlon event.

7.2 EATING AWAY FROM HOME

Very often events are staged away from your home town and you will have to travel to the venue. You may also have to stay over one or two nights or sometimes even longer.

Check out all the eating arrangements you can in advance. This may mean finding out what will be laid on at the event, what the menus are like at your hotel and what other restaurants there are in the vicinity. Find out how late they stay open as many events are held in the evening. This kind of planning ensures that you are not stuck somewhere with the wrong kind of food, not know-ing where to go for something else.

Fast-food restaurants are dealt with on page 56 but other restaurants can also catch out the unwary.

Here are some do's and don'ts for some of the restaurants you might encounter at home or abroad.

Chinese
Do:
- Choose soups to start with
- Choose both rice and noodles or order extra servings of pancakes and steam buns
- Choose steamed or stir-fry dishes
- Avoid oily-looking sauces, try sweet-and-sour or plum sauce instead
- Ask if you can have portions without MSG

Don't:
- Choose deep-fried items. These are often described as 'crispy' or 'in batter'

Indian
Do:
- Choose both rice and plain naan
- Choose Tandoori chicken or lamb
- Choose mild yoghurt-based chicken or vegetable curries
- Include dhal (lentils) or channa (chickpeas)
- Ask for raita (yoghurt) but check that it is not excessively spicy

Don't:
- Choose deep-fried foods like pakoras or samosas
- Choose hot fatty meat curries. Madras and Vindaloo are hot and very hot respectively.

Italian
Do:
- Choose pasta with tomato or vegetable sauces
- Ask for pizza with extra vegetable topping
- Ask for a salad
- Choose plain chicken, liver or fish dishes rather than breaded scallops or steaks

Don't:
- Choose meaty sauces for pasta or creamy carbonara
- Add Parmesan cheese or olive oil to pasta dishes
- Choose fried potatoes

Japanese
Do:
- Choose soup to start with
- Choose both rice and noodles
- Choose sukiyaki or teryaki, grilled chicken or fish

Don't:
- Choose deep-fried foods, often described as tempura

Mexican

Do:
- Choose soup to start with
- Choose both rice and plain (unfried) tortillas or order extra servings of beans
- Choose enchiladas and tacos or tostadas with refried beans and guacamole
- Ask for less cheese than usual in tacos and enchiladas

Don't:
- Eat too many tortilla chips
- Eat too much salsa – it probably contains a lot of chilli

If you are faced with a meal that is all wrong for you, you must still eat. So scrape off all the gravy, remove batter from fish, chicken or mushrooms, drain off the dressing from salads and scoop out as much of the soured cream as you can from a jacket-baked potato.

If you are going abroad and you think there is likely to be a problem, the best answer is to take as much of your own food and drink as you sensibly can. This certainly includes fluid and snacks for the journey and perhaps a supply of breakfast cereals, canned food, cereal bars and dried fruit as well. Remember that the eating habits and food in your place of destination may be very different to those you are used to.

Packed meals for the journey should be simple and familiar. Go for sandwiches in a variety of breads with tuna, salmon, cottage cheese, chicken or turkey fillings. Pack tomatoes and salad vegetables separately and be sure to include plenty of fluids.

Snacks are a good idea to stave off hunger pangs on delayed flights or long journeys. See page 53 for ideas. Avoid coffee, tea and alcoholic drinks as these aggravate the dehydrating effects of the low pressure in the aircraft. Drink plenty of mineral water, sports drinks or juices.

If you are worried about the food on a foreign trip take a selection of the following foods: raisins, dried fruits, nuts and sunflower seeds, muesli bars, good confectionery, breakfast cereals, instant hot cereals, peanut butter, fruit juices, canned soups and stews, fruit and vegetables and instant puddings.

Stomach troubles are commonplace during competition and these can get even worse if you have to go abroad. One way of avoiding this potentially damaging condition is to take great care with everything you eat prior to the competition.

---

12 Rules for Avoiding Stomach Problems Abroad

- Peel all fruit, whether you buy it yourself or consume it in a restaurant.
- Only eat vegetables which are cooked.
- Never eat raw salads.
- Avoid shellfish.
- Avoid all spicy food, but particularly dishes which are likely to contain chilli.
- Select only foods with which you are familiar.
- Never buy from street vendors.
- Try to eat only in places where the standard of hygiene seems reasonable.
- Only drink bottled water.
- Never put ice in your water.
- Avoid rare or undercooked foods, particularly meat.
- Avoid alcoholic drinks of any kind.

7.3 COUNTDOWN FOR A MARATHON OR ENDURANCE SPORT

What you eat and drink in the later stages of training and during the crucial final four days before a marathon or endurance event is a vital part of your preparation for a big race.

Eating and drinking the right things are no substitute for training, nor will they win you the race, but eating and drinking the wrong things can certainly undermine all the hard work you should have put in over several months. The aim is to arrive at the starting-line with your body rested and fully hydrated and your energy stores high.

During the final month training and a high-carbohydrate diet (see page 94) are the keys to combating fatigue. Training increases the ability of the muscles to use fat, allowing the glycogen store to go further. The carbohydrate diet keeps glycogen stores at peak levels.

The Last Week

By the last week of training you should be eating a diet where carbohydrates make up 60 per cent of your food. Examples of menus for typical high-carbohydrate days are given below.

Assuming that the marathon is to take place on a Sunday, here is a count-down to the race.

Monday and Tuesday (Days 1 and 2)
Continue with the intensive programme of training and high-carbohydrate diet you have been pursuing over the last few weeks. If you and your trainer have decided that carbohydrate loading (see Chapter 3) will benefit you, start now. Otherwise continue as before.

High-carbohydrate Menus I

Breakfast:
Fresh fruit juice, muesli with plenty of raisins, dates and chopped apricots with skimmed or semi-skimmed milk, wholemeal toast and jam. Tea or coffee.

Mid-morning:
Banana and wholemeal digestive biscuits, tea or water.

Midday meal:
Tomato and mushroom deep-pan pizza with mixed salad, yoghurt with flapjack and an orange, water.

Mid-afternoon:
Wholegrain cereal and fruit bar, apple and tea or water.

Evening meal:
Vegetable soup, grilled chicken breast with mixed broad beans and peas, carrots and potatoes or pasta, fruit crumble. Water or tea.

Bed-time:
Milky drink and a biscuit.

High-carbohydrate Menus II

Breakfast:
Fresh fruit juice, porridge with honey and skimmed milk, Apple Bran Muffins (page 205) and Wholemeal Rolls (page 303).

Mid-morning
Apple and Date and Nut Halva (page 344) with tea or water.

Midday meal:
Tuna sandwiches with tomatoes, yoghurt, slice of bread and butter pudding and water.

Mid-afternoon:
Date and Orange Squares (page 335) and tea or water.

> **Evening meal:**
> Lentil and Watercress Soup (page 237), monk-fish in Tomato and Basil Sauce (page 253) with Lemon Rice and Bulgar (page 301) and stir-fried vegetables, and pineapple orange yoghurt.

Wednesday (Day 3)

Cut back a little on your carbohydrate intake today. Choose foods which are not excessively starchy or sugary and keep to around 350g/12oz of carbohydrate spread out through the day.

The table on page 100 gives you a run-down on portions of food which provide 50g/2oz of carbohydrate.

You will probably have your last full-scale training run today and this, with the cut-back in starchy and sugary foods, will leave your running muscles fairly low in glycogen stores and 'ripe' for replenishment.

SAMPLE MENUS FOR DAY 3
Breakfast:
Half fresh grapefruit, wholemeal toast with marmalade

Mid-morning:
Pear or apple and tea or water

Midday meal:
Jacket-baked Potato (page 227) with cottage cheese and a green salad followed by fruit yoghurt

Mid-afternoon:
Rock Buns (page 337) with tea or water

Evening meal:
Courgette and Fennel Soup (page 234), trout with almonds with carrots and celery and Pommes Anna (page 323) and Fruit Kebabs with Marmalade Sauce (page 327)

Or if you do not have time to cook very much:
Canned tomato soup with chunks of wholemeal bread,
Crunchy Green salad (page 310) with cottage cheese and
pasta or Rice Salad (page 313) made from leftovers and
ready-made rice pudding with no-soak dried fruit.

Thursday (Day 4)

Training will now be tapering off, but you should increase
the carbohydrate in your diet. For men this could be as
much as 500-600g/1-1¼lb a day. Women will probably not
need to eat so much.

The idea is not to eat large quantities – if you do, your
weight will increase and you will be filling up your gut
with unwanted waste – but to eat mainly carbohydrate-
based foods. Cut right back on meat and fish and all fats.

Try to eat complex or starchy foods – rice, pasta,
potatoes, bread and breakfast cereals – at each meal and
eat simple-carbohydrate or sugary foods as snacks mid-
morning, mid-afternoon and near bed-time. Use fruit and
vegetables to add interest to the meals.

SAMPLE MENUS FOR DAY 4
Breakfast:
Add a glass of milk to one of the high-carbohydrate break-
fasts outlined above.

If you can, avoid tea or coffee at this stage as they both
contain caffeine which has a diuretic effect and makes you
pass water just when you need to conserve it. Try to drink
more water than you usually do and continue to do this
right up to the event.

Mid-morning:
Oatmeal Scone (page 304) and a light fruit drink.

Midday meal:
Build the meal round starchy carbohydrates such as tuna
and bean salad with pasta shapes, baked beans on toast or
with Jacket-baked Potatoes (page 227), tagliatelle with
tomato and basil sauce, Lime and Pineapple Rice (page

294), pitta parcels filled with Turkish falafel or feta cheese and salad.

These dishes are easy to make at home but they are also widely available in restaurants and cafés. Finish off with fruit and yoghurt and a piece of teabread (pages 338-9). Don't forget to drink plenty of liquid.

Mid-afternoon:
A slice of plain cake or some homemade cookies with very weak China tea.

Evening meal:
This meal is very much more of the same complex carbohydrates, perhaps with a small amount of lean meat, chicken or fish to add interest. Choose a starchy food you didn't have at lunch-time. Stick to foods which are familiar to you at this stage. If you are at home, this is fairly easy, but for those who have to travel to the marathon venue and put up at a hotel it can be difficult.

Suggested menus:
1.
Thick vegetable soup with a Wholemeal Roll (page 303), quick Paella (page 287) with salad and fruit crumble and yoghurt

2.
Ravioli with spinach and cottage cheese in tomato sauce, grilled cod steak with potatoes and vegetables, milk pudding and stewed fruits
   If you can manage it, add a little low-fat cheese, such as Brie or Edam, with water biscuits, crispbread or rice cakes.

Eating out:
If you have to eat out, take great care as an upset tummy is the last thing you want. Go for the simplest dishes on the menu such as thick vegetable soup to start with, followed by roast or grilled chicken with a jacket-baked potato and a green salad. Ask for a banana or have a small quantity of

cheese from the cheese board with plenty of biscuits or French bread.

Alternatively try an Italian restaurant and stick to minestrone soup, pasta with tomato (pomodoro) sauce followed by crème caramel.

Saturday (Day 5)

It is even more important today to avoid any kind of food which might upset you, so cut out spicy foods, seafood, fatty food, rare meat and gas-producers such as beans.

Ideally, you should go vegetarian for the day. But, if you must have some meat or it is difficult to find a vegetarian restaurant, avoid hot-dogs, hamburgers, doner kebabs or any kind of unfamiliar food. Upset tummies cause dehydration and this could lead to very serious problems during a marathon.

Cut back on snacks today and take things as easily as possible. Have a breakfast and lunch similar to the previous four days, bearing the above points in mind.

Your evening meal on Saturday does not have to be very heavy, which is probably just as well as you may not be feeling very hungry, either from nerves or excitement. What you should eat – yes, you guessed it – is more starchy carbohydrates such as potatoes, pasta, rice or even a tomato-topped pizza with no cheese.

Remember to keep on drinking plenty of liquid, but take particular care with alcohol at this stage. If you have found in practice that a small drink (up to a pint of beer or lager) helps you to relax, then OK, but avoid spirits and wine, and still have a long non-alcoholic drink too.

Sunday (Day 6)

4-3 HOURS BEFORE THE RACE

It is very important to eat a reasonably large breakfast with plenty of carbohydrates. This will help you to increase your performance by enabling you to make your muscle glycogen stores last as long as possible. If you do not eat much breakfast it is at the 20-mile mark that you will begin to feel the lack!

Choose foods which are low in fat and protein but which are also not too high in fibre. One of the benefits of fibre is that it helps to prevent constipation – not something likely to be bothering you at this stage. In fact you are much more likely to be troubled by the opposite – diarrhoea brought on by nerves.

Another reason for avoiding fibre is that you do not want a bulky meal which will take a while to eat or which might cause gastric discomfort. Plan this last meal very carefully in advance and have a practice run-through prior to the event. Get up very early in the morning, have the planned breakfast and then go for a long run starting about 9.30 or 10.00am.

The sort of food to choose includes bread rolls, crumpets or pikelets, Staffordshire oatcakes, breakfast cereals or porridge, bananas, dried fruits, sugar, honey and jam and milk. These foods should not be too difficult to arrange but do remember that you will be eating around 5.30 in the morning and neither you nor your friends will be able to pop out for something you have forgotten.

Keep up your fluid intake by taking frequent sips of water or whatever you have decided is the best for you in the way of isotonic sports drinks. Carry on doing this all the way to the start area.

30 MINUTES TO THE START
Go to the lavatory during the last 30-minute period. Once you have been you can drink your last drink before the start. You can, if you have trained yourself to tolerate it, drink up to 500ml/16floz without having to worry about needing to pee during the race. There is not time for urine to form before the race starts and once you begin running the blood-flow to the kidneys is reduced and urine formation is minimal.

5 MINUTES TO THE START
If, during training, you have tried out having a high-carbohydrate snack just before you start running, now is the

time to have it (see page 158). Suitable snacks include Turkish delight, mint cake and honeycomb. Avoid chocolate as it contains too much fat.

DURING THE EVENT
Keep topping up your fluids as frequently as you can during the event. Use water or an isotonic sports drink if supplied and you are used to it, or you can carry your own drink (see page 104).

AFTER THE EVENT
Drink as much fluid as you can immediately after you cross the finishing-line and follow this with a snack containing at least 50g/2oz of carbohydrate within two hours of the end of the event. Ideas include six digestive biscuits, two large bananas or a bowl of cereal. If you are not feeling very hungry try a high-carbohydrate drink.

Follow this up with another 50g/2oz of carbohydrate within the next two hours. Ideas include one large Jacket-baked Potato (page 227) filled with baked beans or cottage cheese, a third of a 25-cm/10-inch tomato pizza, 200g/7oz cooked pasta with tomato sauce, three Shredded Wheat with skimmed milk, 175g/6oz cooked rice or a double-decker sandwich filled with prawns or chicken.

7.4 COUNTDOWN FOR SPEED SPORTS

It is just as important for people involved in speed sports to work out a careful eating plan before a major event as it is for endurance sportsmen or women. If you are a sprint runner or cyclist, long or high jumper or fencer, or a participant in karate or judo, you need to build up your glycogen stores just prior to the big event. However, you do not need to load in the carbohydrate in quite the same way as the marathon runner. Indeed, it might well harm your performance to do so, especially if you are competing in weight category sports where you have to control your weight within very fine limits.

You are unlikely to exhaust your body's normal fuel stores in the short time it takes to run the 100-metres sprint or to lift a weight, but for top-class performance you do need to have muscle glycogen stores at the peak.

The Last Week

The answer is to continue with your usual high-carbohydrate, low-fat training diet during the last week up to the event until about 24-36 hours beforehand. During the last day or day and a half, taper your training and exercise regime and pack in plenty of carbohydrate foods the night before and on the morning of the event.

Assuming that it is to take place on a Saturday, here is a countdown to the event.

Sunday to Thursday (Days 1-5)
Take special care during this week to keep strictly to your training diet. Carbohydrate food should account for 60 per cent of total daily energy consumption. Keep fatty foods to a minimum. Have a look at the high-carbohydrate menus set out in Sections 6.2 and 7.5.

Friday (Day 6)
Taper your training programme today. This will allow your muscles to build up and store as much glycogen as they possibly can. Continue with your training diet today but reduce the total number of calories for the day to take account of the fact that you are not training quite so hard.

Build the evening meal round starchy carbohydrate foods such as rice, pasta and potatoes and add only a little low-fat protein to make the food more enjoyable. Ideas include Spanish Rice (page 299), Caribbean Rice and Peas (page 293) and Multi-grain Pilaf (page 297). Serve these dishes as the main attraction rather than as side dishes and add soup or salads to start and a good starch dessert such as Baked Bananas (page 333), Traditional Rice Pudding (page 334) or French Apple Batter Pudding (page 330).

Alternatively look at the recipes in Protein Partners from page 267. These vegetarian recipes use low-fat protein foods which are ideal for high-carbohydrate meals at this stage.

Remember to start building up on your fluid intake in good time and keep drinking as much as you can during the last day before the event. Check your urine to see that it remains very pale in colour – a good indication that you are taking sufficient fluids.

Saturday (Day 7)

4-3 HOURS BEFORE THE EVENT

You must try to eat a reasonably good breakfast to top up your stores of glycogen. Yours may be a short-duration sport but you are still very reliant on carbohydrates for fuel. If there are to be several heats it is vital to ensure a good intake of starchy food. Choose muffins and toast as well as breakfast cereals or porridge with fruit. If you have time, make Oaty Buttermilk Pancakes (page 208); serve with honey, jam or syrup. And have plenty to drink.

The precise organization of meals before a major event will be influenced by the timing. Obviously you will have to plan a slightly different countdown if you are swimming at 8.00 in the morning than if you are sprinting at midday or playing a squash match at 6.00p.m.

Here are some of the options:

Early-morning Events

This can be quite a difficult one because you will need to get up early if you are to have something to eat before the event. Make sure that you have a really good carbohydrate meal the night before and top it up with as large a bed-time snack as you can manage. Make sure you have plenty of fluid at both meals.

Depending on your tolerence, get up between two and four hours before the start of the event and eat really familiar foods such as toast and marmalade or your favourite cereals with skimmed milk. Drink more liquid than you would normally drink and continue to drink fluids on the way to the event.

Mid-Morning Events
Eat a high-carbohydrate meal the night before with extra liquid. Eat a familiar breakfast by about 7.00a.m. to allow all the food to digest.

Afternoon Events
This kind of timing allows you to choose between a large carbohydrate breakfast followed by a light lunch or an early brunch at about 10.30-11.00a.m. This will allow plenty of time for the food to digest. Try out dishes like Indian Toast (page 209), Omelette Brunch Baps (page 211) or Oaty Buttermilk Pancakes (page 208) in advance and if they suit you, use them to make an interesting meal. Drink plenty of liquid.

Evening Events
You will have plenty of time for a hefty carbohydrate breakfast and lunch so you do not need to go quite so heavily on the carbohydrate foods the night before. Depending on the actual time of the event, plan for a light snack in the late afternoon. Drink extra fluids all day.

7.5 COUNTDOWN TO THE BIG MATCH

A good many sports people – both amateur and professional – are involved in weekly matches. If you are one of them, you need to prepare both for the start of your sporting season and for each match.

Between Seasons

If you are really serious about your sporting activities you will not lose your fitness just because you are not playing football, hockey or rugby regularly. Instead you should be exercising in other ways and adjusting your diet to the new levels of activity.

Unfortunately the tendency is to indulge in all the things you have been avoiding during the season and at the same time to be much more lazy about exercising. Weight-category sports people are the worst offenders! To counteract this choose an activity which you enjoy – walking, cycling, jogging, tennis or badminton – it does not matter which, provided that you are prepared to build regular exercise sessions into your off-season lifestyle.

Work out what your new energy requirements are and base your diet on this. You may find that you do not need to fuel your activities with quite as much complex-carbohydrate food as you did when you were training, but you will still need to eat plenty of it. The guidelines for healthy eating (see Chapter 2) call for 55 per cent of daily energy requirements to be met by carbohydrates.

If you continue to exercise and follow these guidelines you will avoid putting on weight. You will also remain pretty fit. When the next sporting season starts, you will be able to pick up your training programme and return to your training diet without any difficulty. This is far better than having to worry about getting rid of fat which you have allowed to build up.

Before the Match

Many team sports like football, basketball, lacrosse, hockey and rugby are characterized by intermittent bursts of exercise. The best way to deal with this is to treat them in the same way as you would continuous activity based on the lengths of time you are actually playing.

You may also need to analyse the requirements of your particular position on the team. Some players are required to run fairly continuously about the pitch during the match, for others play is much more intermittent. The more running around you do the more your energy requirement will increase.

Decide your needs and follow either the countdown for endurance sports on page 181 or the countdown for speed sports on page 189.

Are you guilty of not bothering to eat after a long match because you do not feel hungry?

Your muscle glycogen stores are depleted during exercise and they must be refilled, otherwise you will go into your next match with depleted energy reserves and the predictable result will be a lost match. The best time to refuel is in the first hour after exercise – when you probably feel the least like eating!

8
RECIPES

V = **Vegetarian**
F = **Can be Frozen**

All the recipes have an indication of the number of servings they will make. In some instances this may be variable and the choice will depend upon how you are serving the dish – on its own or with other dishes, and on your own nutritional requirement. If you are loading on the carbohydrates, for example, you may want to eat a larger portion of some dishes.

The recipes have been nutritionally analysed on the basis of the higher number of portions indicated. Thus a recipe which states that it serves 3-4 will be analysed on the basis of four portions. If you only serve three people with it you will all get proportionately more of the nutrients involved.

NB:
Butter rather than margarine has been used as the basis for analysis. Margarines vary in their nutritional make up and you should refer to the details on the label. However, if you use margarine rather than butter the saturated fat content of the dish is likely to fall and the polyunsaturated fat content is likely to rise.

Flour has been analysed as plain white flour unless stated otherwise in the recipe.

Pasta and rice have been analysed as plain white and white respectively. If you use wholemeal pasta or brown rice you will increase the vitamin and fibre content of the dish.

Bread has been analysed as wholemeal in all cases.

Eggs have been analysed as size 2 or 65g in weight.

Optional ingredients and alcohol have not been included in the analysis of a recipe unless the analysis chart indicates otherwise.

All the recipes have been analysed using the Comcard Compute-a-Diet Nutrient Balance System. The percentage energy totals do not always exactly add up to 100 for mathematical reasons.

8.1 STARCHY BREAKFASTS

Most of the time breakfast is a quick and easy meal. There are any number of proprietary breakfast cereals on sale, many of them made from whole grains. Muesli mixes abound and there couldn't be a quicker hot breakfast to make than porridge.

Add some orange juice, milk and fruit and you have a really wholesome meal. Total calories will be around 400-500 depending on the fruit you choose. Substitute toast or muffins from time to time but take care with the butter or margarine, for these can pile on the calories.

Incidentally, it might be worth thinking twice about margarine. Most brands of both ordinary and low-fat margarine contain quite large quantities of hydrogenated fat or trans-fatty acids (see page 22).

Muesli mixes are often eaten straight from the pack with milk and fruit, but in the original Swiss Bircher muesli oat flakes are soaked overnight in water with dried fruit and nuts. The fruit and any other flavourings are added the next morning just before serving.

I always make muesli in this way partly because I find it

quite difficult to find muesli mixes which do not contain sugar and because I prefer the lighter taste of muesli made with water rather than milk. The recipe given below can be kept in the fridge for two to three days. Not only does it make an excellent breakfast dish, it is also very good served as a high-carbohydrate dessert or as an easy-to-eat snack after a late evening run or training session.

Most people rarely tire of a good straightforward breakfast. But if you are trying to increase the complex-carbohydrate content of your diet, eating larger portions of cereal and more toast can become a bit monotonous.

The recipes in this section are designed to add variety and interest to breakfast as well as carbohydrates. Some are quite quick to make and can be cooked when you want them. Others can be prepared or baked in advance and stored in a fridge, freezer or cake tin ready to be taken out and served at breakfast-time – or indeed whenever you are in need of a starchy snack.

Muffins, particularly, make good 'any-time' eats. Like most baked foods they are at their best when they are fresh. Let them cool for 20 minutes or so and eat them warm. However, they do keep well in an air-tight tin. Do not put them in the fridge – they tend to lose their lightness. Muffins can also be frozen. For the best results thaw and reheat in a microwave oven.

Brunch recipes like Omelette Brunch Baps and Savoury Crumpets are useful recovery late breakfasts at around 10.00 or 11.00a.m. if you have had an early weekend workout. They also make good snack meals at other times of the day.

Some people really hate the idea of breakfast and a Blender Breakfast in a glass may be the answer for them.

NUTRITIONAL INFORMATION (PER 100g) BREAKFAST CEREALS

		CORN FLAKES	FROSTIES	CRUNCHY NUT CORN FLAKES	SPECIAL K	RICE KRISPIES	RICICLES	COCO POPS
Energy	kcal	370	380	390	370	380	380	380
Protein	g	8	5	7	15	6	4	5
carbohydrate	g	83	88	82	75	85	90	87
(of which–sugars	g	(7)	(40)	(35)	(15)	(10)	(40)	(40)
–starch)	g	(76)	(48)	(47)	(60)	(75)	(50)	(47)
Fat	g	0.7	0.4	3.5	1	1	0.5	0.9
(of which saturates)	g	(0.1)	(0.1)	(0.6)	(0.4)	(0.4)	(0.2)	(0.4)
Sodium	g	1.1	0.8	0.8	0.9	1.1	0.8	0.8
Fibre	g	1	0.6	1	2.5	0.7	0.5	1
Vitamins								
Vitamin C	mg	–	–	–	–	–	–	–
Vitamin E	mg	–	–	–	–	–	–	–
Niacin	mg	15	15	15	30	15	15	15
Vitamin B6	mg	1.8	1.8	1.8	3.3	1.8	1.8	1.8
Riboflavin (B2)	mg	1.3	1.3	1.3	2.7	1.3	1.3	1.3
Thiamin (B1)	mg	1.0	1.0	1.0	2.0	1.0	1.0	1.0
Folic Acid	μg	250	250	250	500	250	250	250
Vitamin D	μg	2.1	2.1	2.1	4.2	2.1	2.1	2.1
Vitamin B12	μg	1.7	1.7	1.7	3.3	1.7	1.7	1.7
Minerals								
Iron	mg	6.7	6.7	6.7	20	6.7	6.7	6.7
Zinc	mg	0.2	0.1	0.3	1.9	0.9	0.6	0.8
Calcium	mg	10	10	20	70	10	10	20
Potassium	mg	100	70	140	250	160	100	220
Phosphorus	mg	40	30	50	200	140	100	120
Magnesium	mg	10	10	20	60	30	20	40

PUFFED WHEAT	SHREDDED WHEAT	SUGAR PUFFS	WEETABIX	ALL-BRAN	BRAN BUDS	BRAN FLAKES	SULTANA BRAN	COMMON SENSE OAT BRAN FLAKES	COMMON SENSE OAT BRAN FLAKES WITH RAISIN & APPLE	GOLDEN CRACKLES	GOLDEN OATMEAL CRISP
321	325	348	352	270	280	320	310	350	340	380	360
14.2	10.6	5.9	11.5	14	13	12	10	12	11	7	9
67	68	84.5	75	48	50	64	65	66	67	83	69
(0.3)	(0.8)	(56.5)	(5)	(18)	(25)	(18)	(27)	(17)	(22)	(27)	(26)
(66.7)	(67.2)	(28)	(70)	(30)	(25)	(46)	(38)	(49)	(43)	(56)	(42)
1.3	3.0	0.8	2.7	2.5	2.5	1.5	2	4	4	2	6
(0.2)	(0.4)	(0.1)	(0.4)	(0.4)	(0.4)	(0.3)	(0.4)	(0.8)	(0.8)	(0.2)	(1.0)
4	8	9	2.7	0.9	0.6	0.9	0.8	0.8	0.8	1	0.7
5.6	9.8	3.2	9.7	24	22	13	11	10	9	1.5	4
–	–	–	–	–	–	25	–	–	–	–	–
2.0	1.2	0.34	1.0	–	–	–	–	–	–	–	–
8.1	6.6	3.7	13.4	11.3	11.3	15	15	15	15	15	15
0.14	0.24	0.05	0.2	1.3	1.3	1.8	1.8	1.8	1.8	1.8	1.8
0.06	0.05	0.03	1.5	1.0	1.0	1.3	1.3	1.3	1.3	1.3	1.3
–	0.27	–	0.9	0.8	0.8	1.0	1.0	1.0	1.0	1.0	1.0
na	na	na	na	188	188	250	250	250	250	250	250
–	–	–	–	1.6	1.6	2.1	2.1	2.1	2.1	2.1	2.1
–	–	–	–	1.3	1.3	1.7	1.7	1.7	1.7	1.7	1.7
4.6	4.2	2.1	7.4	12	12	20	15	6.7	6.7	6.7	6.7
2.8	2.3	1.5	2.0	6.7	6.2	3.3	2.8	2.5	2.3	0.7	1.4
26	38	14	35	70	70	50	50	60	60	70	50
390	330	160	370	1000	950	600	700	400	450	200	300
350	340	140	290	700	650	400	350	450	350	80	220
140	130	55	120	220	220	120	120	100	100	30	70

Swiss Muesli Bowl

Makes 4-6 servings

V

12 heaped tablespoons rolled oats or mixed cereal flakes of your choice

450ml/15floz water or skimmed milk

2 teaspoons honey (optional)

2 tablespoons raisins or sultanas

2 tablespoons flaked almonds or brazil nuts

2 tablespoons cashew nuts, chopped

Note: For a lower fat content substitute dried fruits for nuts.

Optional extras per serving:

1 eating apple, freshly grated

2 tablespoons plain yoghurt mixed with fresh raspberries, blueberries or strawberries

3 tablespoons soaked and cooked dried apricots or prunes

3 tablespoons stewed gooseberries or plums

1 mashed banana

1. Place all the ingredients in a large bowl and stir to combine.

2. Cover and store in the fridge until required. Stir again and spoon into a bowl.

3. Eat alone or with one or two of the optional extras.

CALORIES PER PORTION			Fats				**211**
	CHO(g)	Prot(g)	Sat(g)	Mono(g)	Poly(g)	Iron(mg)	Ca(mg)
Total	28.5	7	2	4	2	1.5	117
Energy	51%	13%		36%			

Oatbran Breakfast

Makes 1-2 servings

V

5 tablespoons oatbran
450ml/15floz skimmed milk or water
Optional extras per serving:
1 tablespoon honey, molasses or maple syrup
2 tablespoons apple sauce
2 tablespoons mixed chopped dates and raisins
2 tablespoons toasted hazelnuts

1. Make up the oatbran as directed on the pack, gradually bringing to the boil. Cook over a low heat for 3 minutes.

2. Add one of the optional extras just before serving.

Note To toast hazelnuts, place in a dry frying pan over a low heat. Dry-fry until the nuts are well browned. Keep the nuts on the move to prevent burning. Leave to cool and then rub off the brown outer skins. Chop and store in an airtight jar.

CALORIES PER PORTION			Fats				**180**
	CHO(g)	Prot(g)	Sat(g)	Mono(g)	Poly(g)	Iron(mg)	Ca(mg)
Total	33	11	0.5	0.5	0.5	14	290
Energy	69%	24%		7%			

Fruit Semolina

Makes 1-2 servings

V

175g/6oz raspberries, blueberries or strawberries
300ml/10floz skimmed milk
150ml/5floz water
50g/2oz semolina, wholegrain if possible

1. Rub the fruit through a sieve or purée in a blender. This should give about 150ml/5floz fruit purée. If there is more, subtract the extra amount from the amount of water you use at the next stage.

2. Heat the milk and water in a saucepan and bring to the boil.

3. Sprinkle the semolina into the milk and water in a thin stream, stirring all the time to prevent lumps from forming.

4. Continue cooking and stirring until the semolina is thick and cooked through. This will take about 12 minutes

5. If you do not want to stand over the mixture it can be cooked in a double saucepan but this will take longer.

CALORIES PER PORTION			Fats				159
	CHO(g)	Prot(g)	Sat(g)	Mono(g)	Poly(g)	Iron(mg)	Ca(mg)
Total	31	9	–	–	–	1	206
Energy	73%	22%		5%			

Blender Breakfast I

Makes 1 serving

<u>V</u>

1 banana
juice of 2 oranges
2 tablespoons dried skimmed milk powder
water

1. Mash the banana and place in a blender with the orange juice and milk powder.

2. Process until smooth, adding water to give the required consistency.

CALORIES PER PORTION			Fats				219
	CHO(g)	Prot(g)	Sat(g)	Mono(g)	Poly(g)	Iron(mg)	Ca(mg)
Total	49	8	0.5	0.5	0.5	1	218
Energy	84%	14%		2%			

Blender Breakfast II

Makes 1 serving

V

2 kiwifruit
150g/5oz plain yoghurt
1 tablespoon wheatgerm
3 tablespoons skimmed milk

1. Peel and chop the kiwi fruit and place in the blender with the yoghurt and wheatgerm.

2. Process until smooth, adding milk to give the required consistency.

CALORIES PER PORTION			Fats				275
	CHO(g)	Prot(g)	Sat(g)	Mono(g)	Poly(g)	Iron(mg)	Ca(mg)
Total	44	18	1	0.5	1	3	402
Energy	59%	26%		14%			

Marmalade Muffins

Makes 10 muffins

<u>VF</u>

350g/12oz plain flour
25g/1oz sugar
4 teaspoons baking powder
¼ teaspoon salt
1 egg
5 tablespoons orange or grapefruit and ginger marmalade
150ml/5oz plain yoghurt
50g/2oz butter or margarine, melted
25ml/1floz skimmed milk
½ teaspoon vanilla essence (optional)

1. Preheat the oven to 190°C/375°F/Gas 5 and lightly grease muffin pans or deep bun trays.

2. Mix the flour, sugar, baking powder and salt in a mixing bowl. Beat the egg with 3 tablespoons of the marmalade and the yoghurt and melted butter or margarine, milk and vanilla essence. Pour over the dry ingredients and mix.

3. Use half the mixture to half-fill 10 muffin pans. Make a small hollow in the dough and place a heaped teaspoonful of the remaining marmalade in each one. Top with the remaining muffin mixture.

4. Bake for 25-30 minutes. Leave to cool for 5 minutes before removing from the pans, then transfer to a cooling rack. Serve warm or cold.

CALORIES PER PORTION				Fats				**206**
	CHO(g)	Prot(g)	Sat(g)	Mono(g)	Poly(g)	Iron(mg)	Ca(mg)
Total	37	5.5	3	1.5	4	1	105
Energy	67%	10%		23%			

Per muffin

Apple Bran Muffins

Makes 10 muffins

VF

75g/3oz Allbran or bran flakes
350ml/12floz skimmed milk
125g/4oz plain flour
1½ teaspoons baking powder
½ teaspoon salt
½ teaspoon ground cinnamon
40g/1½oz sugar
1 egg, well beaten
2 tablespoons oil
2 apples, peeled and coarsely grated

1. Preheat the oven to 200°C/400°F/Gas 6 and lightly grease muffin pans or deep bun trays.

2. Soak the Allbran or bran flakes in about two-thirds of the milk to moisten.

3. Sift together the flour, baking powder, soda, salt and cinnamon and stir in the sugar.

4. Mix the egg with the remaining milk and the oil and add to the soaked bran mixture. Stir in the grated apple. Fold in the dry ingredients until just moistened.

5. Spoon the mixture into the prepared muffin pans and bake for 15-20 minutes until risen and firm to the touch. Transfer to a cooling rack. Serve warm or cold.

CALORIES PER PORTION			Fats				**134**
	CHO(g)	Prot(g)	Sat(g)	Mono(g)	Poly(g)	Iron(mg)	Ca(mg)
Total	21	4	0.5	1.5	2	1	75
Energy	59%	11%		28%			

Per Muffin

Carrot and Sultana Muffins

Makes 6 muffins

<u>VF</u>

a little vegetable oil
150g/5oz plain white flour
2 teaspoons baking powder
¼ teaspoon each cinnamon and salt
1 large egg, beaten
40g/1½oz light muscovado sugar
75ml/3floz skimmed milk
25g/1oz butter or margarine, melted
50g/2oz carrots, coarsely grated
25g/1oz sultanas or raisins
15g/½oz sunflower seeds or chopped nuts

1. Preheat the oven to 190°C/375°F/Gas 5 and lightly grease muffin pans or deep bun trays.

2. Mix the flour, baking powder, cinnamon and salt in a large bowl.

3. Whisk the egg and sugar and when smooth whisk in the milk and butter or margarine. Pour over the dry ingredients and mix together with the carrots, sultanas or raisins and sunflower seeds or nuts.

4. Spoon into the prepared muffin pans and bake for 25-30 minutes until springy to the touch. Transfer to a cooling rack. Serve warm or cold.

CALORIES PER PORTION				Fats			**198**
	CHO(g)	Prot(g)	Sat(g)	Mono(g)	Poly(g)	Iron(mg)	Ca(mg)
Total	31	5	3	2	1	1	81
Energy	59%	10%		30%			

Per muffin

Monterey Muffins

Makes 10 muffins

VF

200g/7oz plain wholemeal flour
2 teaspoons baking powder
¼ teaspoon freshly grated nutmeg
50g/2oz light muscovado sugar
75g/3oz prunes, stoned and chopped
50g/2oz walnuts, coarsely chopped
1 teaspoon finely grated lemon rind
1 egg, beaten
1½ teaspoons clear honey
200ml/7floz skimmed milk

1. Preheat the oven to 200°C/400°F/Gas 6 and lightly grease muffin pans or deep bun trays.

2. Mix together the flour, baking powder and nutmeg in a bowl. Stir in the sugar, prunes, walnuts and lemon rind.

3. Beat the egg with the honey and milk and stir into the flour mixture. Spoon the mixture into the prepared muffin pans.

4. Bake for about 20 minutes or until golden-brown and well risen. Transfer to a cooling tray. Serve warm or cold.

CALORIES PER PORTION			Fats				**144**
	CHO(g)	Prot(g)	Sat(g)	Mono(g)	Poly(g)	Iron(mg)	Ca(mg)
Total	22	5	0.5	1	2.5	1.5	53
Energy	57%	14%		29%			

Per muffin

Oaty Buttermilk Pancakes

Makes 12 pancakes

<u>VF</u>

25g/1oz instant dried skimmed milk
50ml/2floz water
50g/2oz rolled oats
75g/3oz plain wholemeal flour
½ teaspoon baking powder
½ teaspoon salt
200ml/7floz buttermilk
1 egg, beaten
1 teaspoon clear honey
2 tablespoons toasted sunflower seeds (optional)

1. Mix the dried milk with the water. Mix the remaining dry ingredients in a bowl.

2. Add the dried milk mix, buttermilk, egg and honey. Beat well together. Leave to stand until required (up to 24 hours). When ready to use, mix again.

3. Very lightly grease a heavy-based frying pan. Heat until the pan is hot but not smoking.

4. Use a tablespoonful of mixture for each pancake and drop into the pan. Cook for a minute or so until risen slightly and browned underneath.

5. Turn over and cook for another minute or so. Eat hot or cold.

CALORIES PER PORTION			Fats				133
	CHO(g)	Prot(g)	Sat(g)	Mono(g)	Poly(g)	Iron(mg)	Ca(mg)
Total	21	11	0.5	0.5	0.5	0.5	338
Energy	60%	32%		8%			

Per pancake

Indian Toast

Makes 1 serving

V

1 egg, beaten
50ml/2floz skimmed milk
½ teaspoon curry powder
salt and freshly ground black pepper (optional)
2 slices wholemeal bread
1 tablespoon your favourite chutney
1 tablespoon grated hard cheese

1. Beat the egg, milk, curry powder and seasoning if using together and place in a shallow bowl.

2. Soak the slices of bread in the egg mixture.

3. Heat a non-stick frying pan over a medium heat and fry the slices of bread until lightly browned. Turn over.

4. Mix the chutney and cheese and spread over the toast.

5. When cooked on the second side sandwich together with the cheese and chutney in the centre.

CALORIES PER PORTION			Fats				332
	CHO(g)	Prot(g)	Sat(g)	Mono(g)	Poly(g)	Iron(mg)	Ca(mg)
Total	35	19	5.5	5	1	3.5	233
Energy	40%	23%		37%			

Bean and Potato Hash

Makes 4 servings

<u>V</u>

2 onions, peeled and sliced
1-2 cloves garlic, peeled and chopped (optional)
2 tablespoons vegetable oil
450g/1lb left-over boiled or mashed potatoes
1 × 400-g/14-oz can blackeye, haricot or red kidney beans, drained
4 tablespoons chopped fresh parsley
salt and freshly ground black pepper

1. Fry the onion and garlic if using in the oil in a non-stick frying pan for about 3-4 minutes over a medium heat until just turning to gold.

2. Add the potatoes (diced in the case of boiled potatoes) and beans and continue to fry until the vegetables are heated through.

3. Sprinkle with the parsley and seasoning and press down with a fork or potato masher so that the mixture sticks together.

4. Turn up the heat and brown the base for about 1 minute. Turn out to serve with the browned side up.

Note: Cook extra potatoes at the evening meal and keep in the fridge until required.

CALORIES PER PORTION			Fats				**312**
	CHO(g)	Prot(g)	Sat(g)	Mono(g)	Poly(g)	Iron(mg)	Ca(mg)
Total	49	12.5	1	3	4	3	63
Energy	59%	16%		25%			

Omelette Brunch Baps

Makes 1 serving

V

2 eggs
1 tablespoon water
salt and freshly ground black pepper
1 teaspoon vegetable oil
1 brown bap, split in half
Optional fillings:
1½-2 tablespoons cooked sweetcorn kernels
½ teaspoon mixed dried herbs or 1 tablespoon chopped fresh herbs
1 tomato, finely chopped

1. Beat the eggs in a basin with the water and seasoning.

2. Heat the oil in a small non-stick frying pan. Pour in the eggs and cook for about 1 minute until the base is just set. (If you are really pushed for time you can break the eggs directly into the pan. Cut the yolks with a knife to spread them and proceed as before.)

3. Sprinkle with your chosen filling and fold over. Transfer to the centre of the bap and eat at once.

Note: Baps are fairly soft rolls about the size of a saucer. They are sometimes called teacakes but are not sweet. Sesame or burger buns can also be used for this recipe.

CALORIES PER PORTION			*Fats*				**608**
	CHO(g)	Prot(g)	Sat(g)	Mono(g)	Poly(g)	Iron(mg)	Ca(mg)
Total	74	29	5.5	9	5	6.5	192
Energy	46%	19%		36%			

With all fillings

8.2 SAVOURY SNACKS AND EASY FILLERS

Eating snacks is not necessarily greedy. It can be a way of eating before you get too hungry and start to crave sweet or fatty foods. Snacks can also help to keep you going before a work-out, practice session or run when a regular meal would leave you with too full a stomach. They're also helpful to start the refuelling after a training session before you can get to have a 'proper' meal.

The recipes in this section include quick-to-make snacks, some using a bread base or convenience food such as taco shells, as well as some dishes which can be made when you have a bit of time to spare.

One of the quickest snacks to make is a dip to serve with water biscuits, toast fingers, tortilla chips and raw fresh vegetable crudités such as carrot and cucumber sticks, cauliflower florets, radishes and spring onions. Dips can also be used as sandwich spreads and toppings for jacket potatoes. Thinned down with skimmed milk, they make excellent low-fat salad dressings.

Sandwiches offer endless variety – open, closed, double decker, club and submarines. Sandwiches are an extremely useful way of providing your own food when you are away from home. Packed lunches for school and work and when travelling enable you to control your food and keep to a good high-carbohydrate, low-fat diet.

The problem is that they can get rather boring after a while and it can take some ingenuity to keep the interest up and the wrong foods out. Keep sandwiches interesting by using all the different kinds of bread and rolls on pages 303 to 306 and mix and match them to make layered or club sandwiches. Hollowed out rolls or 'subs' as they are often called can be filled with salad mixtures as well as the more conventional sliced meats, eggs and cheese.

Some ideas are given here for combinations such as rye deckers and nutritious fillings like the two versions of chopped liver. One of the most versatile of bread-based snacks comes from Italy. It is bruschetta, a kind of warm open sandwich with a variety of toppings. Other ideas come from Germany and Denmark as well as from the USA and UK.

Spanish tortilla makes a great standby for quick snacks. It is good hot or cold and can be kept in the fridge for a day or two. Traditional tortilla is made with potato alone but Spanish tapas bar chefs all have their own versions. It doesn't take all that long to make.

Most of the recipes which take longer to prepare can be stored in the fridge, to be sliced or cut into wedges as and when you want them. You can freeze dishes like the Dutch Pepper Loaf. Pack in single serving slices and thaw in the microwave as required.

Jacket-baked potatoes may take an hour to cook but you can go away and leave them to cook on their own while you go for a run or do something else. They only need to be scrubbed, pierced and popped into the oven. The topping may be ready-made or take only a minute or two to prepare.

If you have a microwave oven the preparation of jacket potatoes can be speeded up to qualify them as quick snacks.

Guacamole Dip

Makes 4-6 servings

V

2 large ripe avocados
juice of 2 lemons
1 clove garlic, peeled and crushed
2-3 loaves pitta bread
Optional flavourings:
2 tablespoons chopped fresh coriander
2 small tomatoes, peeled, seeded and finely diced
3-4 spring onions, very finely chopped

1. Blend the avocados, lemon juice and garlic in a blender until smooth and creamy.

2. Stir in one or more of the optional flavourings and serve at once with toasted pitta bread.

Note: This dip will not keep as long as the others as the avocado tends to discolour in contact with the air.

CALORIES PER PORTION			Fats				200
	CHO(g)	Prot(g)	Sat(g)	Mono(g)	Poly(g)	Iron(mg)	Ca(mg)
Total	31	5.5	1.5	4	1	1	53
Energy	57%	11%		32%			

With all flavourings and pitta bread

Middle Eastern Hummus with Pitta Bread

Makes 4-6 servings

VF

1 × 400-g/14-oz can chickpeas, drained
2 tablespoons tahina paste
1-2 cloves garlic, peeled and crushed
juice of 1 lemon
water
salt
2-3 pitta loaves
Garnish:
2-3 tablespoons olive oil (optional)
ground cumin
paprika
sprigs of fresh continental parsley

1. Rub the chickpeas through a sieve or blend in a food processor.

2. Add all the remaining ingredients and blend well together. Thin with a little water if the mixture is too thick.

3. Spoon into a bowl, pour on the olive oil if using and garnish with the spices and parsley.

4. Serve with pitta bread.

CALORIES PER PORTION		Fats				312
	CHO(g)	Prot(g)	Sat(g)	Mono(g)	Poly(g)	Iron(mg)	Ca(mg)
Total	40	12.5	2	4	5.5	3.5	188
Energy	48%	16%		36%			

Without garnish

Rye Deckers I

Makes 2 large deckers

4 thick slices soft wholemeal bread
2 slices pumpernickel rye bread
1 × 125-g/4-oz can sardines, sild or brisling, in oil
a little lemon juice
freshly ground black pepper
75g/3oz cooked beetroot, grated
25g/1oz dill gherkin or cucumber, grated
1 teaspoon Greek yoghurt

1. Cut the wholemeal bread to the same size as the pumpernickel.

2. Drain the sardines well, mix with lemon juice and pepper and spread over half the pieces of wholemeal bread.

3. Mix the grated beetroot, gherkin and yoghurt and spread over the slices of pumpernickel.

4. Place the pumpernickel on top of the sardine-spread bread and top with another slice of wholemeal bread.

5. Cut into 4 smaller squares before wrapping.

Note: The Chopped Liver recipe (page 219) could be used instead of sardines.

CALORIES PER PORTION			Fats				**372**
	CHO(g)	Prot(g)	Sat(g)	Mono(g)	Poly(g)	Iron(mg)	Ca(mg)
Total	47	25	2	3.5	3.5	5	437
Energy	48%	26%		26%			

Rye Deckers II

Makes 2 large deckers

V

4 thick slices soft wholemeal bread
2 slices pumpernickel rye bread
10 green grapes, seeded and diced
2 sticks celery, very finely diced
1 tablespoon ground almonds
freshly ground black pepper
1 tablespoon Greek yoghurt
4 lettuce leaves
75g/3oz Brie

1. Cut the wholemeal bread to the same size as the pumpernickel.

2. Mix the grapes, celery, almonds, seasoning and yoghurt and spread over two of the slices of wholemeal bread. Top with the lettuce leaves.

3. Spread the Brie over the pumpernickel and place on top of the lettuce. Finish off with the remaining slices of wholemeal bread. Cut into 4 smaller squares and wrap.

CALORIES PER PORTION			Fats				428
	CHO(g)	Prot(g)	Sat(g)	Mono(g)	Poly(g)	Iron(mg)	Ca(mg)
Total	54	19	7.5	5.5	2	4	334
Energy	47%	18%		35%			

Chicken and Avocado 'Subs'

Makes 2 'subs'

1 small avocado, peeled, stoned and diced
a little lemon juice
125g/4oz cold cooked chicken, diced
1 tablespoon low-fat mayonnaise
salt and freshly ground black pepper
2 × 20-cm/8-in french sticks
2 tablespoons cranberry sauce
4-6 large lettuce leaves

1. Mix the avocado with the lemon juice as quickly as possible after preparation. Add the chicken, mayonnaise and seasoning.

2. Cut the French sticks in half lengthways and remove some of the dough to make room for the filling.

3. Spread the cranberry sauce over the bread and line with lettuce leaves.

4. Spoon in the chicken and avocado mixture and close up.

CALORIES PER PORTION			Fats				**468**
	CHO(g)	Prot(g)	Sat(g)	Mono(g)	Poly(g)	Iron(mg)	Ca(mg)
Total	56	27	4	8	2	2.5	161
Energy	45%	23%		32%			

Chopped Liver Sandwiches

Makes 4 rounds

F

450g/1lb lamb's liver (ask the butcher to cut it in one piece)
1 onion, peeled and sliced
4 tablespoons water
salt and freshly ground black pepper
8 slices wholemeal bread

1. Preheat the oven to 180°C/350°F/Gas 4.

2. Place the liver in a casserole dish and add the remaining ingredients.

3. Cover with a lid and bake for about 40-45 minutes until the liver is cooked through.

4. Cut the liver into chunks and purée in a food processor or a blender with the onions and cooking juices.

5. Use to make sandwiches.

CALORIES PER PORTION			Fats				356
	CHO(g)	Prot(g)	Sat(g)	Mono(g)	Poly(g)	Iron(mg)	Ca(mg)
Total	32	29	3.5	3.5	2	12.5	56
Energy	34%	33%		33%			

Mushroom Sesame Toast

Makes 1 serving

1 teaspoon sunflower oil
a few drops Chinese toasted sesame oil
1 thick slice wholemeal bread
4 spring onions, trimmed and chopped
salt and freshly ground black pepper
2 teaspoons sesame seeds
1 teaspoon light soy sauce
1 teaspoon freshly grated root ginger

1. Mix the sunflower and sesame oils and brush the bread on both sides with the mixture.

2. Toast on each side.

3. Place all the remaining ingredients in a food processor or blender and process until a smooth paste is formed.

4. Spread this over the toast and fry paste side down.

CALORIES PER PORTION			Fats				225
	CHO(g)	Prot(g)	Sat(g)	Mono(g)	Poly(g)	Iron(mg)	Ca(mg)
Total	22	8	1.5	4	5.5	3	104
Energy	37%	14%		50%			

Pan Bagnat

Makes 2 servings

2 large flat rolls or baps, or 4 ciabatta rolls
2 tablespoons extra-virgin olive oil
6-8 lettuce leaves
1 large continental or beef tomato, thinly sliced
1 × 200-g/7oz can tuna, drained and flaked
1 small onion, peeled and thinly sliced
8-12 black olives, stoned and halved
4 sprigs of fresh basil or continental parsley

1. Cut the rolls into two flat halves and brush the cut sur-faces with the olive oil.

2. Place the lettuce and tomatoes on the base of each roll and top with tuna or eggs. Add onion rings, olives and herbs.

CALORIES PER PORTION				Fats				596
	CHO(g)	Prot(g)	Sat(g)	Mono(g)	Poly(g)	Iron(mg)	Ca(mg)
Total	72.5	36	3	11.5	3	4	189
Energy	46%	24%		30%			

Dutch Hot Open Sandwiches

Makes 1 serving

1 large thick slice bread
½ teaspoon Meaux or Dijon mustard
125g/4oz thick slices cold cooked lean meat (beef, ham or pork)
1 egg
small knob of butter or margarine
coarsely ground black pepper
Garnish:
grilled tomatoes
sprigs of fresh parsley

1. Spread the bread with the mustard and top with the meat.

2. Fry the egg in the butter or margarine and place on top of the meat.

3. Sprinkle with seasoning and serve garnished with grilled tomatoes and sprigs of parsley.

CALORIES PER PORTION			Fats				413
	CHO(g)	Prot(g)	Sat(g)	Mono(g)	Poly(g)	Iron(mg)	Ca(mg)
Total	21	47	6	6	1.5	6	64
Energy	19%	46%		35%			

Bruschetta

Makes 1 serving

V

3-4 thick slices from an Italian ciabatta loaf or 2 ciabatta rolls, split
open (or any good bread could be used)
1 tablespoon olive oil
1-2 large cloves garlic, peeled
sprigs of fresh basil
2 tomatoes, sliced
Optional extras:
2-3 slices aubergine, grilled on each side
6-8 stoned black olives or stuffed green olives
1 small head fennel, sliced and grilled

1. Toast the bread or rolls lightly on each side.

2. Brush with the olive oil and rub briskly with the garlic so that the clove is used up.

3. Top with basil and the sliced tomatoes, and any extra toppings, and return to the grill.

CALORIES PER PORTION							580
	CHO(g)	Prot(g)	Sat(g)	Mono(g)	Poly(g)	Iron(mg)	Ca(mg)
Total	93	17	3	11	2.5	3.5	212
Energy	60%	12%		29%			

Bruschetta With Aubergine

CALORIES PER PORTION							607
	CHO(g)	Prot(g)	Sat(g)	Mono(g)	Poly(g)	Iron(mg)	Ca(mg)
Total	97	18.5	3	11	3	4	229
Energy	60%	12%		28%			

Bruschetta With Olives

CALORIES PER PORTION							609
	CHO(g)	Prot(g)	Sat(g)	Mono(g)	Poly(g)	Iron(mg)	Ca(mg)
Total	93	17	3	13	3	4	229
Energy	57%	11%		32%			

Bruschetta With Fennel

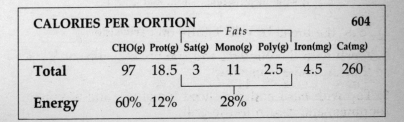

CALORIES PER PORTION							604
	CHO(g)	Prot(g)	Sat(g)	Mono(g)	Poly(g)	Iron(mg)	Ca(mg)
Total	97	18.5	3	11	2.5	4.5	260
Energy	60%	12%		28%			

Potato and Fennel Pancake

Makes 4 servings

V

450g/1lb small heads Italian fennel, trimmed and halved
900g/2lb floury potatoes, peeled and quartered
salt
1 tablespoon oil
1 onion, peeled and finely chopped
1 clove garlic, peeled and finely chopped
1 teaspoon fennel seeds (optional)
freshly ground black pepper
1 large egg, beaten

1. Cook the fennel and potatoes in salted boiling water for 12-15 minutes until almost tender. Drain and slice the vegetables fairly thinly.

2. Heat the oil in a medium-sized, heavy-based frying pan and fry the onion, garlic and fennel seeds, if using, for 3-4 minutes until lightly browned.

3. Layer the sliced vegetables in the pan, sprinkling with salt and pepper as you go. Cook over a medium heat for about 4 minutes.

4. Beat the eggs, pour over the vegetables and cook for a further 2-3 minutes until set on the bottom. Turn the pancake over with a fish slice and cook on the other side until it too is well browned.

CALORIES PER PORTION				Fats			252
	CHO(g)	Prot(g)	Sat(g)	Mono(g)	Poly(g)	Iron(mg)	Ca(mg)
Total	46	8.5	1	1.5	1.5	1.5	63
Energy	68%	14%		18%			

Japanese Pan-fried Chicken Cakes

Makes 4 servings

F

1 tablespoon sesame seeds
4 chicken breast fillets, boned and skinned
3 tablespoons soy sauce
2 teaspoons sherry (optional)
1 teaspoon freshly grated root ginger
2 spring onions, very finely chopped
1 small (size 6) egg
salt and freshly ground black pepper
1 tablespoon vegetable oil
4 sesame buns
2 tomatoes, sliced
sprigs of fresh coriander

1. Toast the sesame seeds in a hot dry frying pan. Keep the seeds on the move as they burn very quickly. When they are lightly browned, remove from the pan and reserve.

2. Mince the chicken or use a food processor until coarsely chopped. Mix with all the remaining ingredients except the cooking oil, sesame seeds, buns, tomatoes and coriander.

3. Shape into 8 small cakes, about 1cm/½in thick. Cook in hot oil for 5 minutes. Turn over, sprinkle with the reserved sesame seeds and cook for a further 5 minutes, until cooked through.

4. Serve in a sesame bun with sliced tomatoes and fresh coriander leaves.

CALORIES PER PORTION							**473**
			Fats				
	CHO(g)	Prot(g)	Sat(g)	Mono(g)	Poly(g)	Iron(mg)	Ca(mg)
Total	34.5	48	3.5	6	5	3.5	149
Energy	27%	41%		32%			

Lentil Tacos

Makes 1 serving

V

3 heaped tablespoons Spiced Lentils (page 275)
3 taco shells
4-6 lettuce leaves, shredded
1 tablespoon grated hard cheese

1. Heat the lentils through in a microwave oven or in a basin over a pan of hot water.

2. Heat the taco shells in the oven as directed on the pack.

3. Spoon a tablespoonful of the lentil mixture into each taco shell and top with shredded lettuce and grated cheese. Serve at once.

CALORIES PER PORTION			Fats				**460**
	CHO(g)	Prot(g)	Sat(g)	Mono(g)	Poly(g)	Iron(mg)	Ca(mg)
Total	55.5	20	5	6.5	6	5	219
Energy	45%	17%		38%			

Dutch Pepper Loaf

Makes 1 loaf or about 6-8 thick slices

F

1 red pepper, seeded and finely chopped
½ green pepper, seeded and finely chopped
25ml/1floz olive oil
175g/6oz self-raising flour
75g/3oz Edam cheese, grated
2 eggs, beaten
50g/2oz rolled oats
salt and freshly ground black pepper
pinch of freshly grated nutmeg

1. Preheat the oven to 190°C/375°F/Gas 5 and grease or line a 450-g/1-lb loaf tin.

2. Gently fry the peppers in the oil for about 3 minutes to soften but not brown them.

3. Place the flour and cheese in a bowl and mix together with the fried peppers. Stir and add the beaten eggs, seasoning and nutmeg.

4. Pour into the prepared loaf tin and bake for 50 minutes. Loosen the sides with a knife and leave to cool in the tin. Turn out and slice to serve.

CALORIES PER PORTION			Fats				**196**
	CHO(g)	Prot(g)	Sat(g)	Mono(g)	Poly(g)	Iron(mg)	Ca(mg)
Total	25	8	2.5	4	1	1	179
Energy	47%	16%		38%			

Jacket-baked Potatoes

Makes 1 serving

1 large potato (225-275g/8-10oz)
salt and freshly ground black pepper

FILLINGS:
Choose from one of the following simple fillings:
a) 2 heaped tablespoons Greek yoghurt with sprigs of fresh parsley
b) 75g/3oz low-fat Cheddar cheese, grated and mixed with 1 tablespoonful chutney
c) 75g/3oz cottage cheese mixed with chopped chives, chervil or tarragon
d) 2 tablespoons Guacamole Dip (page 214) and some crushed corn chips
e) 1 tablespoon tahina paste mixed with crushed garlic and lemon juice

1. Preheat the oven to 220°C/425°F/Gas 7.

2. Scrub and dry the potato and make a cut in the top with a knife. Place in the oven. Bake for 50 minutes to 1 hour until the inside feels soft. Make crosswise slits in the top of the potato and press in at the base until the incisions open.

3. Fill with your chosen filling. For a softer-skinned potato, wrap in foil before baking or prick all over with a fork and brush with a very little oil before placing in the oven. Metal potato bakers speed up the cooking time.

Filling a)

CALORIES PER PORTION			Fats				426
	CHO(g)	Prot(g)	Sat(g)	Mono(g)	Poly(g)	Iron(mg)	Ca(mg)
Total	81	14.5	4	2	0.5	2	140
Energy	71%	14%		15%			

Filling b)

CALORIES PER PORTION			Fats				444
	CHO(g)	Prot(g)	Sat(g)	Mono(g)	Poly(g)	Iron(mg)	Ca(mg)
Total	89	20	2	1	0.5	2	86
Energy	75%	18%		7%			

Filling c)

CALORIES PER PORTION			Fats				413
	CHO(g)	Prot(g)	Sat(g)	Mono(g)	Poly(g)	Iron(mg)	Ca(mg)
Total	81	20	2	1	0.5	2	82
Energy	73%	19%		7%			

Filling d)

CALORIES PER PORTION			Fats				680
	CHO(g)	Prot(g)	Sat(g)	Mono(g)	Poly(g)	Iron(mg)	Ca(mg)
Total	91	23	6	10.5	9.5	3	107
Energy	50%	14%		36%			

Filling e)

CALORIES PER PORTION			Fats				380
	CHO(g)	Prot(g)	Sat(g)	Mono(g)	Poly(g)	Iron(mg)	Ca(mg)
Total	71	10	2	4	1.5	2	60
Energy	70%	11%		19%			

Potato Kedgeree

Makes 4 servings

4 large potatoes
170g/6oz frozen smoked haddock fillet
50g/2oz frozen peas
3 eggs
2 tablespoons chopped fresh parsley
salt and freshly ground black pepper
Garnish (optional):
soured cream or Greek yoghurt

1. Preheat the oven to 220°C/425°F/Gas 7 and cook the potatoes as directed for Jacket-baked Potatoes (page 227).

2. Meanwhile, cook the smoked haddock fillet and peas as directed on the packs and hard-boil the eggs.

3. When the jacket potatoes are cooked, cut in half lengthways and scoop about a third of the potato out of the skins into a bowl.

4. Skin, bone and flake the cooked fish and add to the potato with the drained cooked peas, chopped hard-boiled egg, parsley and seasoning and mix well together with a fork.

5. Pile back into the potato halves and return to the oven for 5-6 minutes to heat through. Serve with soured cream or Greek yoghurt, if liked.

CALORIES PER PORTION			Fats				**319**
	CHO(g)	Prot(g)	Sat(g)	Mono(g)	Poly(g)	Iron(mg)	Ca(mg)
Total	50.5	18	1.5	2	1	2.5	78
Energy	59%	23%		18%			

Potato Eggs Florentine

Makes 4 servings

<u>V</u>

4 large potatoes
1 × 225g/8oz pack frozen creamed spinach
2 tablespoons skimmed milk
knob of butter or margarine
4 eggs, beaten
salt and freshly ground black pepper

1. Preheat the oven to 220°C/425°F/Gas 7 and cook the potatoes as directed for Jacket-baked Potatoes (page 227).

2. Meanwhile, place the creamed spinach in a pan to thaw and heat through.

3. Heat the butter or margarine and milk in another pan and add the eggs. Scramble until just set.

4. When the potatoes are cooked, cut a thin slice or lid lengthways off the top of each potato and scoop out and discard a little of the potato. Fill up with creamed spinach and top with scrambled eggs. Put the potato lid gently in place and serve at once.

CALORIES PER PORTION			_Fats_				368
	CHO(g)	Prot(g)	Sat(g)	Mono(g)	Poly(g)	Iron(mg)	Ca(mg)
Total	44.5	15.0	7	5	1	3	140
Energy	45%	17%		38%			

8.3 SOUPS AND STARTERS

Home-made soups taste delicious, they are also an invaluable part of the sporting cook's repertoire. They can be made quite quickly on the day they are wanted or you can make extra and simply heat up portions as required. Soups can be stored in the fridge for two to three days – most can also be frozen for up to three months. Freeze in individual portions. Soups like Courgette and Fennel Soup, Leek and Mustard Soup with Mushrooms, and American Gumbo freeze well.

Soups are versatile, too. They can be served on their own as a first course. Or they can be eaten as a main course with plenty of crusty bread or with rice (American Gumbo) or buckwheat noodles. In Mexico the Chickpea and Lemon Soup is often served with garlic croutons or even a fried egg. Soups also make easy between-meal snacks or late-night fillers.

The starter or first course recipes, too, are quite substantial and could be used for snack meals and supper dishes in their own right, though you may need to serve a little more of them. The Stuffed Peppers and Lentil Salad keep very well in the fridge.

Greek Potato Soup

Makes 4-6 servings

V

2 onions, peeled and chopped
2 tablespoons olive oil
900g/2lb (4 large) waxy potatoes, cut into small cubes
2 carrots, peeled and chopped
4 ripe tomatoes, chopped
salt and freshly ground black pepper
1 teaspoon dried marjoram or oregano
½-1 teaspoon fennel seeds
150g/5oz plain yoghurt
1.2litres/2pints vegetable stock
juice of 2 lemons
1 tablespoon tomato purée
Garnish:
1-2 tablespoons chopped fresh mint

1. Gently fry the onions in the oil until transparent, then add the potatoes, carrots and tomatoes. Season with salt and pepper, add the herbs and mix well to coat all the vegetables with the oil.

2. Stir in the yoghurt, pour over the stock and bring to the boil. Cover and simmer gently for 30 minutes.

3. Stir in the lemon juice and tomato purée just before serving. Serve sprinkled with fresh mint.

CALORIES PER PORTION			Fats			**229**	
	CHO(g)	Prot(g)	Sat(g)	Mono(g)	Poly(g)	Iron(mg)	Ca(mg)
Total	40	9.5	6.5	4	2	4	128
Energy	66%	12%		21%			

Courgette and Fennel Soup

Makes 4 servings

VF

1 large onion, peeled and sliced
2 heads fennel, trimmed and sliced
350g/12oz courgettes, trimmed and sliced
1 tablespoon olive oil
50ml/2floz sherry (optional)
750ml/1¼pints vegetable stock
salt and freshly ground black pepper

1. Gently fry the onion, fennel and courgettes in the oil for about 2-3 minutes, stirring all the time.

2. Add the sherry if using and bring to the boil. Cook for 1 minute to remove the alcohol.

3. Add the stock and bring back to the boil. Cover, reduce the heat and simmer for about 30 minutes.

4. Serve with plenty of wholemeal bread.

CALORIES PER PORTION			Fats				**91**
	CHO(g)	Prot(g)	Sat(g)	Mono(g)	Poly(g)	Iron(mg)	Ca(mg)
Total	10	3.5	0.5	2.5	0.5	1	69
Energy	40%	16%		45%			

Without sherry

American Gumbo

Makes 4 servings

F

4 rashers streaky bacon, diced
1 large onion, peeled and chopped
1 clove garlic, peeled and crushed

1 red pepper, seeded and chopped
225g/8oz okra, trimmed but not chopped
3 tomatoes, peeled and chopped
900ml/1½pints chicken stock, made by dissolving 2 chicken stock
cubes in boiling water
75g/3oz long-grain rice
salt
a few drops Tabasco sauce
Optional extra:
meat from 2 cooked chicken joints, shredded

1. Fry the bacon in a non-stick pan to release the fat. Fry the onion and garlic in this. Add the chopped pepper and fry for 2-3 minutes.

2. Add all the remaining ingredients except the rice, salt and Tabasco and bring to the boil. Reduce the heat and simmer for 30 minutes.

3. Meanwhile, place the rice in a pan with 175ml/6floz salted boiling water. Cover with a lid and cook for 12-13 minutes until all the liquid is absorbed and the rice is tender.

4. Season the cooked soup to taste with Tabasco and add the shredded chicken if using. Spoon into individual bowls. Place a small mound of rice in the centre of each bowl and serve at once.

CALORIES PER PORTION			Fats				170/228
	CHO(g)	Prot(g)	Sat(g)	Mono(g)	Poly(g)	Iron(mg)	Ca(mg)
Total	27/	9.5/	1	1	1	1.2/	124/
	27	18	2	2	1	2.5	127
Energy	59%	23%		19%			
	44%	32%		24%			

Without chicken/with chicken

Mexican Chickpea and Lemon Soup

Makes 4 servings

F

1 onion, peeled and chopped
3 cloves garlic, peeled and chopped
1 tablespoon olive oil
1 × 400g/14oz cans chickpeas, drained
900ml/1½pints chicken stock
3 tablespoons chopped fresh mint
grated rind and juice of 1 lemon
salt and freshly ground black pepper
Garnish:
fresh mint leaves

1. Fry the onion and garlic in the oil until lightly browned.

2. Add the chickpeas and cook for 1 further minute. Then add the stock, bring to the boil and cook for 5 minutes.

3. Purée the mixture in a blender or food processor. Stir in the mint, lemon rind and juice and season to taste. Serve with a garnish of fresh mint leaves.

CALORIES PER PORTION							**177**
				Fats			
	CHO(g)	Prot(g)	Sat(g)	Mono(g)	Poly(g)	Iron(mg)	Ca(mg)
Total	21	8	1	3	2	2	60
Energy	47%	19%		35%			

Lentil, Carrot & Watercress Soup

Makes 4 servings

F

1 tablespoon olive oil
1 medium onion, peeled and sliced
450g/1lb carrots, peeled and chopped
75g/3oz red split lentils, picked over
75g/3oz watercress, with stalks
½ beef stock cube
1.2litres/2pints water
2 sprigs of fresh parsley
1 sprig of fresh thyme or ¼ teaspoon dried
1 bayleaf
salt and freshly ground black pepper
25g/1oz whole green continental lentils
2 rashers lean smoked bacon, very finely chopped, with rind and fat removed

1. Heat the oil in a pan and gently fry the onion until just beginning to turn gold. Add the carrots and cook over a very low heat for 3-4 minutes, stirring all the time.

2. Add the red lentils, watercress, stock, water, herbs and seasoning and bring to the boil. Reduce the heat and simmer for 30 minutes.

3. Remove the sprig of thyme and the bayleaf. Process in a blender or rub through a sieve.

4. Return to the heat and add the green lentils and the bacon. Simmer for a further 30 minutes until the lentils are just cooked.

	CHO(g)	Prot(g)	Sat(g)	Mono(g)	Poly(g)	Iron(mg)	Ca(mg)
CALORIES PER PORTION				*Fats*			**191**
Total	26.5	10	1	3	1	3	87.5
Energy	52%	22%		27%			

Lentil Salad with Anchovies

Makes 4 servings

125g/4oz whole dried lentils
1 small onion, stuck with a clove
1 very small carrot, peeled
1 bouquet garni
1 tablespoon olive oil
1 teaspoon red wine vinegar
1 teaspoon chopped fresh tarragon
3 spring onions, finely chopped
salt and freshly ground black pepper
2 × 50g/2oz cans anchovy fillets, drained
Garnish:
sprigs of fresh herbs

1. Wash the lentils and drain well.

2. Place in a pan with the onion, carrot and bouquet garni and cover with water. Bring to the boil, reduce the heat and simmer for 25-30 minutes until the lentils are just tender but still whole. Take care not to over-cook them or they will become too mushy to make a good salad.

3. Drain, discarding the onion, carrot and bouquet garni. Mix the lentils with the oil, vinegar, herbs, spring onions and seasoning and leave to cool.

4. Add all the remaining ingredients and pile on to individual plates. Garnish with sprigs of fresh herbs.

Variation: Leave out the anchovies for a vegetarian meal.

CALORIES PER PORTION				*Fats*			**225**
	CHO(g)	Prot(g)	Sat(g)	Mono(g)	Poly(g)	Iron(mg)	Ca(mg)
Total	21	14	0.5	2.5	0.5	5	117
Energy	35%	26%		38%			

Smoked Chicken and Vegetable Salad

Makes 4 servings

125g/4oz broad beans
225g/8oz baby courgettes
125g/4oz sugar peas or mangetout
meat from 2 drumsticks of smoked chicken
4 wholemeal rolls
Dressing:
2-3 tablespoons hazelnut oil
1 teaspoon sherry vinegar
salt and freshly ground black pepper
Garnish:
plenty of sprigs of fresh parsley

1. Cook the broad beans in boiling water until tender.

2. Steam the vegetables: 6 minutes for courgettes and 3 for peas.

3. Leave all the vegetables to cool. Cut the chicken meat into strips and mix with the cold vegetables.

4. Mix the dressing ingredients and pour over the salad. Garnish with sprigs of fresh parsley, dotting them all over the salad.

5. Serve with wholemeal bread rolls.

CALORIES PER PORTION			Fats				**270**
	CHO(g)	Prot(g)	Sat(g)	Mono(g)	Poly(g)	Iron(mg)	Ca(mg)
Total	31	15	1.5	3.5	4.5	3.5	99
Energy	43%	21%		35%			

Stuffed Peppers

Makes 4 servings

V

8 large red peppers
700g/1½lb aubergines
3 cloves garlic, peeled and crushed
1 tablespoon olive oil
4 tablespoons fresh breadcrumbs
50-75g/2-3oz pitted black olives
25g/1oz capers
450g/1lb ripe tomatoes, peeled, seeded and chopped
¼ teaspoon dried oregano
50g/2oz chopped fresh parsley
salt and freshly ground black pepper

1. Preheat the oven to 220°C/425°F/Gas 7. Wash and dry the peppers. Scorch over a flame or under a grill. When they have blackened, carefully scrape off the skin. Cut round the stem and remove the seeds from the inside.

2. Wash the aubergines and cut into thick slices. Grill and cook until well-browned on both sides. Dice.

3. Fry the garlic in the oil for 1 minute. Add the breadcrumbs and fry for 2-3 minutes. Add all the remaining ingredients except the peppers and aubergines, and cook for a further 2-3 minutes.

4. Stir the diced aubergine into the mixture and spoon into the prepared peppers. Place in a greased baking dish. Bake for about 20 minutes.

CALORIES PER PORTION			Fats				200
	CHO(g)	Prot(g)	Sat(g)	Mono(g)	Poly(g)	Iron(mg)	Ca(mg)
Total	27	6	1.5	4	2	3	87
Energy	51%	13%		37%			

Tomatoes Stuffed with Herb Bulgar or Millet

Makes 4 servings

<u>V</u>

125g/4oz bulgar or millet
8 spring onions, finely chopped
½ teaspoon dried mixed herbs
300ml/10floz vegetable stock
25g/1oz pinenuts, or flaked almonds or brazil nuts
3 tablespoons chopped fresh parsley
salt and freshly ground black pepper
juice of ½ lemon
4 large continental or beef tomatoes

1. Place the millet, spring onions, dried herbs and vegetable stock in a saucepan. Bring to the boil and stir once. Reduce the heat, cover and simmer for 25-30 minutes until the millet is cooked. Leave to cool.

2. Toast the nuts in a dry frying pan until well browned. Leave to cool.

3. Mix the millet with the nuts, parsley, seasoning and lemon juice.

4. Cut the tops off the tomatoes. Scoop out the centres and seeds and fill with the millet mixture.

5. Serve cold or bake at 180°C/350°F/Gas 4 for 10-15 minutes and serve hot.

CALORIES PER PORTION							**196**
				Fats			
	CHO(g)	Prot(g)	Sat(g)	Mono(g)	Poly(g)	Iron(mg)	Ca(mg)
Total	32	7	0.5	1.5	3	3	39
Energy	62%	14%		25%			

8.4 PUMPING PASTA

Pasta is one of the quickest and easiest ways of adding complex carbohydrates to your diet. It is also one of the most attractive. A bowl of pasta with a simple but tasty sauce makes a delicious meal in minutes – even the thickest dried pasta cooks within 15 minutes. Fresh pasta cooks in two to three minutes.

Cook the pasta in a large pan in plenty of lightly salted boiling water. This gives the pasta room to expand and prevents it from sticking together. Take care not to overcook. Pasta should be served *al dente* or just tender, with a slight bite to it. Drain as soon as this stage is reached and toss in your chosen sauce.

Stuffed fresh pastas such as ravioli and tortelloni are useful if you are in a hurry for all they need is the addition of a little olive oil, yoghurt or low-fat soft cheese. They are cooked when they rise and float on the top of the cooking water. A handful of fresh herbs such as sage, basil or tarragon sprinkled over the top turns the meal into a feast.

Freshly grated Parmesan cheese is the traditional accompaniment to all but fish-based pasta sauces. Do try to buy a whole piece of Parmesan and grate it yourself. The drums of ready-grated Parmesan on sale in some supermarkets taste just like sawdust! You will find that you do not need to use very much if you buy good Parmesan. Remember it will keep in the fridge in a polythene box for a month or more.

Leftover pasta is not very good reheated but it can be used to make excellent cold salad dishes (see page 315). Alternatively use it up in soups.

Pasta is not only to be found in Italy. The Chinese and Japanese have been eating pasta for at least as long if not longer than the Italians. Chinese egg noodles are very easy to prepare. All you have to do is to bring a large pan of water to the boil and plunge the noodles into this. Remove from the heat, stir and leave to stand for five minutes. Some Japanese noodles can be prepared in the same way. Others need to be gently simmered in stock. Follow the instructions on the pack. Some Japanese noodles are made from buckwheat (soba), others from wheat. The former have an interesting nutty flavour.

Spaghetti with Peanut Butter Sauce

Makes 2-3 servings

V

350g/12oz spaghetti
salt
1 onion, peeled and finely chopped
1 clove garlic, peeled and crushed
1 tablespoon olive oil
1½ tablespoons peanut butter (smooth)
100ml/4floz skimmed milk
freshly ground black pepper

1. Cook the spaghetti in plenty of lightly salted boiling water until just tender. Drain well.

2. Gently fry the onion and garlic in the oil in a small non-stick pan.

3. Gradually stir in the peanut butter and milk and bring to the boil, adding a little more milk if the sauce gets too thick.

4. Season to taste and serve with the spaghetti.

CALORIES PER PORTION							**212**
				Fats			
	CHO(g)	Prot(g)	Sat(g)	Mono(g)	Poly(g)	Iron(mg)	Ca(mg)
Total	27.5	8	2	3.5	3	1	54
Energy	49%	14%		37%			

Tagliatelle with Garlic Cheese Sauce

Makes 1 serving

V

100-125g/3½-4oz dried tagliatelle
salt
1-2 tablespoons skimmed milk or water
75g/3oz Boursin cheese
freshly ground black pepper

1. Cook the pasta in plenty of lightly salted boiling water until just cooked or *al dente*.

2. Heat the milk or water in a small saucepan and stir in the cheese. Continue stirring until the cheese has dissolved into a thick sauce. Season to taste.

3. Drain the cooked pasta and toss with the cheese sauce.

CALORIES PER PORTION				*Fats*			578
	CHO(g)	Prot(g)	Sat(g)	Mono(g)	Poly(g)	Iron(mg)	Ca(mg)
Total	97	23.5	7	3.5	1.5	2.5	91
Energy	63%	16%		21%			

Neopolitan Macaroni

Makes 3-4 servings

V

350g/12oz elbow macaroni
salt
2 tablespoons extra-virgin olive oil
2 cloves garlic, peeled and chopped
4 sticks celery, trimmed and finely chopped
4 tomatoes, peeled and chopped

4 tablespoons chopped fresh parsley
2 tablespoons chopped fresh basil or 1 tablespoon chopped fresh
rosemary
1 × 400g/14oz can beans, drained (haricot, cannellini, flaageolet or
borlotti)
freshly ground black pepper

1. Cook the pasta in plenty of lightly salted boiling water for about 8-10 minutes or as directed on the pack, until just cooked or *al dente*.

2. Heat the oil in a pan and gently fry the garlic and celery for 2-3 minutes. Do not allow to brown. Add the tomatoes and cook for a further 2-3 minutes.

3. Add all the remaining ingredients and toss over a medium heat for 3-4 minutes.

4. Drain the pasta in a colander. Add the bean and tomato mixture and toss well together.

CALORIES PER PORTION			Fats				500
	CHO(g)	Prot(g)	Sat(g)	Mono(g)	Poly(g)	Iron(mg)	Ca(mg)
Total	88	20	1.5	5.5	2	4.5	69
Energy	66%	16%		18%			

Pasta Bows with Fromage Frais

Makes 1 serving

<u>V</u>

100-125g/3½-4oz dried pasta bows
75g/3oz fromage frais
salt and freshly ground black pepper
1 tablespoon chopped fresh parsley
1 tablespoon toasted pinenuts

1. Cook the spaghetti in plenty of lightly salted boiling water until just cooked or *al dente*, then drain.

2. Heat the fromage frais in a small saucepan and stir until the cheese has dissolved into a thick sauce. Season to taste.

3. Toss the hot pasta in the cheese sauce, and sprinkle with the parsley and pinenuts.

CALORIES PER PORTION							616
	CHO(g)	Prot(g)	Sat(g)	Mono(g)	Poly(g)	Iron(mg)	Ca(mg)
Total	98	22.5	4	5	7	3.5	104
Energy	59%	14%		26%			

Chinese Noodles with Stir-fried Beef and Beans

Makes 4 servings

225g/8oz French beans, topped, tailed and halved
salt
300g/10oz uncooked Chinese noodles
3 tablespoons corn oil
2 medium red peppers, seeded and cut into strips
2 medium yellow peppers, seeded and cut into strips
175g/6oz oyster mushrooms, torn into strips
1 bunch spring onions, cut into 2.5-cm/1-in pieces
225g/8oz baby sweetcorn
350g/12oz lean rump steak, cut into long thin strips
4-5 teaspoons horseradish relish
2 tablespoons soy sauce

1. Boil the beans in lightly salted water until just done but still crisp. Refresh in cold water, drain and set aside.

2. Fill a large pan with water and bring to the boil. Plunge the noodles into the water. Remove from the heat. Stir and leave to stand until required.

3. Heat half the oil in a wok or large frying pan. Add the peppers and stir-fry for about 1 minute. Add the oyster mushrooms and spring onions. Stir-fry for 1 further minute. Add the sweetcorn and cooked beans and stir-fry a little longer.

4. Remove the vegetables from the pan and keep warm. Heat the remaining oil until very hot, toss in the beef and stir-fry very quickly.

5. Stir in the horseradish relish and soy sauce. Return the vegetables to the pan and toss again.

6. Drain the noodles and serve with the stir-fried beef and beans.

CALORIES PER PORTION			Fats				**606**
	CHO(g)	Prot(g)	Sat(g)	Mono(g)	Poly(g)	Iron(mg)	Ca(mg)
Total	69	33	5	9	7	5.5	79
Energy	43%	22%		35%			

Pasta Pescatori

Makes 3-4 servings

350g/12oz pasta shells
salt
2 tablespoons olive oil
1 × 212g/7½oz can tuna
2 tablespoons chopped fresh parsley
a little grated lemon rind
½ bunch spring onions, trimmed and finely chopped

1. Cook the pasta shells in lightly salted water until just tender, or *al dente*.

2. Drain and toss in the olive oil.

3. Drain and flake the tuna and add to the pasta with the parsley, lemon rind and spring onions.

4. Toss over a low heat until thoroughly heated. Serve at once.

CALORIES PER PORTION			*Fats*				422
	CHO(g)	Prot(g)	Sat(g)	Mono(g)	Poly(g)	Iron(mg)	Ca(mg)
Total	65	23	1.5	5.5	1.5	2.5	32
Energy	58%	22%		20%			

Tuscan Herby Pasta

Makes 4 servings

25g/1oz basil
25g/1oz fresh parsley
2 cloves garlic, peeled and crushed
50g/2oz toasted pinenuts
3 tablespoons extra-virgin olive oil
salt and freshly ground black pepper
450g/1lb new potatoes
225g/8oz French beans, topped and tailed
350g/12oz spaghetti
25g/1oz freshly grated Parmesan, to serve

1. Chop the fresh herbs finely or process in a blender with the garlic, half the pinenuts and the oil. Leave the mixture to stand for 10-15 minutes.

2. Steam the potatoes and beans until tender. Dice and mix with the sauce.

3. Cook the spaghetti until just tender or *al dente*, then drain. Toss with the vegetables and sauce and the remaining pinenuts.

4. Serve at once with freshly grated Parmesan cheese.

CALORIES PER PORTION			Fats				616
	CHO(g)	Prot(g)	Sat(g)	Mono(g)	Poly(g)	Iron(mg)	Ca(mg)
Total	87	18	3.5	11	7	4.5	116
Energy	53%	12%		35%			

Japanese Buckwheat Noodles with Stir-fried Vegetables

Makes 4 servings

<u>V</u>

300g/10oz Japanese buckwheat noodles
1-cm/½-in piece of root ginger, peeled and grated
1 clove garlic, peeled and crushed
2-3 spring onions, or a shallot or small onion, peeled and very finely chopped
1 tablespoons vegetable oil
a selection of 75g/3oz each of four or five of the following vegetables:
baby courgettes, baby sweetcorn, green beans, mangetout, sugar peas, red or green pepper strips, carrot slices. broccoli or cauliflower florets, beansprouts, sliced mushrooms, half a can of water chestnuts or bamboo shoots
1-2 tablespoons light soy sauce
1-2 tablespoons stock
Additional optional flavourings:
2 kumquats, sliced and with the pips removed, Five Spice Powder, grated orange or lemon rind, Chinese sesame oil

1. Cook the Japanese noodles as directed on the pack.

2. Fry the ginger, garlic and onion in the oil for 30 seconds.

3. Add the vegetables, leaving the quicker-cooking vegetables to the end. Stir-fry for 1-2 minutes.

4. Add the soy sauce, stock and any extra flavourings used. Bring to the boil and cook a further 1-2 minutes. Or cover and cook longer; it depends on how crisp or soft you like your vegetables.

5. Drain the noodles and top with the stir-fried vegetables.

CALORIES PER PORTION			Fats				318
	CHO(g)	Prot(g)	Sat(g)	Mono(g)	Poly(g)	Iron(mg)	Ca(mg)
Total	60	13.5	0.5	1.5	2	3	50
Energy	71%	17%	14%				

Spaghetti with Lemon

Makes 1 serving

V

100-125g/3½-4oz dried spaghetti
salt
1 tablespoon extra-virgin olive oil
grated rind of ½ lemon
2 tablespoons chopped fresh lemon balm, chervil or chives
freshly ground black pepper
1 tablespoon freshly grated Parmesan cheese, to serve

1. Cook the spaghetti in plenty of lightly salted boiling water until just cooked or *al dente*.

2. Drain and toss with the oil, lemon rind, herbs and pepper.

3. Serve with freshly grated Parmesan cheese.

CALORIES PER PORTION			Fats				630
	CHO(g)	Prot(g)	Sat(g)	Mono(g)	Poly(g)	Iron(mg)	Ca(mg)
Total	92.5	21	5.5	12	3	3	211
Energy	53%	13%		32%			

Spaghetti Salerno

Makes 3-4 servings

225g/8oz spaghetti
salt
2 tablespoons olive oil
350g/12oz broccoli, broken into florets
75g/3oz wholemeal breadcrumbs
50g/2oz canned anchovy fillets, drained, washed and chopped
freshly ground black pepper

1. Cook the spaghetti in lightly salted boiling water until just tender or *al dente*. Toss in a teaspoonful of the oil and keep warm.

2. Steam the broccoli florets until just tender. Drain well and chop very coarsely.

3. Fry the breadcrumbs in the remaining oil and add the anchovies.

4. Place a portion of spaghetti on each plate. Sprinkle with the breadcrumb and anchovy mixture and top with broccoli and black pepper. Serve at once.

CALORIES PER PORTION			Fats				364
	CHO(g)	Prot(g)	Sat(g)	Mono(g)	Poly(g)	Iron(mg)	Ca(mg)
Total	51	15	1.5	5.5	2	3.5	110
Energy	53%	17%		30%			

8.5 FISH AND MEAT DISHES

If you want to be really fit, develop a taste for fish. If you are not sure about dealing with fishy smells, choose really fresh fish and there won't be a lot of odour about the kitchen.

The best way to cook fish is to steam it. This can be done in a steamer, on a covered plate placed over a pan of gently boiling water, in a very little water in a pan or in a microwave oven.

Whichever method you use, take care not to overcook fish. It is cooked as soon as the flesh turns from translucent to opaque – or becomes really white in the case of white fish like plaice, sole and cod. The flakes should come apart quite easily.

Fish can also be grilled or baked but it is even easier to overcook it with these methods, so take care. It is a good idea to cook fish in a foil parcel in the oven. Just add one or two flavourings such as a spring onion and a piece of fresh ginger, chopped tomatoes and leeks or fresh herbs and a little extra-virgin olive oil.

Chicken is always an easy standby. It can be cooked in all kinds of ways and takes up the flavour of other ingredients very well. Turkey meat can also be used in many of the same recipes but it does have a more definite flavour of its own. Try it in the satay and stir-fry recipes or in the Japanese cakes in the Snacks and Easy Fillers section.

Much of the fat content of poultry is contained in the skin, so if you are watching your weight or your overall fat intake, skin chicken and turkey meat before cooking or at least discard before serving.

Unless you choose not to eat meat for whatever reason, you should include red meat in your diet from time to time. Red meat is an important and valuable source of iron, but it is also good to vary your source of protein. Austrian Horseradish Lamb, Spanish-style Marinated Grilled Lamb and Indian Kabobs offer three unusual ways with lamb and beef. The latter is really an Eastern version of the American hamburger!

Monkfish with Tomato and Basil

Makes 4 servings

1 clove garlic, peeled and chopped
1 onion, peeled and finely chopped
1 tablespoon olive oil
225ml/8floz thick Italian tomato juice or 1 × 225-g/8oz can peeled and
chopped tomatoes
1 teaspoon tomato purée
1 small glass white wine or stock
salt and freshly ground black pepper
2 small monkfish tails, each cut into 4 fillets and skinned by the
fishmonger
3-4 large sprigs of fresh basil.

1. Gently fry the garlic and onion in the oil to soften it. Do not allow to brown.

2. Pour on the tomato juice or chopped tomatoes and stir in the tomato purée, wine or stock and seasoning. Bring to the boil, then simmer for 5-6 minutes to thicken.

3. Add the monkfish fillets and cook for 8-10 minutes, taking care not to overcook the fish.

4. Tear the basil into shreds and sprinkle over the fish.

5. Serve with rice or noodles.

CALORIES PER PORTION			Fats				**153**
	CHO(g)	Prot(g)	Sat(g)	Mono(g)	Poly(g)	Iron(mg)	Ca(mg)
Total	7	21	0.5	3	1	1	37.5
Energy	17%	55%		28%			

Cardamom Fish Curry With Rice

Makes 4 servings

2 green chillies, seeded and chopped
2 cloves garlic, seeded and chopped
2.5-cm/1-in piece of root ginger, peeled and grated
2 tablespoons vegetable oil
seeds from 4 cardamom pods
450g/1lb cod or haddock fillet, cut into large chunks
1 green pepper, seeded and thinly sliced
1 teaspoon salt
75g/3oz creamed coconut
150ml/5floz boiling water
juice of 1 lemon
1 tablespoon chopped fresh parsley
700g/1½lb cooked rice

1. Fry the chillies, garlic and ginger in the oil for 2 minutes with the cardamom seeds.

2. Add the fish and fry carefully all over. Add the green pepper and salt.

3. Dissolve the creamed coconut in the boiling water and pour over the fish. Add the lemon juice and bring to the boil.

4. Cover, reduce the heat and simmer for 25 minutes. Sprinkle with parsley and serve with rice.

Note: Use coconut milk made with desiccated coconut and water for a lower fat content.

CALORIES PER PORTION			Fats				**461**
	CHO(g)	Prot(g)	Sat(g)	Mono(g)	Poly(g)	Iron(mg)	Ca(mg)
Total	57	26	12	1	1.5	1.5	59
Energy	46%	22%		31%			

Parsley and Tarragon Fish Cakes

Makes 8-10 fish cakes

F

700g/1½lb cod
150ml/5floz skimmed milk
900g/2lb potatoes
125g/4oz breadcrumbs
6 tablespoons Greek yoghurt
1 tablespoon anchovy essence (optional)
6 tablespoons chopped fresh parsley
2 tablespoons chopped fresh tarragon or 2 teaspoons dried
salt and freshly ground black pepper
dried breadcrumbs
vegetable oil

1. Place the fish in a saucepan and add the milk. Bring to the boil, cover and simmer for about 10-15 minutes until cooked through. Flake the fish and mash with a fork.

2. Steam the potatoes, peel and mash. Mix with the fish. Add all the remaining ingredients and beat to a smooth paste.

3. Shape into flat cakes and coat with breadcrumbs.

4. Grill on each side until golden-brown. Serve with a sesame bun and Beetroot with Orange (page 321).

CALORIES PER PORTION		Fats				**179**
CHO(g)	Prot(g)	Sat(g)	Mono(g)	Poly(g)	Iron(mg)	Ca(mg)
Total 22.5	17	1.5	0.5	0.5	1	78.5
Energy 48%	38%		13%			

Per fish cake

Cod Steaks in Lemon, Onion and Ginger

Makes 4 servings

4 cod steaks
2 tablespoons plain wholemeal flour
salt and freshly ground black pepper
1 tablespoon vegetable oil
grated rind and juice of 2 lemons
4 pieces of preserved ginger in syrup, very finely chopped
½ bunch spring onions, trimmed and finely chopped

1. Preheat the oven to 190°C/375°F/Gas 5.

2. Mix the flour and seasoning and use to dust the cod steaks, shaking off any excess.

3. Heat the oil in a non-stick frying pan and brown the fish for 3 minutes on each side. Drain on paper towels.

4. Place the fish in an ovenproof dish and pour on the lemon rind and juice. Sprinkle with ginger and spring onions and cover with a lid. Cook for 30 minutes.

5. Serve with Jacket-baked Potatoes (page 227).

CALORIES PER PORTION			Fats				150
	CHO(g)	Prot(g)	Sat(g)	Mono(g)	Poly(g)	Iron(mg)	Ca(mg)
Total	8.5	19	0.5	1.5	2	1	25
Energy	21%	50%		28%			

Orange Baked Hake with Vegetables

Makes 4 servings

4 hake or cod steaks
4 oranges
75ml/3floz white wine or stock
salt
225g/8oz courgettes, cut into long thin sticks
2 medium carrots, cut into long thin sticks
4-6 spring onions, sliced lengthways
Garnish:
sprigs of fresh parsley

1. Preheat the oven to 190°C/375°F/Gas 5.

2. Place the fish steaks in a shallow ovenproof dish and pour on the juice of 2 of the oranges and the wine or stock. Sprinkle with salt. Cover with a lid or foil and bake for 20 minutes.

3. Meanwhile, cook the vegetable sticks in a little boiling salted water for 10 minutes until just tender. Drain and toss in 15g/½oz of the butter or margarine and a little grated orange rind. Keep warm.

4. When the fish is cooked, drain off all the juices into a saucepan and add the juice from the remaining oranges. Bring the mixture to the boil and continue boiling rapidly for 3-4 minutes to reduce the mixture to about one-third.

5. Pour over the fish steaks and add the vegetables. Garnish with sprigs of parsley. Serve with potatoes steamed in their jackets.

CALORIES PER PORTION				Fats				171
	CHO(g)	Prot(g)	Sat(g)	Mono(g)	Poly(g)	Iron(mg)	Ca(mg)	
Total	10.5	29	–	–	0.5	1	57	
Energy	23%	68%		8%				

Peppered Cod Steaks

Makes 4 servings

4 × 175-g/6-oz frozen cod steaks, thawed
2 tablespoons fresh orange or lemon juice
1 tablespoon vegetable oil
2-3 tablespoons black peppercorns, crushed, or freshly ground black
pepper
4 slices of tomato
Garnish:
chopped fresh parsley
3 stuffed olives, sliced
sprigs of watercress or 3 blanched broccoli florets

1. Preheat the oven to 180°C/350°F/Gas 4.

2. Put the fish into a shallow dish. Mix the fruit juice with the oil and pour over the steaks. Turn the fish over to coat thoroughly, then leave to marinate for 30 minutes, turning once during this time.

3. Remove the cod steaks from the dish with a slotted spoon, reserving the marinade. Coat the steaks on both sides with the peppercorns, or season generously with ground pepper, pressing well so the coating sticks to the fish. Return to the dish and cover with a lid.

4. Bake for 20 minutes. Top the fish with tomato slices and spoon over a little of the marinade. Cook for a further 10 minutes.

5. Place on a serving dish, garnish each cod steak with

parsley and olives and arrange watercress or broccoli in the centre of the dish. Serve with mashed potatoes or Lemon Dill Potatoes (page 325).

CALORIES PER PORTION			Fats				158
	CHO(g)	Prot(g)	Sat(g)	Mono(g)	Poly(g)	Iron(mg)	Ca(mg)
Total	1.5	29	0.5	1.5	2	2	75
Energy	3%	73%		30%			

Coriander Potatoes with Baked Chicken

Makes 1 serving

1 large potato
2 chicken drumsticks or thighs
seasoned flour
1 tablespoon ground coriander
4-6 tablespoons yoghurt or soured cream
sprigs of fresh coriander

1. Preheat the oven to 200°C/425°F/Gas 7.

2. Scrub and dry the potato and bake for 50 minutes to 1 hour, depending on size, until tender.

3. Skin the chicken joints and roll in seasoned flour. Place in a roasting tin. Bake with the potato for about 40-45 minutes until well cooked through.

4. Place the ground coriander in a hot frying pan and toast over a medium heat until it turns a little darker. Leave to cool and reserve.

5. When the potato is cooked, slit in half lengthways, not cutting quite through. Open up and spread with the soured cream or yoghurt and sprinkle with the toasted coriander. Place the baked chicken joints in the potato and press gently together. Serve at once with sprigs of fresh coriander.

CALORIES PER PORTION			Fats				377
	CHO(g)	Prot(g)	Sat(g)	Mono(g)	Poly(g)	Iron(mg)	Ca(mg)
Total	54.5	28	2	2.5	1	2	216
Energy	54%	30%		16%			

Chicken Breasts with Grilled Peppers and Sun-dried Tomatoes

Makes 2 servings

1 small yellow, orange or red pepper
1 small green pepper
2 fully boned chicken breast fillets
salt and freshly ground black pepper
3 spring onions or 2 shallots, peeled and chopped
1 tablespoon vegetable oil
4 tablespoons chicken or lamb stock
2 tablespoons red wine or more stock
3 large pieces sun-dried tomato packed in oil, drained and cut into thin strips

1. Cut the peppers into quarters, remove all seeds and membranes and lay flat, skin-side up, under a hot grill. Grill until lightly browned.

2. Remove to a dish, cover and leave to stand for 15 minutes. Remove the skin and cut the flesh into thin strips.

3. Season the chicken fillets and cook in a steamer for 15-20 minutes, depending on size, until done.

4. Fry the onions or shallots in the oil in a small frying pan for 3-4 minutes until lightly browned.

5. Add the stock and wine, stir, then add the tomato strips. Bring to the boil and reduce. Add the peppers, heat through and serve poured over the cooked chicken fillets.

CALORIES PER PORTION			Fats			**305**
	CHO(g)	Prot(g)	Sat(g)	Mono(g)	Poly(g)	Iron(mg)	Ca(mg)
Total	6.5	39.5	2.5	5	5	1.5	33
Energy	8%	52%		40%			

Chicken and Grapefruit Satay

Makes 4 satay sticks

4 skinned and boned chicken breast fillets, each weighing about
200g/7oz, cut into chunks
Marinade:
1 tablespoon clear honey
200ml/7floz fresh grapefruit juice (from 2 grapefruit)
1 teaspoon ground turmeric
1 small onion, peeled and very finely chopped

1. Whisk together all the ingredients for the marinade.

2. Put the chicken into the marinade and leave for a minimum of 30 minutes – the result will be even better if you can leave it overnight.

3. Thread the marinated chicken on to skewers and grill for 3-4 minutes on each side. Check that the chicken is completely cooked through with no traces of pinkness in the meat before serving with rice.

CALORIES PER PORTION				Fats			272
	CHO(g)	Prot(g)	Sat(g)	Mono(g)	Poly(g)	Iron(mg)	Ca(mg)
Total	10	44	2	2.5	1	1	37
Energy	14%	65%		22%			

Per stick

Stir-fried Chicken with Bulgar and Okra

Makes 4 servings

50g/2oz bulgar
125g/4oz broad beans
300g/10oz okra, washed and trimmed
2 teaspoons polyunsaturated cooking oil
4 spring onions, finely chopped
2 teaspoons freshly grated root ginger
3 chicken breast fillets, cut into strips
2 tablespoons chicken stock or water
1 red pepper, seeded and finely chopped
salt and freshly ground black pepper

1. Put the bulgar into a bowl and cover with cold water. Leave to stand for 30 minutes while you prepare the remaining ingredients.

2. Cook the broad beans in a little boiling salted water.

3. Cut the okra into small rings. Though these vegetables tend to exude a sticky substance, you do not need to worry – the end-result will be dry.

4. Heat 1 teaspoon of the oil in a wok or non-stick frying pan and fry the onion and ginger for 30 seconds. Add the chicken strips, keeping them on the move. When they are sealed, add the stock or water. Stir-fry over a high heat for 2 minutes until all the liquid has evaporated and the chicken is fully cooked. Remove from the pan and keep on one side.

5. Drain the bulgar very well on kitchen paper and drain the beans. Heat another teaspoon of oil in the wok and fry the peppers for 1 minute. Add the okra and stir-fry for 2 minutes. Next add the dry bulgar and seasoning and toss over a very high heat until it begins to brown.

6. Return the chicken to the pan with the beans. Toss together and serve at once.

CALORIES PER PORTION			*Fats*				**315**
	CHO(g)	Prot(g)	Sat(g)	Mono(g)	Poly(g)	Iron(mg)	Ca(mg)
Total	17.5	33.5	2	4	5	2.5	158
Energy	21%	43%		36%			

Chinese Chicken in Foil

Makes 1 serving

2 cloves garlic, peeled and crushed
1 teaspoon freshly grated root ginger
1 teaspoon soy sauce
1 chicken joint, breast or thigh, skinned
Optional extras:
1 small red or green pepper, seeded and thinly sliced
3-4 dried Chinese mushrooms, soaked in boiling water
1 bunch spring onions, trimmed and sliced lengthways
125/4oz broccoli or calabrese, sliced

1. Preheat the oven to 190°C/375°F/Gas 5 and very lightly grease a square of kitchen foil.

2. Mix the garlic, ginger and soy sauce to a paste.

3. Place the chicken on the prepared foil and spread with the vegetable paste.

4. Add one of two or the optional extras and fold the foil into a parcel. Seal so that the air does not escape.

5. Bake for about 35-40 minutes until the chicken is cooked through.

CALORIES PER PORTION				Fats			245
	CHO(g)	Prot(g)	Sat(g)	Mono(g)	Poly(g)	Iron(mg)	Ca(mg)
Total	6	43	2	2	1	2.5	29
Energy	9%	71%		21%			

Chicken With Lentils

Makes 4 servings

1 onion, peeled and sliced
1 clove garlic, peeled and crushed
1 tablespoon vegetable oil
½ teaspoon mild curry powder
½ teaspoon ground cumin
½ teaspoon ground coriander
125g/4oz whole green continental lentils
25g/1oz raisins
4 chicken thighs, skinned, boned and chopped
600ml/1pint chicken stock
75g/30z fresh spinach, shredded
salt and freshly ground black pepper

1. Gently fry the onion and garlic in the oil for 2-3 minutes until softened. Add the spices and cook for another minute or so.

2. Add the lentils, raisins, chicken and stock. Bring to the boil. Cover and simmer for 30 minutes until the chicken and lentils are cooked.

3. Stir in the spinach and cook for a further 3-4 minutes. Season to taste.

CALORIES PER PORTION				Fats			239
	CHO(g)	Prot(g)	Sat(g)	Mono(g)	Poly(g)	Iron(mg)	Ca(mg)
Total	25	21	1	2	2.5	5	81
Energy	40%	36%		24%			

Indian Kabobs

Makes 4 servings

F

275g/10oz very lean beef, minced
1 onion, peeled and finely chopped
1 clove garlic, peeled and crushed
½ green chilli, finely chopped
2 teaspoons freshly grated root ginger
½ teaspoon ground turmeric
pinch of salt
½ bunch fresh coriander leaves, finely chopped
1 tablespoon plain flour
Garnish:
½ onion, peeled and sliced
2 lemons
4 sesame buns

1. Break up the minced beef with a fork and mix in the onions, garlic and chilli until well distributed. Add the ginger, turmeric, salt and coriander leaves and mix again until firm and sticky. Add enough flour to bind the mixture, but do not make it too dry.

2. Turn the mixture on to a well-floured board and, with floured hands, shape into 4 burgers.

3. Heat a non-stick frying pan and fry the kabobs until

browned on both sides, turning two or three times to prevent them from sticking.

4. Garnish with rings of sliced onion and lemon wedges and serve in pitta bread parcels, hamburger buns or Jacket-baked Potatoes (page 227).

CALORIES PER PORTION			Fats				305
	CHO(g)	Prot(g)	Sat(g)	Mono(g)	Poly(g)	Iron(mg)	Ca(mg)
Total	44	21.5	2	2	0.5	3.5	120
Energy	54%	28%		18%			

In sesame buns

Austrian Horseradish Lamb

Makes 4 servings

F

2 onions, peeled and chopped
1 tablespoon vegetable oil
2 bayleaves
¼ tablespoon dried thyme or a sprig of fresh thyme
salt and freshly ground black pepper
100ml/4floz wine or cider vinegar
450g/1lb lean leg of lamb steaks, with all fat removed, cubed
175ml/6floz beef stock
4 tablespoons creamed horseradish sauce
4 tablespoons chopped fresh parsley
350g/12oz egg noodles

1. Fry the onions in the oil in a deep saucepan until lightly browned. Add the herbs, seasoning and vinegar and bring to the boil. Boil for 1 minute.

2. Next add the lamb and stock and return to the boil. Cover and reduce the heat, then simmer gently for 20 minutes until the lamb is cooked.

3. Cook the noodles as directed on the pack.

4. Add all the remaining ingredients to the lamb mixture.

CALORIES PER PORTION			*Fats*				643
	CHO(g)	Prot(g)	Sat(g)	Mono(g)	Poly(g)	Iron(mg)	Ca(mg)
Total	77	36	7	9.5	4	4	83
Energy	45%	23%		32%			

8.6 PROTEIN PARTNERS

If you are vegetarian you may be worried about whether you are getting enough protein. Dairy food is one answer. But there are also plenty of protein-rich vegetables – dried and canned beans, seeds, rice, bread, pasta and oatmeal – which, in the right combination, offer very high levels of usable protein. For the theory of complementary proteins see page 16.

The most effective combinations of protein-rich foods are pulses, sometimes known as legumes (lentils, beans and peas) and seeds, and pulses (lentils, beans and peas) and grains. Grains and low-fat milk products are other useful combinations.

Indeed, adding milk products to any of the above combinations will result in a protein increase. If you are worried about increasing the fat content of the dish use low-fat yoghurt or skimmed milk. Use dried skimmed milk in baked foods.

Here are some examples of quick and easy combinations to make when you are in a hurry. They are followed by some slightly more elaborate recipes.

- Cheddar Ploughman's platter
- Cottage cheese sandwiches
- Hummus with pitta bread
- Baked beans on toast

- Rice cooked with beans or peas
- Succotash: broad beans mixed with sweetcorn kernels
- Ready-made rice pudding
- Spaghetti with peanut butter sauce
- Pizza topped with cheese and tomatoes
- Taco shells filled with lentils or refried beans
- Pitta or flatbread filled with bought falafel
- Ready-made ravioli or tortelloni stuffed with ricotta cheese
- Lentil, bean or pea soup with a bread roll
- Peanut butter sandwiches
- Minestrone soup with added pasta or rice
- Muesli, porridge or unrefined breakfast cereals with skimmed milk

See also:

Savoury Snacks and Easy Fillers:
Italian Bean Dip with toast fingers
Middle Eastern Hummus with pitta bread
Lentil Tacos

Pumping Pasta:
Tagliatelle with Garlic Cheese Sauce
Pasta Bows with Fromage Frais
Neopolitan Macaroni

Cereals on the Side:
Caribbean Rice and Peas
Oatmeal Leek Savoury

Salads and Vegetable Dishes:
Corn and Bean Pudding
Italian Potato Pie

Puddings and Desserts:
Steamed Rice and Cardamom Pudding
Traditional Rice Pudding

Peanut Dip with Baked Garlic Pitta

Complementary Proteins: peanuts* and cheese
Makes 6-8 servings

<u>V</u>

225g/8oz cottage cheese
75g/3oz peanut butter
3 tablespoons plain yoghurt
75-100ml/3-4floz skimmed milk
freshly ground black pepper
2 tablespoons olive oil
2-3 cloves garlic, peeled and crushed
6-8 large pitta breads

1. Preheat the oven to 200°C/400°F/Gas 6.

2. Place the cottage cheese, peanut butter and yoghurt in a blender or food processor. Blend carefully with the milk to form a smooth, thick dip.

3. Mix the oil and garlic. Cut the pitta bread lengthways into long strips about 1cm/½in wide. Brush both sides of the bread all over with the oil and garlic mixture. Place on a baking tray.

4. Bake for about 10 minutes until crisp. Serve piping hot from the oven with peanut dip.

* Peanuts are actually pulses, not true nuts.

CALORIES PER PORTION							367
				Fats			
	CHO(g)	Prot(g)	Sat(g)	Mono(g)	Poly(g)	Iron(mg)	Ca(mg)
Total	53	15.5	3	5	2.5	2	167
Energy	54%	17%		29%			

Lentil Toad in the Hole

Complementary Proteins: lentils, flour and milk
Makes 2 servings

V

50g/2oz whole green continental lentils, rinsed
2 tablespoons vegetable oil
1 small onion, peeled and chopped
1 clove garlic, crushed
75g/3oz mushrooms, wiped and sliced
½ teaspoon dried thyme
salt and freshly ground black pepper
For the batter:
50g/2oz self-raising wholemeal flour
¼ teaspoon salt
1 egg
150ml/5floz skimmed milk

1. Preheat the oven to 220°C/425°F/Gas 7.

2. Cook the lentils in boiling water for 20 minutes or until tender. Drain well.

3. Heat 1 tablespoon of the oil in a saucepan and fry the onion and garlic for 5 minutes or until lightly browned. Add the mushrooms and fry for a further 5 minutes. Stir in the lentils and thyme and season to taste. Keep the mixture hot.

4. To make the batter, sift the flour and salt into a bowl, then add any bran left in the sieve. Make a well in the centre and add the egg and one-third of the milk. Beat vigorously with a wooden spoon, gradually incorporating the flour and the remaining milk. Beat well.

5. Put the remaining oil in a shallow baking tin and heat in the oven for 2-3 minutes. Pour the batter straight into the hot oil, then quickly spoon the lentil mixture on top.

6. Bake for 30 minutes or until risen and golden.

CALORIES PER PORTION				Fats			239
	CHO(g)	Prot(g)	Sat(g)	Mono(g)	Poly(g)	Iron(mg)	Ca(mg)
Total	36	16	1	2	1	4	214
Energy	56%	26%		17%			

Mushroom Stroganoff with Noodles

Complementary Proteins: wheat and milk
Makes 4 servings

<u>V</u>

350-450g/¾-1lb long flat noodles or tagliatelle
salt and freshly ground black pepper
1 onion, peeled and finely chopped
1 clove garlic, peeled and finely chopped
1 tablespoon olive oil
225g/8oz mushrooms, halved or quartered depending on size
3 tablespoons chopped fresh parsley
1 teaspoon Worcestershire sauce
2 tablespoons vegetable stock or water
225g/8oz cottage cheese
150g/5oz plain yoghurt
1 teaspoon cornflour, dissolved in 1 tablespoon water

1. Cook the noodles in plenty of salted boiling water for 8-10 minutes or as directed on the pack.

2. Fry the onion and garlic in the oil for 2-3 minutes.

3. Add the mushrooms and parsley and fry gently over a low heat for a further 2-3 minutes.

4. Add the Worcestershire sauce and stock or vegetable water and cook for a further 5 minutes until the mushrooms are cooked.

5. Meanwhile, blend the cottage cheese, yoghurt and seasoning in a basin with the dissolved cornflour.

6. Add to the pan when the mushrooms are cooked. Return to the heat and bring to the boil. Simmer for 2-3 minutes, then pour over the cooked and drained noodles.

CALORIES PER PORTION				Fats			**521**
	CHO(g)	Prot(g)	Sat(g)	Mono(g)	Poly(g)	Iron(mg)	Ca(mg)
Total	94	25	2	2.5	1.5	3	165
Energy	68%	19%		13%			

Easy Mexican Pan Bread

Complementary Proteins: corns and beans
Makes 4-6 servings

<u>V</u>

1 large onion, peeled and chopped
2 cloves garlic, peeled and chopped
1 tablespoon olive oil
200g/7oz canned red kidney beans (drained weight)
300ml/10floz water or vegetable stock
175g/6oz polenta or cornmeal
25g/1oz wholemeal flour
1 egg, beaten
2 teaspoons baking powder
½ teaspoon each chilli powder, ground cumin and salt
1 green pepper, very finely diced
25g/1oz cheese, grated
50g/2oz black olives, stoned and sliced

1. Preheat the oven to 180°C/350°F/Gas 4.

2. Gently fry the onion and garlic in the oil in a frying pan until just soft.

3. Remove half the vegetables from the pan and mix with the beans and all the remaiming ingredients except the cheese and olives.

4. Sprinkle the reserved garlic and onion over the base of a shallow ovenproof flan dish. Pour the cornmeal mixture into the dish on top of the onion. Bake in the oven for about 30 minutes.

5. Sprinkle the top with cheese and olives and bake for a further 30 minutes. Cut into wedges and serve hot or cold.

CALORIES PER PORTION		Fats				**242**
	CHO(g)	Prot(g)	Sat(g)	Mono(g)	Poly(g)	Iron(mg)	Ca(mg)
Total	36	14	2	3	1	2.5	57.5
Energy	56%	15%		26%			

Pasta Soup

Complementary Proteins: pasta and beans
Makes 3-4 servings

VF

225g/8oz floury potatoes, peeled and cubed
1 onion, peeled and finely chopped
2-3 sticks celery, trimmed and finely chopped
1.2 litres/2 pints chicken stock
1 × 400-g/14-oz can cannellini or haricot beans, drained
2 tablespoons wine vinegar or ½ teaspoon balsamic vinegar
4 tablespoons chopped fresh basil
4 tablespoons chopped fresh parsley
¼ teaspoon mixed dried herbs
salt and freshly ground black pepper
125g/4oz small pasta such as conchiglie (shells)
12-16 whole basil leaves
125g/4oz freshly grated Parmesan cheese, to serve

1. Place the potatoes, onion and celery in a saucepan with the stock and bring to the boil. Cover and simmer for 20 minutes.

2. Purée about two-thirds of the beans in a blender or food processor.

3. Add the puréed and remaining whole beans to the soup with all the remaining ingredients except the cheese and basil leaves.

4. Return to the boil and simmer for a further 10 minutes until the pasta is cooked through. The soup should be quite thick.

5. Ladle the soup into large bowls and garnish with basil leaves. Serve the cheese on the side to sprinkle over the top.

CALORIES PER PORTION			— Fats —				**418**
	CHO(g)	Prot(g)	Sat(g)	Mono(g)	Poly(g)	Iron(mg)	Ca(mg)
Total	58	22.5	7	3	1	3.5	283
Energy	52%	22%		26%			

Flageolets with Bulgar

Complementary Proteins: wheat and beans
Makes 4 servings

VF

1 clove garlic, peeled and chopped
1 bunch spring onions, chopped
½ red pepper, seeded and finely diced
225g/8oz bulgar
1 tablespoon olive oil
225g/8oz canned flageolet beans (drained weight)
1 teaspoon paprika
salt and freshly ground black pepper
1 × 400g/14oz can tomatoes

1. Fry the garlic, spring onions, red peppers and bulgar in the oil in a saucepan for 2-3 minutes, stirring all the time.

2. Add all the remaining ingredients. Cover and bring to the boil.

3. Reduce the heat and simmer for 15 minutes or until all the liquid is absorbed and the bulgar is tender. Stir once during cooking to prevent the mixture from sticking to the bottom of the pan.

CALORIES PER PORTION			Fats				318
	CHO(g)	Prot(g)	Sat(g)	Mono(g)	Poly(g)	Iron(mg)	Ca(mg)
Total	59	13.5	1	3	0.5	3	52.5
Energy	69%	17%		15%			

Spiced Lentils

Complementary Proteins: lentils and rice
Makes 6 servings

VF

2 large onions, peeled and finely chopped
2 cloves garlic, peeled and crushed
1 teaspoon chilli powder
1 teaspoon dried thyme
½ teaspoon ground cumin seeds
½ teaspoon ground allspice
salt and freshly ground black pepper
2 tablespoons vegetable oil
225g/8oz red or yellow split lentils
2 tablespoons tomato purée
2 teaspoons yeast extract
1.75litres/2½pints water

1. Fry the onions, garlic and spices in the oil for 3-4 minutes to soften the vegetables.

2. Add all the remaining ingredients. Stir and bring to the boil.

3. Reduce the heat and simmer for about 40-45 minutes until the lentils are well cooked and the mixture is fairly thick.

4. Serve with boiled rice.

CALORIES PER PORTION							205
	CHO(g)	Prot(g)	Sat(g)	Mono(g)	Poly(g)	Iron(mg)	Ca(mg)
Total	29	11	0.5	2	2.5	3	46
Energy	53%	22%		25%			

Savoury Bread Pie

Complementary Proteins: bread and cheese
Makes 3-4 servings

V

1 onion, peeled and sliced
1 tablespoon vegetable oil
125g/4oz low-fat soft cheese
6 large slices bread
4 tomatoes, sliced
125g/4oz celeriac, freshly grated, or very finely chopped celery
2 eggs, beaten
450ml/15floz skimmed milk
salt and freshly ground black pepper

1. Fry the onion in the oil for 3-4 minutes until it turns transparent.

2. Spread the soft cheese over the slices of bread and cut into squares or triangles.

3. Layer the bread in a pie dish with the onion, sliced tomatoes and celeriac or celery.

4. Beat the eggs with the milk and season. Pour over the pie. Leave to stand until about 1 hour before you want to eat.

5. Preheat the oven to 180°C/350°F/Gas 4. Bake the pie for about 1 hour 10 minutes until lightly browned and set in the centre.

CALORIES PER PORTION			Fats				**306**
	CHO(g)	Prot(g)	Sat(g)	Mono(g)	Poly(g)	Iron(mg)	Ca(mg)
Total	35	16	3	3	2.5	2.5	213
Energy	43%	21%		37%			

8.7 ALL-IN-ONE DISHES

The recipes in this section are useful because they provide a good combination of nutrients all in one dish. Most of them will only need the addition of a good salad and some fruit for everyday healthy eating.

The dishes are also of help if you are a serious sports person trying to increase your carbohydrate intake because they are themselves based on carbohydrates but in most cases can be served with more carbohydrate-rich foods.

For example, serve Italian Bean and Sausage Soup or New England Fish Chowder as a first course with a dish from Quick and Easy Fillers or Cereals on the Side afterwards. Cajun Jambalaya can be served with a side dish of beans or sweetcorn or a combination of the two and Cod Lyonnaise with Corn and Bean Pudding (pages 281 and 319).

Other combinations include Singapore Noodles with Malaysian Potato Curry and Stir-fried Mixed Vegetables, and Potato Stew with Italian-style Butter Beans.

Spanish Tortilla Wedges

Makes 4 servings

1 teaspoon olive oil
1 clove garlic, peeled and minced
1 large potato, peeled and diced
225g/8oz spinach, washed
125g/4oz peeled cooked prawns
3 tablespoons cooked and diced mixed vegetables
4 eggs, beaten
2 teaspoons water
salt and freshly ground black pepper
pinch of freshly grated nutmeg
Garnish:
wedges of lime
sprigs of fresh continental parsley

1. Heat the oil in a 20-cm-/8-in non-stick frying pan and fry the garlic and diced potato for 5 minutes, keeping the potato on the move with a wooden spatula.

2. Meanwhile, cook the spinach in a large pan with no extra water for 5 minutes. Drain well and chop. Add to the potatoes in the pan with the prawns and cooked vegetables.

3. Beat the eggs with the water, seasoning and nutmeg, pour over the vegetables and stir. Cook over a medium heat for 10 minutes. Turn the tortilla over and cook on the other side for 5 minutes, or finish off under the grill. Serve garnished with lime and parsley sprigs.

4. Serve with crusty bread and a green salad.

CALORIES PER PORTION							390
	CHO(g)	Prot(g)	Sat(g)	Mono(g)	Poly(g)	Iron(mg)	Ca(mg)
Total	25.5	22	6	10	3	6	237
Energy	25%	23%		52%			

Mexican Chicken

Makes 1 serving

1 chicken breast, boned and skinned
salt and freshly ground black pepper
1 onion, peeled and sliced
2-3 tablespoons uncooked rice
1 green or red pepper, seeded and chopped
2 ripe tomatoes, peeled and chopped
¼-½ teaspoon chilli powder

1. Preheat the oven to 180°C/350°F/Gas 4.

2. Place the chicken breast in a small, lightly greased oven-proof dish. Season, spread the onion slices over the top and sprinkle on the rice.

3. Mix the remaining ingredients and pile into the dish.

4. Cover with a lid and bake for 45 minutes until the chicken is cooked through and the rice is tender.

CALORIES PER PORTION			Fats				**626**
	CHO(g)	Prot(g)	Sat(g)	Mono(g)	Poly(g)	Iron(mg)	Ca(mg)
Total	92	49	2	3	2	3	140
Energy	55%	31%		14%			

Cajun Jambalaya

Makes 4 servings

F

1 large onion, peeled and chopped
1 clove garlic, peeled and chopped
2 sticks celery, finely chopped
1 tablespoon vegetable oil
225g/8oz long-grain rice

450g/1lb tomatoes, peeled, seeded and chopped
1 tablespoon tomato purée
600ml/1pint fish stock, made with boiling water and 2 fish stock cubes
a few drops of Tabasco sauce
175g/6oz chorizo sausages, sliced
175g/6oz cooked lean ham, diced
1 green pepper, seeded and coarsely chopped
1 red pepper, seeded and coarsely chopped
12 large prawns in their shells
Garnish:
sprigs of fresh thyme

1. Fry the onion, garlic and celery in the oil for 2-3 minutes. Add the rice and continue frying until the grains are well coated with oil.

2. Add the tomatoes, tomato purée, fish stock and Tabasco and bring to the boil. Stir once and cover with a lid. Reduce the heat and cook for 20 minutes.

3. Add all the remaining ingredients except the prawns and continue cooking over a low heat for a further 10 minutes. Check from time to time to see that the rice is not drying out. Add a little more stock if this happens.

4. Add the prawns 3-4 minutes before the end of cooking time. Garnish with sprigs of fresh thyme.

CALORIES PER PORTION			— Fats —				**487**
	CHO(g)	Prot(g)	Sat(g)	Mono(g)	Poly(g)	Iron(mg)	Ca(mg)
Total	61	30	5	5.5	3	2.5	101
Energy	47%	25%		28%			

Cod Lyonnaise

Makes 4 servings

2 large onions, peeled and coarsely chopped
1 tablespoon vegetable oil
2 rashers streaky bacon (optional)
900g/2lb potatoes, peeled and chopped
4 large tomatoes, skinned and chopped
350g/12oz cod fillets, skinned and cut into chunks
4 tablespoons skimmed milk
salt and freshly ground black pepper

1. Gently fry the onions in the oil in a pan with the bacon if using. Cook for 3-4 minutes to soften the onions.

2. Add all the remaining ingredients and bring the mixture to the boil.

3. Reduce the heat, cover with a lid and simmer very gently for 20-30 minutes until the fish and potatoes are cooked through.

4. Add a little more milk if the pan shows signs of drying out during cooking. Stir carefully so as not to mash everything up.

CALORIES PER PORTION			Fats				336
	CHO(g)	Prot(g)	Sat(g)	Mono(g)	Poly(g)	Iron(mg)	Ca(mg)
Total	52.5	22.5	0.5	1.5	2.5	2	81.5
Energy	59%	27%		14%			

Malaysian Potato Curry

Makes 4 servings

<u>V</u>

50g/2oz sesame seeds
1 teaspoon fenugreek seeds

½-1 teaspoon chilli powder
½ teaspoon ground turmeric
½ teaspoon salt
2 cloves garlic, peeled and crushed
2.5-4-cm/1-1½-in piece of ginger root, peeled and grated
1 tablespoon vegetable oil
25g/1oz creamed coconut
150ml/5floz skimmed milk
50ml/2floz water
900g/2lbs waxy or new potatoes, diced
1 red pepper, seeded and diced
1 tablespoon chopped fresh coriander

1. Toast the sesame and fenugreek seeds under the grill. Crush with a rolling pin.

2. Mix the chilli powder, turmeric and salt with a little water to make a paste.

3. Fry the garlic and ginger in the oil for 1-2 minutes. Add the spice paste and the creamed coconut and stir over a low heat until the creamed coconut has dissolved.

4. Stir in the crushed sesame and fenugreek seeds, add the milk and water and bring to the boil.

5. Add the potatoes and pepper. Cover and simmer over a low heat for about 20 minutes until the potatoes are cooked. Stir frequently to prevent the mixture, sticking. Serve with vegetables.

CALORIES PER PORTION			Fats				**332**
	CHO(g)	Prot(g)	Sat(g)	Mono(g)	Poly(g)	Iron(mg)	Ca(mg)
Total	40	8	5	4.5	5.5	2.5	147
Energy	46%	10%		44%			

Plaice Madeira

Makes 4 servings

900g/2lb potatoes
450g/1lb plaice fillets
salt and freshly ground pepper
4 bananas, sliced diagonally
1 onion, peeled and sliced
1 tablespoon vegetable oil
2 tablespoons raisins
3 tablespoons apple, orange or pineapple juice

1. Preheat the oven to 180°C/350°F/Gas 4.

2. Steam the potatoes in a steamer or in a little water until almost tender. Drain, peel and slice the potatoes.

3. Meanwhile, layer the fish and bananas in a casserole dish.

4. Gently fry the onion in the oil with the raisins for 3-4 minutes until soft.

5. Spoon the onion and raisin mixture over the fish and pour on the fruit juice.

6. Top with the sliced potatoes and bake for 20-25 minutes.

CALORIES PER PORTION			*Fats*				**437**
	CHO(g)	Prot(g)	Sat(g)	Mono(g)	Poly(g)	Iron(mg)	Ca(mg)
Total	90	11.5	0.5	1.5	2.5	2	56.5
Energy	77%	11%		12%			

Potato Stew

Makes 1 serving

1-2 rashers smoked bacon, cut into pieces
1 small onion, peeled and chopped
1 teaspoon vegetable oil
1 tablespoon fine oatmeal or rolled oats, ground in a coffee mill
1 teaspoon yeast extract
150ml/5floz water
1 large or 2 medium potatoes, peeled and cut into chunks
1 carrot, peeled and grated, to serve

1. Fry the bacon and onion in the oil in a small non-stick saucepan for 2-3 minutes, then stir in the oatmeal and cook for a further 30 seconds.

2. Add the yeast extract and water. Stir until the yeast extract has dissolved and the sauce is smooth.

3. Add the potatoes and just enough extra water for the sauce to cover the potato.

4. Cover with a lid and bring to the boil. Reduce the heat and simmer for 10-15 minutes until the potato is cooked through. Stir from time to time to prevent sticking.

5. Serve with freshly grated carrot on the side.

CALORIES PER PORTION			Fats				594
	CHO(g)	Prot(g)	Sat(g)	Mono(g)	Poly(g)	Iron(mg)	Ca(mg)
Total	80	26	3	7	8	3.5	108
Energy	51%	18%		32%			

New England Fish Chowder

Makes 4-6 servings

F

50g/2oz streaky bacon, diced
2 large onions, peeled and sliced
600g/1¼lb potatoes, peeled and cubed
125g/4oz cooked sweetcorn kernels
125g/4oz peas
450ml/15floz skimmed milk
200ml/7floz water
1 teaspoon chopped fresh marjoram or ½ teaspoon dried
salt and freshly ground black pepper
450g/1lb white fish fillets (cod, haddock, coley or huss)
125g/4oz peeled prawns

1. Fry the bacon until the fat begins to run. Add the onions and brown slightly.

2. Add the potatoes to the pan with the sweetcorn, peas, milk, water, marjoram and seasoning. Bring to the boil and simmer for 10 minutes.

3. Skin the fish and cut into chunks. Add to the chowder and bring back to the boil. Continue simmering for a further 8-10 minutes until the fish is cooked. Add the prawns and serve in large bowls with plenty of bread.

CALORIES PER PORTION			Fats				**277**
	CHO(g)	Prot(g)	Sat(g)	Mono(g)	Poly(g)	Iron(mg)	Ca(mg)
Total	35	25	1.5	2	1	1.5	164
Energy	47%	36%		16%			

Italian Bean and Sausage Soup

Makes 4 servings

F

50g/2oz smoked bacon, very finely chopped
125g/4oz pork fillet, very finely diced
150g/5oz (4 small) Italian pork sausages, skinned and diced
1 large onion, peeled and chopped
1 clove garlic, peeled and finely chopped
1 small head fennel, sliced
1 carrot, peeled and diced
1 small sprig of fresh sage
1 small sprig of fresh mint
1 tablespoon coarsely chopped fresh parsley
salt and freshly ground black pepper
1.75 litres/2½ pints beef stock
1 × 400g/14oz can white kidney beans or cannellini beans

1. Fry the bacon in a non-stick frying pan, then the pork and then the sausage until each is well browned. Transfer each with a slotted spoon to a large pan or casserole, draining off any excess fat.

2. Quickly brown the onion and garlic in a very little of the remaining fat and add to the pan with the fennel, carrots, herbs, seasoning and stock.

3. Bring to the boil and simmer for 30 minutes. Stir in the beans and return to the boil. Cook for a further 5 minutes before serving.

CALORIES PER PORTION			*Fats*				**250**
	CHO(g)	Prot(g)	Sat(g)	Mono(g)	Poly(g)	Iron(mg)	Ca(mg)
Total	22	25.5	1.5	1.5	1	3	96
Energy	33%	41%		25%			

Quick Paella

Makes 6-8 servings

1 large onion, peeled and chopped
2 cloves garlic, peeled and chopped
4 tablespoons olive oil
1 red pepper, seeded and chopped
1 green pepper, seeded and chopped
500g/1lb 2oz long-grain rice
125g/4oz petits pois
2 bayleaves
large pinch of saffron powder
300ml/10floz white wine and 700ml/26floz chicken stock (or use all stock)
450g/1lb cooked chicken meat, cut into large pieces
225g/8oz mixed cooked shellfish

1. Gently fry the onion and garlic in the oil in a paella pan or large frying pan for 3-4 minutes. Add the peppers and cook for further 2-3 minutes.

2. Next stir in the rice, petits pois, bayleaves and saffron. Pour on the wine and stock and bring to the boil. Stir and cover with a lid.

3. Cook over a low heat for about 14-15 minutes. The rice should be just cooked and all the liquid absorbed.

4. Add all the remaining ingredients, stir carefully and re-place the lid. Cook for a further 2-3 minutes to warm everything through and serve from the pan.

CALORIES PER PORTION				Fats			438
	CHO(g)	Prot(g)	Sat(g)	Mono(g)	Poly(g)	Iron(mg)	Ca(mg)
Total	60	24	2.5	7	2.5	1.5	96
Energy	51%	22%		27%			

8.8 CEREALS ON THE SIDE

Despite the title of this section many of the recipes in it are good enough to eat on their own with a side salad. However, they can also be served with other dishes from Meat and Fish Dishes, Savoury Snacks and Easy Fillers, and for carbohydrate loaders, All-in-One Dishes.

There is a very wide range of cereals available in the shops today, either in grain form or in flaked or ground form. Here is a quick run-down on how to cook them as a simple side dish to use in the same way as rice or potatoes.

This is followed by some more or less elaborate recipes using a variety of cereals, sometimes alone and sometimes together.

Breads have also been included in this section.

How to Cook Cereals

Bulgar is made from wheat. The grains are boiled and then dried and cracked. It can be cooked in water to make a fluffy side dish rather like a lighter version of rice; or it can be soaked in water, drained and used as it is in salads.

To cook: Place in a saucepan with double its volume of water. Bring to the boil and stir once. Cover with a lid and cook for about 15-20 minutes. Do not lift the lid or stir for 15 minutes. Then check to see if all the liquid has disappeared and the bulgar is cooked. If not, replace the lid and cook for a little longer. Fluff up with a fork and serve.

To soak and use cold: Place in a basin and cover with twice its volume of water. Leave to stand for 15 minutes. Pour into a sieve and drain very well before using in recipes like tabbouleh.

Couscous is usually made from semolina (wheat) though it is possible to buy whole-grain couscous from some health food stores.

To cook: Soak in a bowl of warm water for 10 minutes. Drain well and place in the top half of a steamer or in a metal colander placed over a pan of gently boiling water. Cover and cook for about 20-30 minutes until light and fluffy. For a different flavour gently roast the couscous in a dry frying pan before soaking and cooking.

Millet is on sale in health food shops. Do not buy bird millet – it has not been cleared for human consumption!

To cook: Place in a saucepan and cover with two and a half times its own volume of water. Bring to the boil and stir once. Cover with a lid, reduce the heat and simmer very gently for 25-30 minutes. Do not lift the lid or stir for 25 minutes. Check to see if all the liquid has been absorbed and the millet is light and fluffy like bulgar or couscous. If not, replace the lid and cook for a little longer. Fluff up with a fork and serve. For a different flavour gently roast the millet in a dry frying pan before cooking.

Oatmeal or quick porridge (rolled) oats are usually made into muesli or porridge but they can also be used in recipes like Oat and Leek Savoury, Potato Stew and Oat Pancakes, and in baking.

To cook porridge using oatmeal: Slowly add one part of medium oatmeal to four and a half parts of very hot salted water, stirring with the straight end of a wooden spoon. Bring to the boil, stirring all the time, and simmer for 30 minutes.

To make porridge with quick porridge oats: Place one part of rolled oats to two and a half parts of salted water in a saucepan. Place over a medium heat and bring to the boil, stirring all the time. Simmer for 2-3 minutes and serve.

Polenta or yellow cornmeal is used to make a mush which can be served like mashed potatoes or can be cooked, left to go cold and sliced to use in casseroles and other dishes.

To cook: Slowly add one part of polenta to three to four parts of very hot water (depending on the thickness required). Bring to the boil, stirring all the time. Continue cooking until the mixture is very thick. Leave to cook over a low heat for about 15-20 minutes, stirring occasionally.

This may not be necessary with quick-cook polenta. Check the pack.

Rice is probably the most familiar of the grains. It is available as brown rice with part of the husk remaining and as white polished rice.

To cook: Place in a saucepan with double its volume of water. Bring to the boil and stir once. Cover with a lid and cook for about 12-15 minutes. Do not lift the lid or stir for 12 minutes. Then check to see if all the liquid has disappeared and the rice is cooked. If not, replace the lid and cook for a little longer. Fluff up with a fork and serve. Brown rice takes longer to cook and may need more water. Allow about 25-30 minutes.

Quinoa is a South American grain which is now on sale in health food shops and some supermarkets. It tastes rather like millet.

To cook: Place in a saucepan with a little more than twice its volume of water. Bring to the boil and stir once. Cover and simmer for 10-12 minutes. Fluff up with a fork to serve.

You can vary the taste of these cereals by cooking in stock rather than plain water. Fruit juices work well too. Extra flavour can be added by using herbs or spices, flaked nuts, chopped onion or peppers or freshly grated root ginger in the mix.

Good combinations are toasted couscous with ground cinnamon and toasted flaked almonds or brazil nuts, rice with spring onions and pinenuts, millet with whole cumin seeds and fresh coriander, and quinoa with grated lemon rind and chopped fresh parsley.

Cooked cereals can also be used in salads (see page 313) or they can be cooked in advance and frozen in individual portions. Thaw in a microwave oven or in a double saucepan. You can improvise the latter by placing a pudding basin over a pan with about 5cm/2in of gently simmering water. Cover the pudding basin with the lid. Stir once or twice during thawing.

American-style Apple Rice

Makes 2 servings

VF

4 medium spring onions, finely chopped
1 tablespoon olive oil
1 tablespoon raisins
125g/4oz long-grain rice
200ml/8floz vegetable stock
salt and freshly ground black pepper
1 teaspoon shredded lemon zest
1 apple, cored and diced
1 tablespoon chopped fresh coriander

1. Fry the onions in 1 tablespoon of the oil until lightly browned. Add the raisins and fry for a further minute or so. Next add the rice and stir until well coated. Add the stock and seasoning and bring to the boil.

2. Stir once, cover and cook for about 15 mintues until all the liquid is absorbed and the rice is cooked (longer if using brown rice).

3. Meanwhile, fry the lemon zest in the remaining oil for about a minute. Add the apple and cook for a further minute or two until it begins to soften. Do not allow it to cook fully or the cubes will go mushy.

4. When the rice is cooked, fluff up and stir in the apples and the coriander. Serve at once.

CALORIES PER PORTION			Fats				**363**
	CHO(g)	Prot(g)	Sat(g)	Mono(g)	Poly(g)	Iron(mg)	Ca(mg)
Total	67	5	1.5	6.5	1	1	47
Energy	70%	6%		25%			

Rice with Peas and Pimento

Makes 1 large serving

<u>VF</u>

½ small onion, peeled and finely chopped
1 small red pepper, seeded and finely chopped
25g/1oz peas
75g/3oz long-grain rice
1 teaspoon toasted sesame seeds
150ml/5floz water or vegetable stock
salt and freshly ground black pepper

Top of the stove method:

1. Mix all the solid ingredients together in a saucepan.

2. Pour on the water or stock and bring to the boil. Stir once and cover with a lid.

3. Reduce the heat and cook for about 15 minutes until all the liquid has been absorbed and the rice is tender.

4. Fluff up with a fork and serve.

Oven method:

1. Preheat the oven to 190°C/375°F/Gas 5.

2. Mix all the solid ingredients together and place in an ovenproof dish.

3. Pour on *boiling* water. Stir once, cover with a lid and bake for about 40-45 minutes.

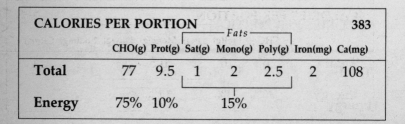

CALORIES PER PORTION							383
	CHO(g)	Prot(g)	Sat(g)	Mono(g)	Poly(g)	Iron(mg)	Ca(mg)
Total	77	9.5	1	2	2.5	2	108
Energy	75%	10%		15%			

Caribbean Rice and Peas

Makes 4 servings

VF

475ml/16floz boiling water
175g/6oz desiccated coconut
1 onion or 1 bunch spring onions, peeled and finely chopped
1 fresh green chilli pepper, seeded and chopped
1 clove garlic, peeled and crushed
1 tomato, peeled, seeded and chopped
225g/8oz long-grain rice
¼ teaspoon dried thyme
225g/8oz canned red kidney or blackeye beans

1. Pour the boiling water over the coconut and leave to cool.

2. Strain off the liquid, squeezing the coconut well. Make up to 475ml/16floz with more water.

3. Place all the remaining ingredients except the beans in a saucepan and mix well. Add the liquid from the coconut and pour over the rice mixture. Bring to the boil and stir once.

4. Cover with a lid and cook for 12 minutes (longer if using brown rice).

5. Stir in the beans and cook for a further 5 minutes before serving.

CALORIES PER PORTION			Fats				317
	CHO(g)	Prot(g)	Sat(g)	Mono(g)	Poly(g)	Iron(mg)	Ca(mg)
Total	63	10	2	0.5	1	2	54
Energy	76%	13%		12%			

Lime and Pineapple Rice

Makes 4 servings

VF

1 tablespoon freshly grated root ginger
1 clove garlic, peeled and crushed
1 tablespoon polyunsaturated cooking oil
25g/1oz creamed coconut
475ml/16floz vegetable stock
1 × 225g/8oz can pineapple rings in natural juice
2 tablespoons lemon juice
225g/8oz American long-grain rice or half plain and half brown rice
2 tablespoons raisins
2 tablespoons pinenuts, toasted
6 spring onions, cut into short lengths
¼ red pepper, seeded and cut into short thin strips
rind of 1 lime, thinly shredded

1. Fry the ginger and garlic in the oil and then stir in the coconut. When all the coconut has dissolved, add the stock and the juice from the pineapple, the lemon juice, rice and raisins.

2. Bring to the boil and stir once. Cover with a lid. Reduce the heat and simmer for 20-25 minutes until all the liquid is absorbed.

3. Leave to stand for 5 minutes. Add two-thirds of all the remaining ingredients, and sprinkle the remaining third on top.

CALORIES PER PORTION							**392**
	CHO(g)	Prot(g)	Sat(g)	*Fats* Mono(g)	Poly(g)	Iron(mg)	Ca(mg)
Total	65	6	5	3	5	1.5	46
Energy	62%	6%		31%			

Polenta Plus

Makes 4 servings

<u>VF</u>

900ml/1½ pints water
125g/4oz polenta or yellow cornmeal
½ teaspoon salt
½ teaspoon freshly ground black pepper
25ml/1floz olive oil
Optional extras:
50g/2oz freshly grated Parmesan cheese
a little freshly grated nutmeg

1. Bring the water to the boil in a large non-stick saucepan. Pour in the polenta or cornmeal in a thin, continuous stream, stirring all the time.

2. Add the seasoning and continue stirring until the mixture thickens.

3. Cook over a low heat for a further 20 minutes, stirring regularly. The finished mixture should be thick and smooth.

4. Beat in the oil.

5. Add the Parmesan cheese and nutmeg, if using, to make a dish on its own to serve with salad.

6. If serving with other recipes, leave out the Parmesan cheese and nutmeg and put into a non-stick or lined 450-g/1-lb loaf tin. Leave to cool.

CALORIES PER PORTION				*Fats*			**170**
	CHO(g)	Prot(g)	Sat(g)	Mono(g)	Poly(g)	Iron(mg)	Ca(mg)
Total	24	2.5	1	3.5	1	1	1.5
Energy	53%	6%		36%			

Oatmeal Leek Savoury

Makes 4 servings (8 slices)

VF

1 small onion, peeled and finely chopped
350g/12oz leeks, trimmed and finely chopped
1 tablespoon vegetable oil
2 teaspoons yeast extract
225g/8oz quick porridge oats
50g/2oz mature Cheddar cheese, grated
3 tablespoons chopped fresh mixed herbs (such as parsley, tarragon)
2 large eggs, beaten
freshly ground black pepper

1. Preheat the oven to 190°C/375°F/Gas 5. Line a 450-g/1-lb loaf tin with baking paper.

2. Gently fry the onion and leeks in the oil for 3-4 minutes until soft. Do not allow to brown.

3. Stir in the yeast extract and tip into a large bowl.

4. Add all the remaining ingredients and mix well together.

5. Spoon into the prepared loaf tin and bake for about 40 minutes until firm and lightly browned on top.

6. Cut into slices to serve with potatoes and vegetables or allow to go cool. Eat cold or use in the same way as cold polenta slices.

CALORIES PER PORTION							**378**
	CHO(g)	Prot(g)	Sat(g)	Mono(g)	Poly(g)	Iron(mg)	Ca(mg)
Total	41.5	16.5	5	5.5	4.5	4	169
Energy	42%	18%		41%			

Multi-Grain Pilaf

Makes 4 servings

VF

50g/2oz millet
1 tablespoon olive oil
125g/4oz long-grain brown rice
50g/2oz bulgar
4 spring onions, finely chopped
2 sticks celery, finely chopped
4 tabléspoons chopped fresh parsley
2 tablespoons chopped fresh mint
salt and freshly ground black pepper
550ml/18floz water
50g/2oz pinenuts
2 hard-boiled eggs, quartered (optional)
Garnish:
sprigs of fresh herbs and extra chopped spring onions

1. Fry the millet in the oil in a saucepan for about 2 minutes until lightly browned and giving off a nutty aroma. Add the rice and bulgar and toss over a low heat for 30 seconds.

2. Add all the remaining ingredients except the pinenuts and hard-boiled eggs, if using.

3. Bring to the boil and stir once. Cover and reduce heat; simmer for 25 minutes.

4. Toast the pinenuts in a dry frying pan until browned. Stir into the cooked grains and top with hard-boiled eggs, if using.

CALORIES PER PORTION				*Fats*			**287**
	CHO(g)	Prot(g)	Sat(g)	Mono(g)	Poly(g)	Iron(mg)	Ca(mg)
Total	45	7	1	2.5	5.5	2.5	37
Energy	59%	10%		31%			

Spicy Aubergine Bulgar or Millet

Makes 4 servings

VF

2 tablespoons vegetable oil
1 tablespoon cumin seeds
½ teaspoon coriander seeds
2 tablespoons sesame seeds
1 teaspoon medium curry powder
1 small onion, peeled and finely chopped
225g/8oz aubergine, finely diced
225g/8oz bulgar or millet
475ml/16floz vegetable stock or water
salt and freshly ground black pepper
2 tablespoons chopped fresh parsley

1. Heat the oil in a deep saucepan and fry the cumin, coriander and sesame seeds for about 2 minutes, until lightly browned. Take care not to let them burn.

2. Stir in the curry powder and onion and fry for 1-2 minutes. Add the aubergine and cook for about 3-4 minutes, until brown all over.

3. Stir in the millet and pour on the stock or water. Season and add half the parsley. Bring the mixture to the boil. Reduce the heat, cover with a lid and simmer very gently for about 30-40 minutes or until all the liquid is absorbed and the millet is tender.

4. Serve sprinkled with the remaining parsley.

CALORIES PER PORTION			_Fats_				**312**
	CHO(g)	Prot(g)	Sat(g)	Mono(g)	Poly(g)	Iron(mg)	Ca(mg)
Total	47	9	1	4	5	2	68
Energy	56%	11%		33%			

Spanish Rice

Makes 2-3 servings

<u>VF</u>

2 tablespoons vegetable oil
pinch of saffron powder
225g/8oz long-grain rice
1 × 400g/14oz can tomatoes
150ml/5floz water
2 Spanish onions, peeled and sliced into rings
salt and freshly ground black pepper

1. Heat the oil in a saucepan and fry the saffron for a minute or so. Add the rice and continue frying and stirring until it is very lightly browned.

2. Add the tomatoes and the water. Stir once and bring to the boil.

3. Arrange the onion and pepper slices on the top and season. Cover with a lid and cook over a gentle heat for 30 minutes until the rice and vegetables are tender and all the liquid has been absorbed.

4. Serve at once without stirring.

CALORIES PER PORTION				*Fats*			**465**
	CHO(g)	Prot(g)	Sat(g)	Mono(g)	Poly(g)	Iron(mg)	Ca(mg)
Total	82	9	1.5	4	6	1.5	99.5
Energy	67%	8%		26%			

Mexican Green Rice

Makes 3-4 servings

VF

2 small onions, halved but not peeled
6 large cloves garlic, unpeeled
1 green pepper, quartered and seeded
2 small fresh chillies, halved and seeded
75g/3oz fresh coriander leaves, coarsely chopped
600ml/1pint vegetable stock
350g/12oz long-grain brown rice
salt and freshly ground black pepper

1. Grill the onions, garlic, peppers and chillies on all sides until well roasted and slightly charred.

2. Peel all the roasted vegetables and chop.

3. Blend or liquidize in a blender with the coriander and stock to make a purée.

4. Mix with the rice and bring to the boil. Reduce the heat, cover and cook for 20-30 minutes.

CALORIES PER PORTION			Fats				376
	CHO(g)	Prot(g)	Sat(g)	Mono(g)	Poly(g)	Iron(mg)	Ca(mg)
Total	82.5	8.5	0.5	0.5	1	2	101
Energy	82%	9%		9%			

Lemon Rice with Bulgar

Makes 4 servings

VF

1 tablespoon vegetable oil
1 teaspoon whole cumin seeds
150g/5oz long-grain brown rice
75g/3oz bulgar
475ml/16floz vegetable stock
grated rind of 2 lemons
¼ teaspoon ground allspice
salt and freshly ground black pepper

1. Heat the oil in a pan and fry the cumin seeds until they pop. This only takes about 30 seconds so take care not to burn them.

2. Add the rice and fry gently for a further 30 seconds. Add all the remaining ingredients and bring to the boil.

3. Stir once and cover with a lid. Reduce the heat and simmer for about 25 minutes until the grains are soft and all the liquid has been absorbed. Fluff up with a fork and serve.

CALORIES PER PORTION			Fats				231
	CHO(g)	Prot(g)	Sat(g)	Mono(g)	Poly(g)	Iron(mg)	Ca(mg)
Total	45	5	0.5	1.5	2	1	10
Energy	72%	8%		20%			

Portuguese Cornbread

Makes 1 loaf or 12 slices

VF

1 sachet (¼oz/2½ teaspoons) active dried yeast
1 teaspoon sugar
300ml/10floz lukewarm water

200g/7oz fine yellow cornmeal
1½ teaspoons salt
1 tablespoon olive oil
175ml/6floz lukewarm skimmed milk
500g/1lb 2oz plain wholemeal flour

1. Mix the yeast, sugar and water and leave to stand for 15 minutes until frothy.

2. Mix the cornmeal and salt with the oil and milk. Mix well. Add the yeast mixture and mix again, gradually adding the flour to give a soft but manageable dough.

3. Turn out on to a floured board and knead for about 5-8 minutes until elastic.

4. Put the dough in a greased bowl, cover with a cloth and keep in a warm place for about 1 hour until risen to double its size.

5. Punch down and knead again for 5 minutes. Shape into a round loaf and place on a greased baking tray. Cover and allow to rise a second time to double its bulk. This will take about another 1½ hours.

6. Preheat the oven to 180°C/350°F/Gas 4. Bake for about 45 minutes or until the loaf sounds hollow when rapped on the base. Transfer to a wire rack to cool.

Note: White flour can be used in place of wholemeal for a lighter, drier loaf. You will only need 450g/1lb flour. The second rising time will be 1 hour and the baking time 40 minutes.

CALORIES PER PORTION			*Fats*				**207**
	CHO(g)	Prot(g)	Sat(g)	Mono(g)	Poly(g)	Iron(mg)	Ca(mg)
Total	41	7	–	1	0.5	2.5	34
Energy	74%	14%		11%			

12 portions

Irish Soda Bread

Makes 1 loaf or 10 slices

VF

200g/7oz plain wholemeal flour
200g/7oz fine oatmeal
175g/6oz self-raising flour
1 teaspoon salt
1 teaspoon bicarbonate of soda
1 tablespoon brown sugar
450ml/15floz skimmed milk or buttermilk

1. Preheat the oven to 200°C/400°F/Gas 6.

2. Mix all the dry ingredients together in a mixing bowl with a knife. Mix in the buttermilk to make a dough, but do not knead.

3. Turn the dough into a 1.2-litre/2-pint casserole dish. Cover with a lid and bake for 1 hour 10 minutes.

4. Transfer to a wire rack to cool.

CALORIES PER PORTION			*Fats*				**212**
	CHO(g)	Prot(g)	Sat(g)	Mono(g)	Poly(g)	Iron(mg)	Ca(mg)
Total	41	8.5	0.5	0.5	1	2.5	78
Energy	73%	16%		12%			

Per slice

Wholemeal Rolls

Makes 10-12 rolls

VF

325-350ml/11-12floz warm water
12g/½oz dried yeast
450g/1lb plain wholemeal flour
1 teaspoon salt

1. Preheat the oven to 230°C/450°F/Gas 8.

2. Warm the water to blood-heat and mix with the yeast. Leave in a warm place for about 10 minutes until creamy.

3. Sift the flour and salt into a mixing bowl. Add the water and yeast mixture and knead in the bowl for 5-10 minutes.

4. Shape into rolls and place on a greased baking tray. Cover with a cloth and leave in a warm place to rise to double their size (about 1 hour).

5. Bake for 10-12 minutes. Test to see if the rolls are ready by rapping the base with your fingernails. It should sound firm.

6. Transfer to a wire rack to cool.

Note: This recipe can also be used to make a loaf of bread. Simply put the dough into the tin to rise and increase the baking time to 30-40 minutes.

CALORIES PER PORTION			Fats				**117**
	CHO(g)	Prot(g)	Sat(g)	Mono(g)	Poly(g)	Iron(mg)	Ca(mg)
Total	24	5	–	–	0.5	1.5	15
Energy	76%	17%		6%			

Per roll

Oatmeal Scones

Makes 8 scones

VF

175g/6oz plain flour
50g/2oz fine oatmeal
4 teaspoons baking powder
large pinch of salt
50g/2oz butter or margarine
50ml/2floz water
50ml/2floz skimmed milk

1. Preheat the oven to 220°C/425°F/Gas 7.

2. Place the flour, oatmeal, baking powder and salt in a mixing bowl and mix well together. Rub in the fat until the mixture resembles fine breadcrumbs.

3. Mix the milk and water together.

4. Make a well in the centre of the dry ingredients and pour in some of the milk and water. Mix quickly to make a firm, soft dough.

5. Place on a floured surface and knead gently for a couple of minutes.

6. Shape into two rounds about 5cm/2in in depth and place on a baking tray. Make 2 diagonal slashes in the top of each round with a knife.

7. Bake for 15 minutes. Transfer to a wire rack to cool.

CALORIES PER PORTION			Fats				**139**
	CHO(g)	Prot(g)	Sat(g)	Mono(g)	Poly(g)	Iron(mg)	Ca(mg)
Total	18.5	4	3.5	1.5	0.5	1	20
Energy	50%	11%		39%			

Per scone

Olive Bread

Makes 1 large loaf or approximately 10 slices

<u>**VF**</u>

1 sachet (¼oz/2½ teaspoons) Easy Bake yeast
450g/1lb strong white flour
½ teaspoon salt
250ml/9floz tepid water
2 tablespoons olive oil
200g/7oz black olives, stoned and chopped

1. Mix the yeast, flour and salt in a mixing bowl. Make a well in the centre and stir in the water and olive oil. Mix to a stiffish dough.

2. Knead on a floured surface for 10 minutes. Leave to rise in a greased mixing bowl covered with clingfilm.

3. After about 1-1½ hours, knock back the dough, roll out and spread with olives. Roll up and cut fairly deep diagonal slashes across the top of the loaf with a knife.

4. Cover and leave to rise again for about 30 minutes.

5. Preheat the oven to 230°C/450°F/Gas 8. Brush the loaf with water and bake for 30-35 minutes until the loaf is well browned and the base sounds hollow when rapped. Transfer to a wire rack to cool.

CALORIES PER PORTION			Fats				202
	CHO(g)	Prot(g)	Sat(g)	Mono(g)	Poly(g)	Iron(mg)	Ca(mg)
Total	40	5.5	1	3	1	1.5	75
Energy	63%	11%		26%			

Per slice

8.9 SALADS AND VEGETABLE DISHES

This chapter includes ideas for substantial salads and vegetable dishes which offer quite high levels of carbohydrate.

High-energy salads can often be more attractive than a cooked meal, particularly if you are tired after a work-out or an event. They are easy to eat late at night or just at odd times of the day.

Use carbohydrate-rich vegetables such as corn, peas, beetroot, carrots and potato. Cooked pulses such as chickpeas, kidney beans and haricot beans contribute both carbohydrate and protein. You can also add interest and calories with fruit and toasted (not fried) croûtons. Small amounts of meat, fish or cheese are useful too but vegetarians and vegans can easily manage without by boosting some of the other protein-rich foods.

Serve salads with a hunk of bread but remember not to spoil the whole effect by plastering the bread with butter or margarine or the salad with mayonnaise or salad dressing.

Salads are excellent for vitamins C and A and potassium and magnesium. Broccoli, not usually eaten raw, pays real dividends here with 110mg vitamin C, 2500mg vitamin A, 24mg magnesium and 415mg potassium in one 12.5-cm/5-in stalk.

Some of the salads in this section such as Broccoli, Carrot and Bean Salad and Lentil Salad are based on pulses. Others are based on potatoes, rice or pasta. They can all be served as light lunch or supper dishes, as part of the central course at a main meal or as a starter or snack.

Obviously, the amount you serve will vary depending on the meal. The servings given here are for a light supper dish or part of a main meal with other salads.

The vegetable dishes concentrate on interesting ways to cook potatoes but there are also some recipes for using other vegetables which contain carbohydrates. Some of these dishes also make good starters or snacks. Pan-fried Corn with Peppers, for example, and Potatoes and Chickpeas in Tomato Sauce make good light meals when served with soda bread.

Italian Potato Pie and Corn and Bean Pudding can be served with salad. The Italian bean recipes make good starters and Rosti makes a substantial snack with a poached egg or grated cheese on top.

Chicken and Mango Salad

Makes 4 servings

1 small onion, peeled and sliced
2.5-cm/1-in piece of root ginger, peeled and grated
1 clove garlic, peeled and crushed
½ tablespoon vegetable oil
1 tablespoon mild curry powder or garam masala
2 teaspoons ground coriander
salt and freshly ground black pepper
3 chicken breast fillets, cubed
150g/5oz plain yoghurt
125g/4oz canned chickpeas, drained
1 mango, peeled, stoned and chopped
2-3 tablespoons low-fat mayonnaise
Garnish:
1 mango, peeled and sliced
sprigs of continental parsley

1. Fry the onion, ginger and garlic in as little oil as possible until lightly browned. Stir in the spices and seasoning and fry for 1 further minute.

2. Add the chicken and yoghurt with the chickpeas and bring to the boil. Stir, reduce the heat and cover with a lid. Simmer gently for 45 minutes until fairly dry.

3. Leave to cool, then stir in the mango and mayonnaise.

4. Spoon on to a serving plate and garnish with sliced mango and sprigs of parsley.

CALORIES PER PORTION							287
	CHO(g)	Prot(g)	Sat(g)	Mono(g)	Poly(g)	Iron(mg)	Ca(mg)
Total	18	32	1.5	2.5	2	1.5	109
Energy	24%	44%		32%			

Broccoli, Carrot and Bean Salad

Makes 4 servings

V

1 large carrot, peeled and coarsely grated
125g/4oz broccoli, chopped
2 tablespoons lemon juice
1 tablespoon salad oil
175g/6oz canned haricot beans, drained
1 tablespoon raisins or sultanas
1 tablespoon toasted cashew nuts
2 tablespoons chopped fresh parsley

1. Toss the carrot and broccoli in the lemon juice and oil.

2. Add all the remaining ingredients and toss well together.

CALORIES PER PORTION			Fats				**161**
	CHO(g)	Prot(g)	Sat(g)	Mono(g)	Poly(g)	Iron(mg)	Ca(mg)
Total	17.5	7	1	3	3	2	42
Energy	40%	17%		43%			

Gypsy Rice Salad

Makes 4-6 servings

V

450g/1lb cooked rice (from 150-175g/5-6oz raw rice)
3 cooked carrots, diced
175g/6oz cooked peas
125g/4oz cooked sweetcorn kernels
125g/4oz raw mushrooms, finely chopped
1 small red pepper, seeded and diced
2 tablespoons olive oil

Dressing;
4 tablespoons olive oil
1 tablespoon wine vinegar
pinch of paprika
salt and freshly ground black pepper

1. Place all the ingredients except those for the dressing in a bowl and mix well together.

2. Mix all the dressing ingredients and pour over the salad. Toss everything well together and serve.

3. Any leftovers can be stored in the fridge for 2-3 days.

CALORIES PER PORTION							213
	CHO(g)	Prot(g)	Sat(g)	Mono(g)	Poly(g)	Iron(mg)	Ca(mg)
Total	51.5	8	1	4	1	0.5	25
Energy	61%	10%		30%			

Crunchy Green Salad with Apricots

Makes 4 servings

V

150g/5oz baby spinach leaves
½ bunch watercress
2 tablespoons raw peanuts
1 tablespoon pumpkin or sunflower seeds
1 small cucumber, diced
½ green pepper, seeded and diced
4 fresh apricots, stoned and diced
50g/2oz mangetout, sliced
2 tablespoons plain low-fat yoghurt
1 tablespoon lemon juice
1 tablespoon chopped fresh chives or spring onions

1. Place the spinach and watercress in a bowl and tear any very large leaves into smaller pieces.

2. Add the peanuts, seeds, cucumber, pepper, apricots and mangetout and toss well together.

3. Mix the yoghurt with the lemon juice and chives or spring onions and pour over the top.

CALORIES PER PORTION				Fats				101
	CHO(g)	Prot(g)	Sat(g)	Mono(g)	Poly(g)	Iron(mg)	Ca(mg)	
Total	6.5	5	1	2	2.5	1.5	88.5	
Energy	23%	21%		56%				

For lower fat content use Yoghurt Dressing

Spiced Country Salad

Makes 1 serving

150g/5oz very small new potatoes
50g/2oz French beans, topped and tailed
1 medium well-flavoured tomato, cut into wedges
10-12 small Italian pickled onions in oil, drained and washed
(optional)
Optional Flavourings:
a little smoked chicken, sliced sausage, salami, or ham
Garnish:
1 tablespoon chopped fresh coriander
Dressing:
1 tablespoon olive oil
a few drops of oriental sesame oil or half and half olive oil and light
sesame oil
1 tablespoon sesame seeds
1 teaspoon freshly grated root ginger
1 tablespoon lemon juice
pinch of cayenne pepper

1. Steam the new potatoes in a steamer for 5 minutes. Add the beans and steam together for a further 5 minutes. Leave to cool.

2. Next make the dressing: heat the oils in a pan and fry the seeds until lightly browned. Stir in the ginger, lemon juice and cayenne, then leave to cool.

3. Arrange the potatoes and beans on a plate with the tomato, onion and flavourings if using. Sprinkle with the coriander and pour on the cold dressing.

CALORIES PER PORTION			_Fats_				400
	CHO(g)	Prot(g)	Sat(g)	Mono(g)	Poly(g)	Iron(mg)	Ca(mg)
Total	29	8.5	4	14	7	4.5	202
Energy	29%	9%		62%			

Waldorf Rice Salad

Makes 1 serving

<u>V</u>

1 small eating apple, cored and chopped
juice of ½ lemon
1 stick celery, chopped
15g/½oz walnuts, chopped
75g/3oz cooked long-grain rice
freshly ground black pepper

1. Place all the ingredients in a bowl and mix well together.

CALORIES PER PORTION			_Fats_				239
	CHO(g)	Prot(g)	Sat(g)	Mono(g)	Poly(g)	Iron(mg)	Ca(mg)
Total	31	5	1	2	7.5	1	72
Energy	48%	8%		43%			

Orange Spiced Tabbouleh Salad

Makes 4 servings

V

225g/8oz bulgar
10 tablespoons chopped fresh parsley (1 large bunch)
grated rind of 2 oranges
1 small red pepper, seeded and very finely chopped
4 tablespoons olive oil
4 tablespoons lemon juice
½ teaspoon ground cinnamon
½ teaspoon ground coriander
salt and freshly ground black pepper
1 × 225g/8oz can mandarin orange segments, well drained and chopped

1. Place the bulgar in a bowl and cover with plenty of water. Leave to stand for 30 minutes.

2. Drain very well, squeezing out all the water with your hands.

3. Mix with all the remaining ingredients.

CALORIES PER PORTION				Fats			289
	CHO(g)	Prot(g)	Sat(g)	Mono(g)	Poly(g)	Iron(mg)	Ca(mg)
Total	49	8	1	5	1	2	44.5
Energy	64%	11%		26%			

Sushi Rice Salad

Makes 6 servings

V

225g/8oz long-grain brown rice
600ml/1 pint vegetable stock or water

1 tablespoon olive oil
4 tablespoons vinegar
3 tablespoons sugar
1 teaspoon salt
2 tablespoons sherry or lemon juice
6 mushrooms, diced
½ × 225g/8oz can bamboo shoots, cut into thin sticks
½ × 225g/8oz can water chestnuts, sliced
1 small cucumber, finely diced
1 medium carrot, coarsely grated
50g/2oz mangetout, cut into thin lengths
Garnish:
½ bunch spring onions, shredded lengthways

1. Place the rice, stock or water and the oil in a saucepan and bring to the boil. Stir, cover and simmer over a low heat for 30 minutes until all the liquid is absorbed and the rice is tender. Leave to cool.

2. Meanwhile, heat the vinegar, sugar and salt in a small saucepan over a high heat, stirring until the sugar is dissolved. Leave to cool a little, then add the sherry or lemon juice. Bring to the boil and continue boiling until reduced by half.

3. Pour this mixture over the cold cooked rice and stir once or twice. Leave to cool completely.

4. Toss the vegetables together with the rice, retaining a few to sprinkle on top.

5. Spoon into a serving dish and garnish with the shredded spring onions and the reserved vegetables.

CALORIES PER PORTION			Fats				**217**
	CHO(g)	Prot(g)	Sat(g)	Mono(g)	Poly(g)	Iron(mg)	Ca(mg)
Total	44.5	6	0.5	2	0.5	1	21.5
Energy	77%	8%		16%			

Pasta Salad

Makes 4 servings

V

350g/12oz mixed pasta shapes
salt and freshly ground black pepper
2 tablespoons salad oil
1 small green pepper, seeded and finely chopped
1 small red pepper, seeded and finely chopped
7.5-cm/3-in piece of cucumber, finely chopped
2 sticks celery, finely chopped
1 tablespoon lemon juice
1 tablespoon chopped fresh parsley
¼ teaspoon oregano

1. Cook the pasta in lightly salted boiling water until tender, drain and mix with the oil. Leave to cool.

2. Mix the pepper, cucumber and celery with the pasta, lemon juice and parsley and season to taste.

3. Turn into a bowl and sprinkle with the oregano just before serving.

CALORIES PER PORTION							**384**
				Fats			
	CHO(g)	Prot(g)	Sat(g)	Mono(g)	Poly(g)	Iron(mg)	Ca(mg)
Total	67	11	1	5	1.5	2.5	45
Energy	66%	12%		22%			

Curried Pasta Salad

Makes 4 servings

225g/8oz pasta twists or fusilli
salt and freshly ground black pepper
1 tablespoon olive oil

150ml/5floz low-fat mayonnaise
2 teaspoons light curry powder
350g/12oz cooked diced chicken
1 tablespoon mango chutney
3 tablespoons cooked peas
3 tablespoons cooked sweetcorn kernels
2 sticks celery, very finely chopped
salad leaves, to serve

1. Cook the pasta in lightly salted boiling water until tender. Drain and toss in the oil. Leave to cool.

2. Mix the mayonnaise and curry powder with the chicken. Stiring all the remaining ingredients, including the cold pasta.

3. Serve on a bed of green salad leaves.

CALORIES PER PORTION			Fats				**489**
	CHO(g)	Prot(g)	Sat(g)	Mono(g)	Poly(g)	Iron(mg)	Ca(mg)
Total	56	28	1.5	4	1.5	2	38.25
Energy	43%	23%		34%			

LOW-FAT SALAD DRESSINGS

1. Yoghurt Dressing

Makes 4-6 servings

8 tablespoons plain yoghurt
1½ tablespoons cider or white wine vinegar or 2 tablespoons lemon
juice
salt and freshly ground black pepper
Optional flavourings:
25g/1oz strong blue cheese such as Roquefort or Stilton
2 tablespoons chopped fresh chives, chervil, parsley, tarragon or
basil

1. Mix all the ingredients with a fork to give a smooth consistency and pour over the salad.

2. If using one of the optional flavourings, finish in a blender or food processor.

3. Store in the fridge for 2-3 days.

CALORIES PER PORTION			Fats				38/27
	CHO(g)	Prot(g)	Sat(g)	Mono(g)	Poly(g)	Iron(mg)	Ca(mg)
Total	3/	3/			12/	0.5/	85/
	3	2		0.5	0.5	0.5	71
Energy	28%/	30%/		42%/			
	50%	37%		13%			

With/without blue cheese

2. Tofu Dressing

Makes 4-6 servings

125/4oz silken tofu
2 teaspoons water
1 tablespoon lemon juice or white wine vinegar
salt and freshly ground black pepper
Optional flavourings:
25g/1oz strong blue cheese such as Roquefort or Stilton
2 tablespoons chopped fresh chives, chervil, parsley, tarragon or basil

1. Place all the ingredients in a food processor or blender and blend until smooth and creamy.

2. Store in the fridge for 2-3 days.

CALORIES PER PORTION			Fats				30
	CHO(g)	Prot(g)	Sat(g)	Mono(g)	Poly(g)	Iron(mg)	Ca(mg)
Total	1	2.5	–	–	1	1	43
Energy	12%	43%		54%			

Pan-fried Corn with Peppers

Makes 2-3 servings

V

4 large corn on the cob
1 green chilli pepper, seeded and chopped
1 red pepper, seeded and chopped
freshly ground black pepper
25g/1oz plain wholemeal flour
1 tablespoon vegetable oil
grated cheese (optional)

1. Cut the corn from the cobs with a sharp knife and place in a bowl. Add the peppers, black pepper and flour and mix well together.

2. Heat the oil in a non-stick frying pan. Add the corn mixture and cook for about 10 minutes. Turn the mixture over to expose the browned pieces at the bottom of the pan and stir into the mixture.

3. Cook for a further 10 minutes, and again stir in the crispy bits. Cook for a final 8-10 minutes. Serve with grated cheese on top, if using.

CALORIES PER PORTION			Fats				208
	CHO(g)	Prot(g)	Sat(g)	Mono(g)	Poly(g)	Iron(mg)	Ca(mg)
Total	35	4.5	0.5	2	3	1	11.5
Energy	63%	9%		28%			

Corn and Bean Pudding

Makes 2 servings

V

2 corn on the cob
50g/2oz cream crackers, crushed
1 small onion, peeled and grated
½ small green pepper, seeded and sliced
125g/4oz cooked broad beans, skins removed
1 egg, beaten
150ml/5floz skimmed milk
½ teaspoon Worcestershire sauce (optional)
salt and freshly ground black pepper

1. Preheat the oven to 180°C/350°F/Gas 4.

2. Cut the corn from the cobs with a sharp knife. Mix with the crackers, onion, pepper and beans. Place in an oven-proof dish.

3. Beat the egg with the milk, Worcestershire sauce, if using, and seasoning and pour over the vegetables.

4. Bake for about 1 hour until set in the centre and golden on the top.

CALORIES PER PORTION							**278**
	CHO(g)	Prot(g)	Sat(g)	Mono(g)	Poly(g)	Iron(mg)	Ca(mg)
Total	35.5	17	1	1.5	1	3	195
Energy	48%	24%		28%			

Italian-style Beans

Makes 3-4 servings

V

1 × 400g/14oz can haricot, cannellini or butter beans
1 tablespoon olive oil
1-2 cloves garlic, peeled and crushed
3 tablespoons chopped fresh parsley

1. Drain the beans and heat through in the top of a double steamer with boiling water underneath. Or heat gently in their own liquid and drain.

2. Heat the oil in a pan and add the garlic. Fry gently over a low heat for 1 minute.

3. Add the drained, warmed beans and the parsley. Toss well together and serve.

CALORIES PER PORTION				Fats				114
	CHO(g)	Prot(g)	Sat(g)	Mono(g)	Poly(g)	Iron(mg)	Ca(mg)
Total	13.5	6	0.5	2.5	0.5	2	20
Energy	44%	22%		34%			

Beetroot with Orange

Makes 3-4 servings

<u>V</u>

15g/½oz butter or margarine
1 bunch spring onions, chopped
450g/1lb cooked beetroot, diced
50ml/2floz orange juice
freshly ground black pepper

1. Melt the butter or margarine in a saucepan and gently fry the spring onions until they begin to soften. Add the beetroot and toss the mixture well together. Pour on the orange juice.

2. Turn up the heat and cook for about 10 minutes, stirring fairly frequently, until all the liquid has disappeared.

3. Season with pepper and serve at once.

CALORIES PER PORTION			Fats				**73**
	CHO(g)	Prot(g)	Sat(g)	Mono(g)	Poly(g)	Iron(mg)	Ca(mg)
Total	10	2.5	1.5	0.5	–	1.5	31
Energy	52%	13%		35%			

Potatoes and Chickpeas in Tomato Sauce

Makes 4 servings

V

2 tablespoons tomato purée
150/5oz plain yoghurt
1 small onion, peeled and finely chopped
1 small green chilli, seeded and finely chopped
1 small clove garlic, peeled and crushed
salt and freshly ground black pepper
450g/1lb potatoes, peeled and cubed
1 × 400g/14oz can chickpeas, drained

1. Mix the tomato purée with the yoghurt and place in a heavy-based saucepan. Bring the mixture to the boil.

2. Add the onion, green chilli and garlic and boil for a further 2 minutes.

3. Add the seasoning and potatoes and cook over a low heat for 10 minutes.

4. Add the chickpeas and cook for a further 5-10 minutes until the potatoes are tender.

CALORIES PER PORTION			Fats				**241**
	CHO(g)	Prot(g)	Sat(g)	Mono(g)	Poly(g)	Iron(mg)	Ca(mg)
Total	42.5	12.5	0.5	0.5	1.5	2.5	134
Energy	66%	21%		13%			

Quick 'Rosti'

Makes 2 servings

V

2 large potatoes, peeled and grated
½ small onion, peeled and grated
1 small egg (size 6)
salt and freshly ground black pepper

1. Mix all the ingredients together in a bowl.

2. Heat a non-stick frying pan over a low heat and pour in the potato mixture.

3. Cook on one side for about 10 minutes until the base is well browned.

4. Turn over in one piece and brown on the other side. Check that the potato in the centre is well cooked, then serve at once.

CALORIES PER PORTION				Fats				**246**
	CHO(g)	Prot(g)	Sat(g)	Mono(g)	Poly(g)	Iron(mg)	Ca(mg)
Total	47.5	9	0.5	1	0.5	1.5	42
Energy	73%	15%		12%			

Pommes Anna

Makes 2 servings

V

350-450g/12oz-1lb potatoes, peeled and sliced
15g/½oz butter or vegetable oil
salt and freshly ground black pepper
100ml/4fl oz semi-skimmed milk
freshly grated nutmeg

1. Preheat the oven to 190°C/375°F/Gas 5.

2. Layer the potatoes in an ovenproof casserole dish, adding a little butter or oil and seasoning as you go.

3. Pour in approximately 100ml/4floz milk to come three-quarters of the way up the potatoes.

4. Sprinkle with nutmeg. Cover and bake for about 1 hour, until the potatoes are tender.

5. If you like really well-browned potatoes, remove the lid 10 minutes before the end of the cooking time.

Note: For a change, omit the butter or oil and the milk and add a little chopped spring onion and chicken stock instead.

CALORIES PER PORTION			Fats				240
	CHO(g)	Prot(g)	Sat(g)	Mono(g)	Poly(g)	Iron(mg)	Ca(mg)
Total	41	6.5	4	1.5	–	1	72
Energy	64%	11%		25%			

Italian Potato Pie

Makes 1 serving

225g/8oz potatoes, peeled
4 spring onions, sliced
¼ clove garlic, peeled and crushed
50g/2oz strongly flavoured cheese (suchas Pecorino Sardo, Gruyère or Cheddar), grated
1 egg
50g/2oz plain yoghurt
salt and freshly ground black pepper

1. Preheat the oven to 200°C/400°F/Gas 6.

2. Grate the potatoes into a colander and squeeze thoroughly with a paper towel to remove all the water.

3. Mix with all the remaining ingredients in a bowl and spoon into a greased shallow baking dish.

4. Bake for 1 hour until crispy on top.

CALORIES PER PORTION			Fats				506
	CHO(g)	Prot(g)	Sat(g)	Mono(g)	Poly(g)	Iron(mg)	Ca(mg)
Total	43.5	29	13	7	2	3	517
Energy	32%	23%		45%			

Lemon Dill Potatoes

Makes 1 serving

V

8-10 new potatoes
salt and freshly ground black pepper
1 teaspoon extra-virgin olive oil
1 tablespoon chopped fresh dill
1 teaspoon grated lemon rind
a very little lemon juice

1. Steam the potatoes and toss with all the remaining ingredients.

CALORIES PER PORTION			Fats				151
	CHO(g)	Prot(g)	Sat(g)	Mono(g)	Poly(g)	Iron(mg)	Ca(mg)
Total	24.5	2.5	1	3.5	0.5	0.5	10
Energy	61%	7%		32%			

8.10 PUDDINGS AND DESSERTS

Fresh fruit is often the best choice for dessert. But you can get bored with looking at the same fruit bowl at each meal. Accordingly the first recipes in this section concentrate on some interesting ways to serve fruit.

But there is no reason why you shouldn't add to your carbohydrate intake via the dessert course instead of in an earlier course. Starchy puddings are also useful when you really need to pile on the carbohydrates.

Strawberries Aphrodite

Makes 3-4 servings

350g/12oz strawberries
175g/6oz Greek yoghurt
1 tablespoon clear honey (optional)
½ teaspoon grated lemon rind
Garnish:
toasted flaked almonds

1. Cut the strawberries into halves or quarters.

2. Mix the yoghurt with the honey if using and stir in the lemon rind.

3. Mix in the strawberries and serve sprinkled with flaked almonds.

CALORIES PER PORTION				Fats			**74**
	CHO(g)	Prot(g)	Sat(g)	Mono(g)	Poly(g)	Iron(mg)	Ca(mg)
Total	6	3.5	2	1	0.5	0.5	79
Energy	31%	18%		50%			

Fruit Kebabs with Marmalade Sauce

Makes 4 servings

2 pears, peeled, cored and cut into chunks
2 green-skinned apples, cored and cut into chunks
juice of 1 lemon
8 strawberries
8 apricots, halved and stoned
Sauce:
4 tablespoons Seville orange marmalade
juice of 2 oranges
pinch of ground mixed spice

1. Dip the pear and apple chunks in the lemon juice as soon as they are prepared. This will help to prevent them from discolouring on contact with the air.

2. Thread the fruit on to 4 long or 8 short wooden skewers, arranging them so as to obtain the most attractive colour combinations.

3. To make the sauce, place all the ingredients in a sauce-pan and add any remaining lemon juice. Bring the mixture to the boil and pour over the fruit kebabs. Serve at once.

CALORIES PER PORTION		Fats				**144**
	CHO(g)	Prot(g)	Sat(g)	Mono(g)	Poly(g)	Iron(mg)	Ca(mg)
Total	35.5	2		–		1	52
Energy	93%	5%		2%			

Pineapple and Orange Yoghurt

Makes 2 servings

1½ tablespoons raisins
1 tablespoon orange juice
flesh of 1 very small or ½ medium pineapple, chopped
a little grated orange rind
125g/4oz plain low-fat yoghurt
Topping:
toasted flaked almonds, wheatgerm or crunchy breakfast cereal

1. Soak the raisins in the orange juice.

2. Toss with the remaining ingredients in a bowl and spoon into glass dishes.

3. Mix the topping ingredients and sprinkle over the top.

Note: For a change, use grated apples or pears in place of pineapple.

	CHO(g)	Prot(g)	Sat(g)	Mono(g)	Poly(g)	Iron(mg)	Ca(mg)
CALORIES PER PORTION				— Fats —			**165**
Total	37	4.5	0.5	0.5	–	0.5	164
Energy	84%	11%		5%			

Without toppings

Tropical Surprise

Makes 4 servings

2 tablespoons desiccated coconut
1 mango, peeled and chopped
1 papaya, peeled and chopped
1 banana, peeled and sliced
175g/6oz seedless grapes, halved
juice of ½ lemon

400g/14oz low-fat soft cheese (fromage frais or quark)
4 tablespoons light muscovado sugar

1. Toast the coconut under the grill until lightly browned. Leave to cool.

2. Mix all the fruits with the coconut and lemon juice and spoon into a heatproof dish.

3. Cover with fromage frais or quark and then sprinkle with the sugar. Make sure that the sugar completely covers the surface of the dessert.

4. Place under a hot grill for 3-4 minutes, until the sugar starts to bubble.

CALORIES PER PORTION			Fats				**264**
	CHO(g)	Prot(g)	Sat(g)	Mono(g)	Poly(g)	Iron(mg)	Ca(mg)
Total	38.5	8	6.5	2	–	1	108
Energy	55%	12%		33%			

Bananas with Cumberland Sauce

Makes 4 servings

150ml/5floz orange juice
1 × 150g/5oz jar redcurrant jelly
juice of ½ lemon
25g/1oz softened butter or margarine
4 bananas
Garnish:
1 kiwi fruit
1 kumquat

1. Place the orange juice, redcurrant jelly and lemon juice in a saucepan. Bring the mixture to the boil, stirring all the time.

2. Reduce the heat and simmer for 4-5 minutes until reduced by half. Cut the butter or margarine into small pieces and beat into the sauce. Leave to cool a little.

3. Arrange the bananas on serving plates and pour the sauce over. Decorate with slices of kiwi fruit and kumquat.

CALORIES PER PORTION			— Fats —				200
	CHO(g)	Prot(g)	Sat(g)	Mono(g)	Poly(g)	Iron(mg)	Ca(mg)
Total	38	1.5	3	1	–	0.5	10
Energy	71%	3%		25%			

French Apple Batter Pudding

Makes 4 servings

450g/1lb cooking apples, peeled, cored and sliced
1 tablespoon raisins or mixed candied peel
50g/2oz plain flour
3 eggs
50g/2oz granulated sugar
300ml/10floz skimmed milk
2 tablespoons apple brandy (calvados), cider or apple juice

1. Preheat the oven to 190°C/375°F/Gas 5. Lightly grease a heatproof dish.

2. Arrange the apple slices in the base of the dish and sprinkle with raisins or candied peel.

3. Beat the flour with the eggs and sugar and gradually stir in the milk and brandy, or apple juice.

4. Pour the mixture over the apples. Bake for about 1 hour until well-risen and golden-brown.

CALORIES PER PORTION			Fats				247
	CHO(g)	Prot(g)	Sat(g)	Mono(g)	Poly(g)	Iron(mg)	Ca(mg)
Total	42	10	1.5	2	1	1.5	143
Energy	63%	17%		21%			

Cake and Apple Pudding

Makes 4 servings

1 large cooking apple, peeled, cored and sliced
8 thin slices fruit cake or teabread
1 egg, beaten
125g/4oz plain flour
300ml/10floz skimmed milk

1. Preheat the oven to 190°C/250°F/Gas 4 and lightly grease a pie dish.

2. Layer the apple slices with the cake or teabread, ending with the cake.

3. Beat the remaining ingredients together and pour over the top. Leave to stand for 15-20 minutes.

4. Place in the pre-heated oven and bake for 45 minutes until golden on top and set in the centre.

CALORIES PER PORTION			Fats				343
	CHO(g)	Prot(g)	Sat(g)	Mono(g)	Poly(g)	Iron(mg)	Ca(mg)
Total	60	10	3.5	3.5	1	2	171
Energy	65%	12%		23%			

Steamed Rice and Cardamom Pudding

Makes 4 servings

F

600ml/1pint semi-skimmed milk
125g/4oz short-grain or pudding rice
2 tablespoons raisins
seeds from 3 cardamom pods

1. Place all the ingredients in the top half of a double saucepan with gently simmering water in the base.

2. Simmer for 1¾ hours until the mixture is thick and creamy. Stir from time to time.

Note: Semolina, ground rice and tapioca can be cooked in the same way.

CALORIES PER PORTION			Fats				**219**
	CHO(g)	Prot(g)	Sat(g)	Mono(g)	Poly(g)	Iron(mg)	Ca(mg)
Total	42	7.5	2	1	–	0.5	201
Energy	72%	14%		15%			

Banana Walnut Crumble

Makes 4 servings

50g/2oz butter
50g/2oz plain wholemeal flour
50g/2oz brown sugar
50g/2oz porridge oats
4 medium bananas, peeled and sliced

juice of 2 lemons
25g/1oz chopped walnuts
plain yoghurt, to serve

1. Preheat the oven to 200°C/400°F/Gas 6.

2. Rub the butter or margarine into the flour in a bowl. Add the sugar and porridge oats and mix well.

3. Place the bananas in an ovenproof dish. Sprinkle with the lemon juice and chopped walnuts. Spread the crumble mixture over the top.

4. Bake in the oven for 20 minutes. Serve with yoghurt.

CALORIES PER PORTION			*Fats*				**366**
	CHO(g)	Prot(g)	Sat(g)	Mono(g)	Poly(g)	Iron(mg)	Ca(mg)
Total	53	5	7.5	3.5	4	1.5	33
Energy	54%	6%		40%			

Baked Bananas

Makes 1 serving

1 banana
25g/1oz soft brown sugar
lemon juice
1 tablespoon plain yoghurt, to serve

1. Preheat the oven to 200°C/400°F/Gas 6.

2. Place the unpeeled banana on a baking tray and bake for 20 minutes until the skin is absolutely black.

3. Split the banana open along its length with a knife and sprinkle with soft brown sugar and lemon juice to taste. Serve with yoghurt.

CALORIES PER PORTION			Fats				207
	CHO(g)	Prot(g)	Sat(g)	Mono(g)	Poly(g)	Iron(mg)	Ca(mg)
Total	51	2.5		–	–	–	67
Energy	93%	5%		2%			

Traditional Rice Pudding

Makes 4 servings

F

very small knob of butter or margarine
125g/4oz short-grain or pudding rice
1 litre/1¾pints milk
50-75g/2-3oz caster sugar
pinch of salt
freshly grated nutmeg

1. Preheat the oven to 150°C/300°F/Gas 2.

2. Lightly grease a 1.75 litre/2½ pint ovenproof dish with the butter or margarine.

3. Sprinkle the rice over the base of the dish. Pour on the milk and sprinkle with the sugar, salt and nutmeg.

4. Bake for 2-2½ hours. The pudding should be thick and creamy and brown on the top.

Note: For a change, substitute raisins for some of the sugar.

CALORIES PER PORTION			Fats				314
	CHO(g)	Prot(g)	Sat(g)	Mono(g)	Poly(g)	Iron(mg)	Ca(mg)
Total	60	10	3	1.5	0.5	–	316
Energy	70%	13%		16%			

8.11 SIMPLE CAKES AND SWEET SNACKS

It is much better to bake your own cakes and sweet snacks if you possibly can. The problem is that cakes and biscuits are difficult to make without a certain amount of fat and sugar. However if you do your own home baking you can control the amount of fat and sugar that you use and you can experiment with wholemeal flour and other cereals such as oatmeal.

The recipes in this section include easy to make tea-breads and some simple cakes. There are also some ideas for homemade sweets and snacks. The teabreads are a good choice when you are watching your fat intake. Only about 32-37% of the calories come from fat. This compares with a similar figure for bought fruit cake. Other cakes such as Battenburg and Victoria Sponge cakes reach the 43-45% mark.

The sesame biscuits and sesame snacks are high in fat but you should only be eating a small amount at any one time and they are good sources of calcium.

Date and Orange Squares

Makes 9 squares

F

225g/8oz boxed dates, stoned and chopped

75g/3oz raisins or sultanas

grated rind of 1 orange

juice of 1 orange

juice of 1 lemon

75ml/3floz vegetable oil

50ml/2floz clear honey

50g/2oz light muscovado sugar

1 egg

a little vanilla essence

175g/6oz plain wholemeal flour

125g/4oz rolled oats

½ teaspoon baking powder
½ teaspoon salt
1 teaspoon ground cinnamon

1. Preheat the oven to 180°C/350°F/Gas 4 and grease and flour a 23-cm/9-in square baking tin.

2. Mix together the dates, raisins or sultanas, grated orange rind and orange and lemon juice. Leave to stand.

3. Beat together the oil, honey and sugar in a bowl until creamy. Beat in the egg and add a little vanilla essence.

4. In another bowl, mix together the flour, rolled oats, baking powder, salt and cinnamon. Add the egg mixture and mix to a dough.

5. Divide the dough into two equal portions. Press one portion into the prepared tin. Spread the date mixture on top.

6. Form the remaining dough into a ball and grate over the top, making sure that the date mixture is completely covered.

7. Bake for 30 minutes. Leave to cool in the tin before cutting into squares.

CALORIES PER PORTION			*Fats*				**308**
	CHO(g)	Prot(g)	Sat(g)	Mono(g)	Poly(g)	Iron(mg)	Ca(mg)
Total	49.5	6	1.5	4	5	2	40
Energy	60%	8%		32%			

Per square

Rock Buns

Makes 12 buns

225g/8oz plain flour
pinch of salt
2 teaspoons baking powder
75g/3oz butter or block margarine
75g/3oz granulated sugar
75g/3oz mixed chopped dried fruit (raisins, apricots, candied peel)
pinch of ground mixed spice
2 eggs, beaten

1. Preheat the oven to 200°C/400°F/Gas 6 and lightly grease a baking tray.

2. Sift the flour, salt and baking powder into a bowl.

3. Rub in the butter or margarine until the mixture resembles breadcrumbs.

4. Stir in the sugar, mixed fruit and spice. Make a well in the centre and add the eggs. Mix to a thick paste.

5. Drop tablespoonfuls of the mixture on to the prepared baking tray. Bake for 15-20 minutes.

6. Transfer to a wire rack to cool.

CALORIES PER PORTION			Fats				166
	CHO(g)	Prot(g)	Sat(g)	Mono(g)	Poly(g)	Iron(mg)	Ca(mg)
Total	25	3	4	2	–	0.5	42
Energy	57%	8%		35%			

Per bun

Banana Teabread

Makes 1 loaf, approximately 8 portions

75g/3oz butter or block margarine
125g/4oz light muscovado sugar
2 eggs
3 bananas
25g/1oz raisins or sultanas
150g/5oz plain wholemeal flour
75g/3oz wheatgerm
50g/2oz fine oatmeal
2 teaspoons baking powder

1. Preheat the oven to 180°C/350°F/Gas 4 and line a 700-g/1½-lb loaf tin with baking paper.

2. Cream the butter or margarine and sugar until light and fluffy.

3. Sieve or purée the bananas and add to the creamed mixture with the raisins or sultanas.

4. Stir in the flour, wheatgerm, oatmeal and baking powder and spoon into the prepared loaf tin.

5. Bake for about 50 minutes to 1 hour until a skewer pushed into the centre comes out clean.

6. Leave to cool in the tin for 5 minutes. Then turn out on to a wire rack, peeling off the lining paper. Leave to cool completely.

CALORIES PER PORTION				_Fats_			**314**
	CHO(g)	Prot(g)	Sat(g)	Mono(g)	Poly(g)	Iron(mg)	Ca(mg)
Total	48	8	6	4	1	2.5	48
Energy	57%	10%		32%			

Apple and Apricot Teabread

Makes 1 loaf, approximately 8 slices

225g/8oz self-raising wholemeal flour
125g/4oz butter or soft margarine
125g/4oz mixed raisins and chopped no-soak apricots
50g/2oz light muscovado sugar
1 large cooking apple, peeled, cored and very finely diced
2 eggs
2 tablespoons skimmed milk
1 teaspoon ground mixed spice

1. Preheat the oven to 180°C/350°F/Gas 4. Grease and line a 450-g/1-lb loaf tin with baking paper.

2. Place all the ingredients in a bowl and mix well until thoroughly blended.

3. Spoon into the prepared loaf tin and smooth the top level with a spoon.

4. Bake for 45 minutes until risen. Check that the teabread is cooked through by pushing a skewer into the centre of the loaf. It should come out clean.

5. Leave to cool in the tin for 5 minutes. Then turn out on to a wire rack, peeling off the lining paper. Leave to cool completely.

CALORIES PER PORTION							**244**
	CHO(g)	Prot(g)	Sat(g)	Mono(g)	Poly(g)	Iron(mg)	Ca(mg)
Total	34	6	5.5	2.5	0.5	2	35
Energy	53%	10%		37%			

Hazelnut Bread

Makes 1 large loaf, approx. 12 portions

225g/8oz plain flour
175g/6oz hazelnuts, peeled and chopped
50g/2oz granulated sugar
2 teaspoons baking powder
3-4 tablespoons skimmed milk
1 egg, beaten
pinch of salt

1. Preheat the oven to 180°C/350°F/Gas 4 and lightly grease a baking sheet.

2. Sift the flour into a bowl and add the hazelnuts, sugar and baking powder. Make a well in the centre.

3. Add the milk to the egg and pour into the well. Add the salt and stir the liquid to gradually incorporate all the flour. A little more flour or milk may have to be added at this stage so as to get the right consistency.

4. Knead the dough well in the bowl and shape into a round loaf.

5. Place on the prepared baking sheet and bake for 50-55 minutes. After this time, rap the loaf on the base and if it rings hollow, it is done. Transfer to a wire rack to cool completely.

CALORIES PER PORTION				Fats			186
	CHO(g)	Prot(g)	Sat(g)	Mono(g)	Poly(g)	Iron(mg)	Ca(mg)
Total	20	5	1	7.5	1	1	63
Energy	41%	10%		49%			

Mary Berry's Swiss Carrot Cake

Makes 8-10 servings

200g/7oz plain white flour
2½ teaspoons baking powder
25g/1oz fine oatmeal
125g/4oz muscovado sugar
50g/2oz mixed toasted pinenuts and sunflower seeds
125g/4oz grated carrot
2 ripe medium bananas
2 size 1 eggs, beaten
100ml/4floz olive oil

1. Heat the oven to 180°C/350°F/Gas 4 and grease a 20-cm/8-in loose-based cake tin. Coat with a little mixed flour and sugar.

2. Place the flour and baking powder in a bowl and stir in the oatmeal, sugar, nuts and seeds, carrots and banana. Mix well.

3. Make a well in the centre, then pour in the eggs and oil. Beat well until blended.

4. Spoon into the prepared cake tin and bake for 1¼ hours, covering lightly with foil after about 45-50 minutes. Test by pushing a skewer through the centre; it should come out clean.

5. Remove from the tin and leave on a wire rack to cool completely (about 2-3 hours).

CALORIES PER PORTION							**292**
				Fats			
	CHO(g)	Prot(g)	Sat(g)	Mono(g)	Poly(g)	Iron(mg)	Ca(mg)
Total	37	5.5	2	8	3	1.5	65
Energy	48%	7%		45%			

Old-fashioned Ginger Cake

Makes a 22.5 × 17.5cm/19 × 7in cake, approx. 12 pieces

225g/8oz self-raising flour, white or wholemeal
1½-2 teaspoons ground ginger
25g/1oz candied peel
25g/1oz raisins
½ teaspoon baking powder
225g/8oz black treacle
125g/4oz butter or block margarine
65g/2½oz dark muscovado sugar
1 egg
150ml/5floz skimmed milk

1. Preheat the oven to 180°C/350°F/Gas 4.

2. Mix the dry ingredients in a large bowl.

3. Place the treacle, fat and sugar in a saucepan and heat gently until the fat and sugar has dissolved. Do not let the mixture boil.

4. Leave to cool a little, then beat in the egg and milk.

5. Pour over the dry ingredients and mix well. Pour into the prepared tin and bake for 20 minutes. Reduce the heat to 160°C/325°F/Gas 3 and continue baking for about 1 hour until cooked through in the middle. Test by pushing a skewer through the centre; it should come out clean. Transfer to a wire rack to cool completely.

CALORIES PER PORTION			Fats				**227**
	CHO(g)	Prot(g)	Sat(g)	Mono(g)	Poly(g)	Iron(mg)	Ca(mg)
Total	33	4	6	2	0.5	3	125
Energy	56%	7%		38%			

Date and Yoghurt Cake

Makes 1 cake, 10 servings

1 tablespoon black treacle
3 tablespoons golden syrup
50g/2oz light muscovado sugar
100ml/4floz sunflower oil
150g/5oz plain yoghurt
2 eggs, beaten
75g/3oz stoned dates, finely chopped
½ teaspoon ground mixed spice
½ teaspoon bicarbonate of soda
225g/8oz plain wholemeal flour

1. Preheat the oven to 180°C/350°F/Gas 4.

2. Place the treacle, golden syrup and sugar in a saucepan. Stir over a low heat until the sugar has melted. Take care not to overheat.

3. Beat in the oil and the yoghurt and then the eggs.

4. Place all the remaining ingredients in a mixing bowl and mix well together.

5. Make a well in the centre and add the liquid ingredients. Stir together and pour into a 17.5-cm/7-in cake tin.

6. Bake for 1 hour 10 minutes, until a skewer pushed into the centre of the cake comes out clean.

7. Transfer to a wire rack to cool. Keep in an airtight tin for 2-3 days before eating.

CALORIES PER PORTION			Fats				297
	CHO(g)	Prot(g)	Sat(g)	Mono(g)	Poly(g)	Iron(mg)	Ca(mg)
Total	38	6	2	3	8	1.5	68
Energy	48%	8%		44%			

Sesame Biscuits

Makes 14 biscuits

1 egg
15g/½oz granulated sugar
75g/3oz plain wholemeal flour
75g/3oz sesame seeds
grated rind of ½ lemon
25g/1oz butter or margarine, melted

1. Preheat the oven to 180°C/350°F/Gas 4 and lightly grease a baking tray.

2. Beat the egg with the sugar with a wire whisk.

3. Add the remaining ingredients and knead to a firm dough. Place in the fridge to chill for 30 minutes.

4. Roll out on a lightly floured board to about 5mm/¼in thick. Cut 5.5-cm/2¼-in diameter circles with pastry cutters and place on the prepared baking sheet.

5. Bake for 15 minutes until lightly browned. Transfer to a wire rack to cool.

CALORIES PER PORTION							**72**
				Fats			
	CHO(g)	Prot(g)	Sat(g)	Mono(g)	Poly(g)	Iron(mg)	Ca(mg)
Total	4.5	2	1.5	1.5	1.5	1	37.5
Energy	24%	12%		64%			

Date and Nut Halva

Makes 32 pieces

350g/12oz stoned dates, finely chopped
50g/2oz chopped pistachios
50g/2oz chopped almonds
icing sugar

1. Mix the dates and nuts together in a bowl, using your hands.

2. Sprinkle a 20 × 20cm (8 × 8in) square tin with icing sugar and press the date mixture evenly into it. Turn out and cut into squares.

3. Store in a tin until required.

CALORIES PER PORTION			Fats				48
	CHO(g)	Prot(g)	Sat(g)	Mono(g)	Poly(g)	Iron(mg)	Ca(mg)
Total	7.5	1	–	1	0.5	–	10
Energy	57%	8%		34%			

Brown Sugar Fudge

Makes 32 pieces

225g/8oz dark muscovado sugar
225g/8oz white sugar
1 × 200g/7oz can evaporated milk
50g/2oz butter or margarine
150ml/5floz water

1. Line a 20 × 20-cm (8 × 8-in) tin or tray with baking paper.

2. Place all the ingredients in a large saucepan. Stir over a medium heat until all the butter has melted and the sugar dissolved.

3. Bring to the boil and simmer until the mixture reaches the soft ball stage (if you have a sugar thermometer it should register 113°C/235°F). Test by dropping a teaspoonful of the mixture into iced water. It should form a soft, sticky ball.

4. Remove the fudge mixture from the heat and beat with

a wooden spoon until the mixture starts to thicken and crystallize. Pour into the prepared tin and leave to cool.

5. Cut into squares and store in an airtight container.

Note: If you overboil this recipe it makes a deliciously sticky toffee.

CALORIES PER PORTION			Fats				76
	CHO(g)	Prot(g)	Sat(g)	Mono(g)	Poly(g)	Iron(mg)	Ca(mg)
Total	15	0.5	1	0.5	–	–	22
Energy	75%	3%		22%			

Pistachio Nut Fudge

Makes about 450g/1lb

350g/12oz granulated sugar
75ml/3floz water
1 × 200g/7oz can evaporated milk
50g/2oz butter or margarine
50g/2oz pistachio kernels
seeds from 3 cardamom pods, crushed
butter or vegetable oil, for greasing

1. Butter or oil a small square tin.

2. Place the sugar and water in a pan with the milk and butter and heat slowly, stirring until the sugar has dissolved.

3. Raise the heat and bring the mixture to the boil. Continue boiling until the mixture reaches the soft ball stage (or registers 113°C/235°F on a sugar thermometer).

4. Remove the pan from the heat and dip the base in cold water. Add the pistachios and crushed seeds and beat the fudge with a wooden spoon. When it begins to stiffen, pour into the prepared tin.

5. Mark the top into squares with the point of a knife and leave to cool. When completely cool cut into squares and store in an airtight tin.

CALORIES PER PORTION			Fats				**72**
	CHO(g)	Prot(g)	Sat(g)	Mono(g)	Poly(g)	Iron(mg)	Ca(mg)
Total	12	–	1	1	1	–	20
Energy	63%	4%		32%			

Index